GOD—
THE QUESTION AND
THE QUEST

GOD—
THE QUESTION AND
THE QUEST

Toward a Conversation
Concerning Christian Faith

PAUL R. SPONHEIM

FORTRESS PRESS   PHILADELPHIA

Library of Congress Cataloging-in-Publication Data

Sponheim, Paul R.
  God, the question and the quest.

  Bibliography: p.
  Includes index.
  1. God. 2. Faith 3. Apologetics—20th century.
I. Title.
BT102.S628 1985   231   85–47737
ISBN 0–8006–0756–2

1740E85 Printed in the United States of America 1–756

To sisters and brothers
in the venture—
Harlon, Irwin, Marion, Ronald,
Carol, Don . . . and others

CONTENTS

CONTENTS

PREFACE

If a personal word is in place in a preface, I want to comment on how this book seems to me to differ from much of my other writing. In the 1960s I published a book on Soren Kierkegaard, *Kierkegaard on Christ and Christian Coherence,* which attempted a systematic reading of the enigmatic Dane by charting the ordering course of certain christological tendencies in his thought. In the 1970s in *Faith and Process* I sought the wisdom that could be found for Christian faith in the metaphysical writings of A. N. Whitehead. Earlier in the present decade I was one of the six authors of *Christian Dogmatics,* a work the editors aptly described as seeking to speak "from the church to the church, by way of disciplined reflection on the sources of its faith and traditions."[1]

In all these works there is a sense of the determinate. It is clear what one is doing: one is reading or writing about Kierkegaard, or Whitehead, or classical dogmatic teachings. Such determinateness seems linked reciprocally with an appeal to authority. But as I send these last words of this new work to the press, it is not the determinateness of what I have written that strikes me.

What I have written here does not constitute a settled account of how things are in the world, with humankind. There are determinate elements, to be sure, but how they are to be understood together is not clear. Thus Kierkegaard still seems to me to speak perceptively of selfhood, as chapter 5 in particular makes clear. And Whitehead's cosmology is at work in what I have to say of the world, in chapter 6. But can self and world come together coherently? That has to do materially with the question and quest of this book for a "third." Journey is not destination; inquiry not answer. This book has the indeterminateness of that which is incomplete. Furthermore, when

1. *Kierkegaard on Christ and Christian Coherence* (New York: Harper & Row, 1968); *Faith and Process: The Significance of Process Thought for Christian Faith* (Minneapolis: Augsburg Pub. House, 1979); *Christian Dogmatics,* ed. Carl E. Braaten and Robert W. Jenson (Philadelphia: Fortress Press, 1984). The quotation from the last work is from p. xvii.

convincing descriptions are carried beyond their natural terrain in the hope that they can coexist and contribute to a common venture, any appeal to authority must be carefully circumscribed.

Also prescriptively, in speaking of God and of faith, I find this book to carry a diminished appeal to authority. There is still some determinateness. The book is subtitled "toward a conversation concerning Christian faith," even though I hope an awareness of the reality of other faiths is evident in its pages. And the book focuses on God—who is not everything—as does the Christian faith, in my view. But such determinateness sets up the conversation; it does not settle it. There has been something of that dialogical character in my earlier writing as well. Kierkegaard's coherence was not a matter to be judged only by those committed to his Christian word of the infinite qualitative difference between God and us. *Two* realities were understood to be drawn together in *Faith and Process,* and they were not both Christian faith. And as far as that faith itself is concerned, *six* authors were sought for *Christian Dogmatics,* as our situation in the last decades of this century suggested making a virtue out of the necessity of theological pluralism. We six agreed, moreover, that each "locus" of the book ought to relate to the contemporary situation.

But that work was dogmatics and not apologetics. Similarly, Christian faith could be rather cleanly distinguished from and then enthusiastically related to process thought. With Kierkegaard it was more a matter of relating him to himself. I think that in this book the claims of faith and the challenges to faith meet on more equal ground. For that reason I do not use the word "apologetics" on the title page. While there is much that would be apt in that term, matters seem too secure, too neat, when done under that rubric.

Perhaps these comparisons do not, after all, convey a merely personal account. In the sixties, while there was talk in *Time* of the death of God, it still seemed best to many to let the solitary voice of Christian particularity be heard. In the seventies such a move seemed less convincing, but—and—there was much interest in schools offering "holistic" views. Process thought seemed and seems prominent among the alternatives. And what is now clear? Perhaps the indeterminate and incomplete character of my work is not so idiosyncratic. Today otherwise diverse authors converge in the recognition of the problematic status of faith. I see myself in this company.

Robert Scharlemann, in *The Being of God: Theology and the Experience of Truth,* clearly recognizes the drive of human reflection toward unfaith. Yet I think that, ironically, unfaith has too clear, too determinate, a place in his thought, as he moves ahead to trump reflective atheism with reflexive faith. In *Erring,* Mark C. Taylor seems to stay closer to the chaos, disavowing ordering appeals to God, history, self, and book. In my pages these "modern" categories are still employed. I do not believe I am more optimistic than Taylor. To the contrary, it is precisely the Holocausts—the one that gave the lie to modernity's optimism and the one that threatens to give death to life on this planet—that call me back from the intoxicating play of the carnival. Here I appreciate Harvey Cox's concern in *Religion in the Secular City* to combine talk of carnival with moral seriousness, but I do not find the issues of faith's cognitive claims adequately addressed by the liberation theologians to whom he repairs. Those issues focus, as I understand them, on the Christian faith's claims concerning God. This might link me with James Gustafson's *Ethics from a Theocentric Perspective*. But there still seems to be in Gustafson a great deal of H. Richard Niebuhr's "radical monotheism." His confidence seems to exceed mine. My burden is rather to speak of God's transcendence in relationship to us.[2]

I hope I have not in one broad stroke managed arrogantly to claim membership in this circle of important studies and yet to diminish this book's actual prospect by still more arrogantly differing with their approaches. I aim to indicate that there is some significant convergence in the conversation I seek to join. Jürgen Habermas has spoke of how it is essentially human for people to talk to each other.[3] I am glad that Christian theologians seem increasingly to agree that it is Christian to do so as well. Christian faith recognizes that we are pilgrims. On the way we do well to talk together and it is not strange that we should differ with each other. It may even be promising. The outcome is simply not clear. But while appeals to authority may diminish, the conversation authorized by our humanity and our Christianity may flourish.

This book is not a merely personal venture in other ways as well. Much of the writing was done on sabbatical leave in Cambridge, England. The governing board of Luther Northwestern Theological Seminary generously authorized the leave and the community at Clare Hall, Cambridge, graciously received me during it. Additional support was extended by the Aid Association for Lutherans in the form of the Fredrik A. Schiotz fellowship. Throughout the several years devoted to the preparation of the manuscript, the administration of Luther Northwestern has never left me uncertain of their commitment to this effort. I am grateful for all of this assistance.

2. Robert P. Scharlemann, *The Being of God: Theology and the Experience of Truth* (New York: Seabury Press, 1981); Mark C. Taylor, *Erring: A Postmodern Atheology* (Chicago: Univ. of Chicago Press, 1984); Harvey Cox, *Religion in the Secular City: Toward a Postmodern Theology* (New York: Simon & Schuster, 1984); James M. Gustafson, *Ethics from a Theocentric Perspective: Theology and Ethics* (Chicago: Univ. of Chicago Press, 1981).

3. Jürgen Habermas, Axel Hanneth, Eberhard Knodler-Bunte, and Arno Widman, "The Dialectics of Rationalization: An Interview," *Telos* 49 (Washington University, St. Louis, 1981).

I also want to thank many individuals who worked on these pages with me. Dean Arthur Peacocke (my host at Clare), Terence Fretheim, Randy Nelson, Ron Marshall, Jonathan Strandjord, Curt Thompson, Donald Sponheim, and Steven Paulson all helped me with their criticism, though each might well seek further changes. Alma Roisum, Diane Huso, and Karen Schaefer competently converted my chaotic lines into an intelligible text and cheerfully met many difficult deadlines. At the press Norman Hjelm, Davis Perkins, and Barry Blose were helpful at different stages in the development of the manuscript. Mark Mattes has opened up the book at its close by providing a thorough index.

I am glad to dedicate this book to my sisters and brothers. Growing up, I learned we were different from each other. But we were together as we had to be and as we wanted to be. It is not minimalizing to say that the dinner table of such a family is not dull. And it does not detract from the crucial importance of the family of origin to recognize other sisters and brothers in life's venture. It is good that there is One who sets the solitary in families and is the ground for our questioning and the goal of our quest.

PART ONE:
COMING TO
THE CONVERSATION

1 TO CONSIDER CHRISTIAN BELIEF IN GOD

CONTENTION: THE CONTEMPORARY BURDEN
OF CHRISTIAN FAITH

Christian claims concerning God call for consideration:

> That there is One who is other than all the others, marking a measure for everything else;
> That this One is active in the world so that life both as gift and as task is to be lived out before this One;
> That this One has acted decisively in Jesus of Nazareth so that the final meaning of life is thereby determined.

Such claims may be said to be in contention: persons who make these claims and persons who do not at least should agree about this. Careful thought is required of both those who question such God-claims and those whose faith is a quest for and before the God about whom the claims are made.

Christian faith holds that God is real quite apart from anyone's believing or disbelieving. Christians stake out a claim on reality.[1] Moreover, the Christian faith understands that the truth of which it speaks is not trivial; it obliges its adherents to witness to all. Christian claims are made for hearing, since believing them will make a difference. "Woe to me, if I preach not the gospel!" Faith bears this burden: to spread the word that all may believe. Terms like "contention" and "burden" do not come up with reference to common-sense statements about ordinary reality. But these terms do apply to the claims of Christian faith, for claims such as those made in the opening paragraph can hardly be said to convey what all reasonable persons take to be true.

Those who reject these claims do not speak with a single voice. To some it seems that Christian belief is simply no longer needed. Human maturity removes the reasons that once brought people to seek, or speak of, God. We stand today without the crutch of faith.[2] For others such belief is not any longer permissible, for it offends our fundamental understanding of self and world. In this loss of faith there is genuine gain. Wallace Stevens's poetry makes the point eloquently and emphatically:

It was when I said,
"There is no such thing as the truth,"
That the grapes seemed fatter,
The fox ran out of his hole.

You . . . You said,
"There are many truths,
But they are not parts of a truth."
Then the tree, at night, began to change,

Smoking through green and smoking blue,
We were two figures in a wood,
We said we stood alone.

It was when I said,
"Words are not forms of a single word.
In the sum of the parts, there are only the parts.
The world must be measured by eye."

It was when you said,
"The idols have seen lots of poverty,
Snakes and gold and lice,
But not the truth";

It was at that time, that the silence was largest
And longest, the night was roundest,
The fragrance of the autumn warmest,
Closest and strongest.[3]

Still others may settle simply for saying less stridently—almost wistfully—that Christian faith is not now possible for them. They may lack eloquent alternatives or emphatic objections, but the claims of faith simply no longer work to organize their world.

These different voices come together to agree that Christian claims about God are in contention because they stand against or apart from—and so in effect against—the grain of things. They are hardly to be taken for granted. Some adjudication is needed and the burden of proof—or, more aptly, the need to contend, to commend—seems to lie with the Christian. Christians may wish to claim that unfaith is always parasitic, that it depends for dear life on that which it attacks. While that may be suggested by the word "atheism" and may illumine the logic of faith, the self-understanding of many nontheists is quite otherwise. Many persons manage to get through the day without Christian faith in God and without having to burn up psychic energy in consciously rejecting such faith.

Christians should be wary of rejoicing about such an absence of explicit rejection of their contentions. People do not argue about that which does not concern them. Who needs to bear extra burdens? Moreover, the absence of angry controversy may speak quietly of a change in church as well as in world. Alasdair MacIntyre has argued that theists have themselves to thank for this dubious blessing:

> [T]he lack of confrontation is due not only to the directions in which secular knowledge is advancing but to the directions in which theism is retreating. Theists are offering atheists less and less in which to disbelieve. Theism thereby deprives active atheism of much of its significance and power and encourages the more passive atheism of the indifferent.[4]

It is almost as if the Christian faith will have to supply its own dispute, if it is to be in contention. No easy road leads that way. Thus the call to reach all cannot be dispatched by the Christian church by declaring its shrinking numbers and decaying influence to be a witness to the narrowness of the way. Rather, the external difficulties may reveal precisely an inner weakness. If MacIntyre is right about the "less and less in which to disbelieve," Christians may already have a burden of faith even before looking outside the flock.

Perhaps the weakness is not that Christians believe too little but that they believe too much. At least the subject matter of theology seems to spread out into assorted theologies of/and this-and-that. Different persons professing to be Christian compass such wide differences among their number that a distinguishable core can hardly be discerned. In turn this inner pluralism contributes to a certain vagueness about the outer borders of belief. Indeed, the individual Christian may at times sense a closer alliance with the advocate of an apparently non-Christian view—at least as far as particular components are concerned—than with other members of the flock.

There surely are other faiths abroad, other "frameworks of orientation and devotion," to use Erich Fromm's words.[5] Specifically theistic religious alternatives abound, and people evince religious attitudes toward such diverse realities as science, art, and education. Such religious pluralism may seem to the Christian little better than secularism. If to be Christian is to stake out a claim on reality, and if these pluralists effectively give up disputing the truth of the Christian's claims, then indeed this pluralism is essentially as atheistic as secularism. To say that in the face of such pluralism we have a "heretical imperative" to choose on the basis of our own experience makes a significant difference only if the claims of the Christian "option" can be intelligibly stated and considered along with others in some common idiom.[6]

Thus it seems desirable for the Christian to seek to enter dialogue concerning God. Even the non-Christian in the West may sense some burden at this point. Can one be so cleanly done with the Christian faith, with its view of self and its world? This question does not arise merely from the fact that emancipation from faith and its superstitions has not clearly been converted into satisfactory psychic and social capital, or that no other comprehensive world view seems any more competent to point the way to a resolution of the nuclear threat facing the planet. One will not, after all, be bullied or bribed back into faith. But reflecting on the way Christian faith apparently once organized the lives of individuals and societies, one may wonder if we are so different from our predecessors that there is no unfinished business here. Even the non-Christian may be burdened, unable to live with or without faith.

The distinguished Columbia University physicist Isidor Isaac Rabi was raised in an Orthodox Jewish home whose piety did not sustain him. And yet Rabi acknowledged that his break was not completely clean:

> So we reached a sort of modus vivendi where at home I conformed to every-thing. I didn't try to persuade them of anything else. They would have really suffered from that. They didn't ask very much what I did outside. So I was a good son in that respect. I tried to help with the holidays—to make them joyful occasions. I have a great respect and a great feeling for those things. It's part of a culture, a way of life, an outlook. Sometimes I feel I shouldn't have dropped it so completely—I'm talking about the way of life. There's no question that basically, somewhere way down, I'm an Orthodox Jew. In fact, to this day, if you ask for my religion, I say "Orthodox Hebrew"—in the sense that the church I'm not attending is that one. If I were to go to a church, that's the one I would go to. That's the one I failed. It doesn't mean I'm something else.[7]

Are the piety and culture, the "somewhere way down," of Judaism stronger than those of Christianity, or only more prominently exposed through persistence under duress? Perhaps we do not know yet. Perhaps Rabi speaks also for a growing number whose background is Christian, when he speaks of "the church I'm not attending" and adds, "It doesn't mean I'm something else." Perhaps, however, we are on the edge of a truly new time that does not permit us to carry forward our parents' faith. But if we are to enter fully into this new time, we can only do so when we have put to rest the historic Christian faith and its claims.

Both meanings of burden seem thus to apply: *because* of this faith, something must be said; *about* this faith, something must be said. It is timely to consider the Christian claims concerning God in relation to fundamental experience shared by believer and unbeliever alike. Thus we do well to ask: According to the Christian faith, how is God to be understood in relation to my struggle to understand self, other, and world? Does that understanding make sense? To get at that will be of interest to persons on either side of the boundary between belief and unbelief—and as may well be the case with most of us, to every person who is on both sides at once. First we must attend to our condition in and for the conversation.

CONDITION: MODERNITY'S ELLIPTICAL REALITY OF SELF AND WORLD

I seek here to build on the several solid studies of the development of modern consciousness over the last four centuries.[8] With the work of scholars like Peter Gay, Ernst Cassirer, and Basil Willey already at hand I can indicate two crucial components in that consciousness: (1) the identification of the self-world relationship (maybe more naturally called the subject-object relationship) as constitutive of reality, and (2) the celebration of the terms of the relationship. Who are we? Selves with others in the world, surely! What is this? The world in which we may know and create! It is good that it is so! I also wish to suggest that while the relationship is very well established in the modern consciousness, one may yet detect a certain inner instability, in that each term in the relationship bids to center reality independently and even exclusively. It is as if an ellipse is too complicated for a consciousness seeking the simplicity of a circle. Self and world: that these two together are real is clear. And that is good; but would not One be better?

René Descartes is a dramatic early instance of the self-world relation's controlling role in Western thought. Cartesian thought also illustrates the instability in the relationship. While Descartes aspired to know "what might be found within myself or in the great book of the world," that self-world parallelism gives way to a priority of the self. In spite of, and yet through, radical skepticism the desired certainty is to be found in the knowledge of the self. Only thereafter is reality assigned to the world and even then only by appeal to the idea of a God who would not deceive the knower.[9] If this favored self is understood as the sure repository of clear and distinct ideas, it will not surprise us that in turn Descartes's ideal for natural science is mathematical and geometrical clarity.

Thus one can employ this relationship to chart the prevailing tendencies in Western philosophy. With respect to theories of knowledge, if the self's identification with the act of thinking is accepted, one can distinguish empiricist theories stressing the relatively passive reception of the world, from views such as those of Descartes and Spinoza, where the mind's priority and autonomy are emphasized. As the modern consciousness develops, the self-world relationship is sustained, though it is drawn now in this direction, now in that, depending upon which pole of the relationship dominates.

In such development a valuation comes into view. Peter Gay discerns this already in the "prehistory of the Enlightenment":

> Augustine's pious formula that the creature cannot create was now overcome; it was eroded, as it were, from within. Man remains God's creature—of that few Renaissance philosophers had any doubt. But he is a creative creature; he creates, in his art, in his civic life, his scholarship, and his moral philosophizing, that noblest of creatures—himself.[10]

It is common to emphasize the exuberant "turn to the subject" in the seventeenth and eighteenth centuries. But the other pole is accommodated. It should be noted that this subject was changing a world that science and technology found to be remarkably responsive to human ingenuity. Science, medicine, engineering, transportation tell the tale of human sovereignty over an obedient nature.[11]

Given such momentum, it is little wonder that the self-world structure is not only identified but affirmed—celebrated. If one accepts the evidence of political absolutism (whether the power is wielded by the monarch or by the revolutionary) and cultural and aesthetic achievement, one seems to be swept toward Karl Barth's diagnosis of the spirit of the age:

> Absolutism in general can obviously mean a system of life based upon the belief in the omnipotence of human powers. Man, who discovers his own power and ability, the potentiality dormant in his humanity, that is, his human being as such, and looks upon it as the final, the real and absolute, I mean as something "detached," self-justifying, with its own authority and power, which he can therefore set in motion in all directions and without any restraint—this man is absolute man.[12]

Was this praise for the human purchased at the price of divine dignity? Interpreters have disagreed. Carl Becker stressed the "heavenly city" of these thinkers, who are found to be only "half-emancipated from the superstitions they scorn."[13] Peter Gay, on the other hand, argues that what the Enlightenment figures adopted from Christian theology and philosophy were the least distinctively Christian themes; indeed, that what is involved here is a pitting of the classical pagan heritage against the Christian inheritance.[14] Ernst Cassirer reaches back to the Renaissance to stress the differences undercutting apparent commonality:

> The Reformation seems to agree with the Renaissance in giving new value and new sanction to life on earth. . . . But if humanism and the Reformation in this sense meet on the same plane, they are nevertheless miles apart. Faith as understood by the Reformation remains alien to the religious ideals of human-

ism both in its origin and its aim. The core of this opposition lies in the radically different attitude of humanism and the Reformation toward the problem of original sin.[15]

I defer my own judgment as to whether the logic of Enlightenment affirmations needs to include an atheistic implication, in order to continue the characterization of the conditions bequeathed by the Enlightenment for our conversation. If the Enlightenment may be summed up in two words, "criticism" and "power," perhaps that combination may be best understood as criticism for power.[16] I speak of the power of the human self taking up the method of criticism. Descartes's skepticism illustrates this in a more rationalistic style, but a more empirical one is to be found as well. Cassirer speaks of "analysis" as

> the staff which a benevolent nature has placed in the blind man's hands. Equipped with this instrument he can feel his way forward among the appearances, discovering their sequence and arrangement; and this is all he needs for his intellectual orientation to life and knowledge.[17]

Accordingly, Ben Franklin emerges as the quintessential Enlightenment practical man, forging ahead to discover and create a new world.[18] A new world it was to be, with the plausibility structure of the old eroding as the creative human will worked.[19]

One may grant that for many Enlightenment thinkers the new temper reflected the idea of residence in a world without benefit of deity. Peter Gay closes his first volume's study of *The Rise of Modern Paganism* with an eloquent tribute to such a thinker, David Hume:

> [H]e followed his thinking where it led him, and he provided through his own life . . . a pagan ideal to which many aspired but which few realized. He was willing to live with uncertainty, with no supernatural justifications, no complete explanations, no promise of permanent stability, with guides of merely probable validity. . . . Without melodrama but with the sober eloquence one would expect from an accomplished classicist, Hume makes plain that since God is silent, man is his own master: he must live in a disenchanted world, submit everything to criticism, and make his own way.[20]

It surely is clear that the venture and daring of the Enlightenment would combine poorly with what Cassirer calls a religion of "mere receptivity":

> Man is not merely seized and overwhelmed by this activity as by a strange power, but he in turn influences and shapes the activity from within. It is not supranatural power nor divine grace which produces religious conviction in man; he himself must rise to it and maintain it.[21]

There will be opportunity in the remainder of this book to inquire whether the disjunctions within Cassirer's distinctions must stand. Here we can briefly observe how the Enlightenment celebration of self and world came together explicitly with Christian faith. The optimism of the time prevailed, with the result that the elements of classical Christian faith representing the discontinuity between God and humankind were deemphasized. The impression of the deemphasis abides even if one inspects widely varying instances of the faith of the period.

Thus one might trace the accommodation in the seventeenth century of the Christian notion of revelation to a conception of reason as the organ of truth. In England, for example, the Cambridge Platonists (who accepted inner, intuitive reason as the "candle of the Lord"), the "supernatural rationalists" (who, like Samuel Clarke, thought that reason may anticipate revelation and is needed to confirm it), and the deists (who appealed to a universal assent to basic religious notions) come together to illustrate the point.[22] In the same connection one might cite the very different work of Spinoza, even in his apparent attempt to show that

> [p]hilosophy has no end in view save truth: faith, as we have abundantly proved, looks for nothing but obedience and piety. Again, philosophy is based on axioms which must be sought from nature alone: faith is based on history and language, and must be sought for only in Scripture and revelation. . . . [23]

The separation between the spheres of faith and philosophy closes if the good to be sought in obedience is subsequently defined as the guiding of conduct by "adequate"—that is, self-grounded—ideas unavailable in appeals to authority.[24]

One can see in the eighteenth century the process by which moral idealism accommodates distinctive Christian teachings regarding sin and redemption. Kant's *Religion Within the Limits of Reason Alone* is a lovely illustration. Despite the reference to radical evil, one senses some alteration from classical Christian teaching in the following descriptions of incarnation and justification by faith:

> Now it is our universal duty as men to *elevate* ourselves to this ideal of moral perfection, that is, to this archetype of the moral disposition in all its purity— and for this the idea itself, which reason presents to us for our zealous emulation, can give us power. Just because we are not the authors of this idea, and because it has established itself in man without our comprehending how human nature could have been capable of receiving it, it is more appropriate to say that this archetype has *come down* to us from heaven and has assumed our humanity. . . .
>
> Man may then hope to become acceptable to God (and so be saved) through *a practical faith in this Son of God* (so far as He is represented as having taken upon Himself man's nature). In other words, he, and he alone, is entitled to look upon himself as an object not unworthy of divine approval who is conscious of

such a moral disposition as enables him to have a well-grounded confidence in himself and to *believe* that, under like temptations and afflictions (so far as these are made the touchstone of that idea), he would be loyal unswervingly to the archetype of humanity and, by faithful imitation, remain true to his exemplar.[25]

Those words do, indeed, seem to be "other" in a sense different from the one Kant acknowledges! One might further suggest that the work of Friedrich Schleiermacher in the decades at the turn of the century combines Kant's turn to the subject via the independence and priority of "practical" reason's moral imperative with the influence of the "God-intoxicated" Spinoza. Even in the move from the *Speeches* concerning religion to *The Christian Faith* and the concern to deal responsibly with the historical tradition of the church, the content of the faith is to be explicated "always and everywhere on this same basis, namely, the direct description of the religious affections themselves." This churchly theologian who preached regularly from his Berlin pulpit emphasizes that the knowing process is located very firmly within the subject. Perhaps equally significant, God is defined in such Spinozistic independence that whatever there is to be known must happen within the confines of an absolutely dependent humanity.[26]

Or one can trace the movement from the self to a developing world consciousness. One can follow through Hegel's refusal to invest "the finite with the character of an absolute" inasmuch as God, "far from being a being, even the highest, is *the* Being." Thus the early Hegel, the ministerial candidate, can have Christ prophesy:

When ye cease merely to see the divine in me and outside yourselves, then will the divine come to consciousness in you also, because you have been with me from the beginning, because our natures are one in love and in God.[27]

It is not far to the work of David Strauss, for whom the Idea in all its richness and manifoldness will not limit itself to a particular individual.[28] A more empirical form of world consciousness is to be found elsewhere in the nineteenth century, as in the shift from Newtonian to Darwinian paradigms in natural science. Accommodation continues as the argument from design gives way to a description of natural selection, or as the burgeoning science of geology in its discovery of time comes increasingly to stress lawlike processes (as the "Uniformitarians" did) rather than appeal to forces no longer operating (as the "Neptunists," the "catastrophists" did).[29]

I have been inquiring how the Enlightenment identification and celebration of the realities of self and world came to bear on (or take form within) the formulations of Christian theism. A shape does begin to appear even in so brief a sketch.[30] The development to which we have been attending is in fact that of theological liberalism. Here we find an emphasis on immanence in theology, on rationalism in epistemology, on personalism in anthropology, and on meliorism in ethics.[31] The self-world structure underlies these themes and may be seen in varying interactions with theological influence, as when God's immanence is understood to warrant the connection between mind and nature.

If our task today is that of the liberals, it will entail somehow taking up the self-world ellipse as a condition for the consideration of Christian claims concerning God. I believe that their task is ours, since we are children of the Enlightenment, even though their conclusions cannot be ours in any unreconstructed way. Even if one harbors some skepticism about heady proclamations of the postmodern character of our time, one may well recognize the critique and collapse of the liberal synthesis. Wherever God may dwell on earth, humans now seem disinclined to house themselves comfortably in these "accommodations." Self and world abide, but weakened by the absence of a God for whom there seems to be insufficient place reserved. While the conclusions of the classical theological liberal seem jejune, the conditions of their work remain ours.

There seems to be little reason for doubt about the theological collapse. To be a human being in this century is by no means to know that God dwells in this world. Nor is it to be confident that reason can chart our path forward in the chaos that meets us. Personalism and meliorism fare no better. For many concerned with ethical issues the valuing of the individual personality's development and the confidence that life can be bettered may actually obscure our situation and so function as impediments to knowing and doing what needs to be done in a bleak postpersonal world. We need not try to decide how far the theological critique of the liberal adjustment actually contributed to this collapse. It seems more to the point to remark that the passionate and prodigious work of the "neo-orthodox" critics does not itself provide what liberalism once did, a basis for the integration of that which is human and that which is Christian.

It seems too obvious to say that such integration was precisely not sought by the Niebuhrs, Barth, and all their following at midcentury. What is gained, then, by pointing to their alleged deficiency? It still remains the case that the protest they presented seems more informative than constitutive, for despite its dramatic power, it has not uncovered a new theological consensus. It will not do, on the other hand, to dismiss the criticism as an episode internal to the liberal movement. Yet it does seem that the effect of much of the neo-orthodox criticism was still to present yet another illustration of the underlying structure informing the liberal consensus: the self-world relationship.

Moreover, the instability in the targeted structure may still be discerned in the critique. Consider, for example, the tendency in the critique to isolate the individual self. This was not a simple or undialectical personalism, of course. Already Kierkegaard—to whom the neo-orthodox reached back— put a check on the slogan so beloved to college philosophy students, that "subjectivity is the truth." He did that with a doctrine of original sin that went beyond the reality of the individual. And yet the call to the individual is reinstated at another level. In Kierkegaard's view it remained the task of the individual to synthesize the pathetic (the human) and the dialectical (the Christian), so that while subjectivity was not the truth in a simple sense, it was yet the truth dialectically.[32]

I am suggesting that modernity's descriptive vision of self and world, then, is still to be seen in spite of, and even within, the theological criticism of the liberal accommodation. I shall later argue that we still discern and organize reality in terms of the self-world structure—though with an ever-softer hyphen separating the two. Moreover, we manifest as well the tendency of each of the foci of the ellipse to deny the role of the other or to invade its realm.

So self and world come together to constitute our consciousness and compete with each other there. But one discerns fewer instances of celebrating our circumstance. We may agree with Nietzsche that the world—and the self, too—has grown colder.[33] Perhaps the vaunted postmodern person still *sees* the world as the modern did, but *feels* rather different about what is seen. Liberal optimism is unconvincing even on nontheological grounds. A new construction is needed. How then are Christian claims concerning God to be made in relationship to the elliptical reality of self and world?

ORIENTATION: GOD'S COMMITMENT AND HUMAN CAPACITY

I propose a conversation concerning God. Two speakers are needed, each with full speaking and voting privileges, and these two speakers must also be listeners. The conversation is their common burden. But someone must speak first, lest we have indistinguishable babble. Of the two major parts of the book the first is the one in which the Christian hears that which speaks against the faith. But some preliminary brief statement of faith may suggest something of the content and the terms of the conversation. I do not intend that these remarks control the discussion. Direct it they may, but not control, for that to which they direct us entails hearing fully those human voices that speak powerfully of reality without affirming God. These statements will be unseemly bare until they take flesh, and perhaps truer form as well, in the dialogue to which they direct us. We who are Christian do not really know what we believe about our God until we are in dialogue with those who do not believe and with that within us which does not believe.

We begin with God. That is not a matter of choice. To speak significantly of Christian faith is always to speak of God. It is not only to speak of God; indeed all the "only"s (faith, Scripture, grace, . . .) reach out to speak as well of that which is not God. But in whatever else we say as Christians, we speak of God. There are many ways to speak of God, in some of which we may not utter "God" as the all-determining subject of the sentence. But somehow, some way, if Christians are to speak of their faith, they will speak of God. That does not become less true when the speech is intended for dialogue with those who are not Christian. There is no other, no more gradual or less jarring, way actually to begin.

In this beginning it will not do to substitute Jesus for God. Of course Christians are the ones to be found at Bethlehem and Golgotha, but they cannot declare what they find there or how they are found there, without speaking of God. The death-of-God movement in twentieth-century theology shows how Christian reference to this particular Jew, without talk of God, becomes either trivial or fantastic, depending on whether or not the universal and ultimate dimensions of God-talk are retained.[34] To tie God and this man together has its own difficulties: How can this be? Why is this not hopelessly arbitrary? For that matter, what does it mean? But for now it must be said that even those Christians who would speak most strongly of Jesus only manage to do so when they speak of God. There is a natural centripetal tendency in Christian speech about God, as surely as it is in this Jesus that the promise of all words about God is realized. But the image of implosion is inappropriate if it is taken to imply that talk of God disappears in testimony to Jesus. That is not the case, precisely since Christians resist any "unitarianism of the second article." One tactic in that resistance is to employ the law/gospel dialectic to observe that the surprising specific word of salvation does depend on knowing something about ourselves, however hidden that may be.[35] Another is to suggest with Justin that all those who have lived with the logos of God are Christians, so that "whatever among all men has been well said belongs to us Christians."[36] These formulations no doubt still seem at best highly compressed and at worst imperialistic. But they point us (back) in the right direction, for they make clear that precisely the one who most fervently utters "Jesus, Jesus, only Jesus" means to speak of God.[37]

What is it Christians say of God? God is other than we are. Moreover, this is not the ordinary otherness needed to sustain indifferently any particular one among the many ones making up reality. Rather, God's otherness is that of categorical supremacy, as Charles Hartshorne puts it:

"God" is a name for the uniquely good, admirable, great, worship-eliciting being. Worship, moreover, is not just an unusually high degree of respect or admiration; and the excellence of deity is not just an unusually high degree of merit. There is a difference in kind. God is "perfect," and between the perfect and anything as little imperfect as you please is no merely finite, but an infinite, step. The superiority of deity to all others cannot (in accordance with established word usage) be expressed by indefinite descriptions, such as "immensely good," "very powerful," or even "best" or "most powerful," but must be a superiority of principle, a definite conceptual divergence from every other being, actual or so much as possible.[38]

Hartshorne seems right in linking God's unique otherness with worship. We may respect, love, obey, and serve other human beings; but worship is for God alone.

How is this categorical supremacy to be formulated? It is possible to seize upon the otherness directly and seek to render it by metaphysical description. If we do that we are apt to end up with a notion of God as the necessary being, as pure form, as self-sufficient simplicity.[39] That has been done often enough in the church's reflection, as well as in the musings of the metaphysicians, and I will later argue that there is something very sound in what is said in this approach. But I choose to do that later, because it is not in such talk that faith best begins to speak of God. Rather, at bottom God is for Christians the one who has made them to be a people who were no people. That is, Christians speak of one who makes and keeps covenant. It seems best for Christian talk about God to start with the life of faith in relationship to God and indeed to refuse to retreat from that rootedness when it must puzzle over what formal and metaphysical statements are to be made about God.

It is crucial to see that in speaking of God in relationship we have not somehow settled for speaking of a lesser form of God. The temptation to think so abides. But at the very heart of Christian confession lies the confidence that there is no other God than this one, from whom no one can separate us and in whom we more than conquer. Thus, to speak of God's transcendence is not to speak of God before or beyond or beneath God's relatedness to us. The one whom we worship is quite simply *God* for us. We are not speaking of a relationship with one who once was God. God has not stopped being God by being God for us. There is much work to be done in describing how this reality—that God is for us—is to be understood. But that it is this claim that is to be understood Christians have no reason to doubt. Luther could make this point with characteristic earthiness in specifying the divine glory:

It is the honor and glory of our God, however, that, giving himself for our sake in deepest condescension, he passes into the flesh, the bread, our hearts, mouths, entrails, and suffers also for our sake that he be dishonourably handled, on the altar, as on the cross.[40]

Despite his vaunted Calvinism, Barth could say:

The God of the Gospel is no lonely God, self-sufficient and self-contained; He is no "absolute" God (in the original sense of absolute, i.e., being detached from everything that is not himself). To be sure, he has no equal beside himself, since an equal would no doubt limit, influence, and determine him. On the other hand, he is not imprisoned by his own majesty, as though he were bound to be no more than the personal (or impersonal) "wholly other." By definition, the God of Schleiermacher cannot show mercy. The God of the Gospel can and does.[41]

This cheerful appeal to Christian consensus does not do the hard work needed to show how this God who is fully for us is related to the "all-everything" God of metaphysical abstraction. That clarifying work will not necessarily leave everything quite as it was. For example, such dogmatic old reliables as the distinction between the immanent and the economic trinity may come into question.[42] Or the Chalcedonian formulation regarding the person of Christ may be seen to recede from predominance, given its formal character.[43] Yet even if the gap between faith's assurance and theology's abstraction cannot be closed without reconstruction, one needs to account for how Christian thinkers have managed to move from the one to the other. I will later comment on the qualitative link between the religiously salvific and the ontologically unique by suggesting that the radical difference between God and us lies in something that is held in common: volition. The Christian theologian is thus invited to formulate the ontological uniqueness in categories that have to do with the personal, such as possibility, freedom, and decision.

Such a God as I have described will not be unknowable or unknown. The relationship with God includes knowing God. The finite is capable of bearing such an infinite as this, and so the human is possessed by the haunting knowledge of God. Yet the clear Christian consensus that God is known does not carry through to agreement about how God is known. At the very least one would need to distinguish the illuminationist and empiricist traditions, as Tillich did in a famous passage:

One can distinguish two ways of approaching God: the way of overcoming estrangement and the way of meeting a stranger. In the first way man discovers *himself* when he discovers God; he discovers something that is identical with himself although it transcends him infinitely, something from which he is estranged, but from which he never has been and never can be separated. In the second way man meets a *stranger* when he meets God. The meeting is accidental. Essentially they do not belong to each other. They may become friends on a tentative and conjectural basis. But there is no certainty about the stranger man has met. He may disappear, and only *probable* statements can be made about his nature.[44]

Tillich's statement of the distinction nicely reveals his leaning toward the illuminationist's certainties; in the next chapter I will follow the more empirical path.

The assertion that God is known may require qualification. Does not human arrogance need to be cautioned by the apophatic recognition of our ignorance? Perhaps. Still, it is not vain ambition but the gospel that requires us to say that we do know God. There is mystery enough in what we know; but we ought not to back away from the claim to know. Of course it will be important to acknowledge that even in its clearest focus the knowledge of God is not unmediated. Soren Kierkegaard put the point in terms of the direct becoming indirect:

> When one says directly, "I am God; the Father and I are one," that is direct communication. But when he who says it is an individual man, quite like other men, then this communication is not just perfectly direct; for it is not just perfectly clear and direct that an individual man should be God—although what he says is perfectly direct. By reason of the communicator the communication contains a contradiction, it becomes indirect communication.[45]

All persons are capable of knowing God and, more than that, in some sense do know God.[46] To hold this is not at all to deny human depravity. Sin is not ignorance, and salvation is not knowledge. Nevertheless, this bald assertion of the breadth of the human knowledge of God faces difficulties. Does it not smack of Christian imperialism? ("Let us tell you who it really is you know!"), if it does not dribble itself away in religious indifferentism ("Since all already know, what's the point of telling?")? And yet there are crucial claims at stake, such as that we can hear the gospel intelligibly whether or not we believe it, and that when we do believe it, when we are surprised by the joy of the gospel, we nonetheless recognize it as just the good word for which we were unknowingly looking.

Thus we must consider how such gospel-knowing can be connected— whether as supplementation or even in opposition—to a broader knowing of the true God. The Christian Scriptures themselves put that task before us, and do so far more concretely than the metaphysical musings of even portions of these very Scriptures themselves—for instance, the first chapters of Colossians and John.[47]

It is Christian claims concerning God that are to be considered. I have been arguing that those claims insist that the object of knowledge is not some isolated x to be pointed out and given the name God but is one who is relentlessly for us and so in relationship with us. Thus, to talk about God, to argue about God, necessarily is to speak of us: ourselves, our communities, our world.[48] These are not God, but so surely are they related to God that any perceptive speech about them is pertinent to the conversation we seek. In turn, it follows that the human capacity to contribute to the dialogue concerning God is not limited to Christians. Atheists cannot be disqualified from this dialogue or demeaned as junior partners, unless we are prepared to argue that their statements about, say, self and world lack full value. Moreover, as a matter of fact, atheists do speak of God, for they speak against God. Again, my sense is that more than occasionally they do so not as an item of independent interest but in order to speak more fully or more intelligibly about self and world. So we begin this conversation by considering in the next three chapters specific objections made to Christian claims concerning God. In our trying to attend to these objections, the claims themselves may be recast. Only when that movement of active reception is in place will the active commendation of Christian claims be appropriate (chapters 5 through 7). Even then it will be clear that the quest to commend God does not exclude the questioning of God. We begin with questions and we live with questions, though their substance and standing may change.

In this conversation the Christian holds no privileged position. The dialogue is among human beings who together find themselves burdened by a disagreement about Christian claims concerning God. While Christians may seek to argue that their understanding is the more comprehensive one, it must be remembered in the conduct of the debate that it is our common humanity-in-the-world that provides the basis for significant exchange.

But if that is the case, the selection of the claims will itself be affected. This is not to abstract from specifically Christian faith, as if to move people first into the antechapel of bare belief and its possibility. That seems to risk the destruction of the faith by dissection, if it does not unfairly settle the controversy by the structure implied in its staging. What Christian faith has in common with other faiths and what it does not both need to be held together, and the radical human possibility of recognizing no God at all remains something to be considered in connection with the specifically Christian claims. But within the organic reality of Christian faith some claims may be said to bear mainly or even exclusively upon other claims for which a clearer logical priority may be discerned. Given such "layering," it will be natural that the more considerable attention in our discussion be given to those elements that bear most directly upon, and that may indeed most fundamentally offend, common human sensibilities.[49]

We must seek to hold together the issues of the meaning and the truth of the Christian faith.[50] Thus both more general criteria (fruitfulness and faithfulness in relation to human experience, clarity, coherence) and more specific ones (fidelity to the Christian tradition) remain pertinent at each stage in our investigation. The dialogue must proceed without pretending that the outcome is certain.

PART TWO:
CONDUCTING
THE CONVERSATION

To Attend and
to Commend

2 TO ATTEND TO THE QUESTIONS CONCERNING BELIEVING

Can This Be to Know?

The matter of knowing interests both the one who believes in God and the one who does not. The believer is interested because the Christian faith claims to speak of something that is true in the world and for the self. It informs. If this high ground is given up, the Christian is fighting a different battle and may already have lost the decisive one. There is, of course, some risk in Christians' claiming to know. Harold Pinter's Lenny states the dilemma:

> How can the unknown merit reverence? In other words, how can you revere that of which you're ignorant? At the same time, it would be ridiculous to propose that what we *know* merits reverence. What we know merits any one of a number of things, but it stands to reason reverence isn't one of them. In other words, apart from the known and the unknown, what else is there?[1]

Lenny is right that in these matters a third way is not given. To be Christian is to revere the known. There is something special about this knowing, something so special that Christians may even call their way of knowing the way of negation. But there is learning in this ignorance.[2] Within what we know there is a good word of One who does merit reverence.

The unbeliever is interested in this claim as well. We are regularly bewildered by all there is to know. The "information revolution" heightens our sense of ignorance as surely as it increases our fund of knowledge. But perhaps the sense that there is more than we can know may hint that there is also something other than we know, that the quality and not just the quantity of our knowledge is limited. In any case we do want to know. But we are also aware of our potential for being mistaken in claiming to know. Fortunately we can and do know something about knowing. We often can know that we know and how we know.

Given that capacity, the question for the Christian is, Can believing this—this confession, this liturgy, this moral instruction, this experience—be to know? In some instances the question is asked of the "how" of the Christian claim: "If *that* is how you know whatever it is you claim to know, you don't know it at all!" At other times the question is generated by the content of the claim: "How could you ever know such a matter as that?" In both cases it is the modern interest in method that speaks. Believer and unbeliever meet here. While these questions are put from beyond the circle of faith, the person of faith accepts them and even asks them. Of that which we do not know we should keep silent! The Christian agrees, but does not keep silent.

DOES KNOWING GOD RESPECT
THE SELF'S EXPERIENCE?

We learn from experience. Indeed, we learn in experience. In experience one receives the world into oneself in actual encounter. Errors may occur, of course; but there is no higher way to knowledge, no clearer conduit of truth for the self. And it is the self of which we speak. For we moderns seem very clear that the experience of knowing is something that is done by selves. That which I know has to do with me, as surely as who I am has to do with what I know. At bottom, then, if I say that I know something, I must somehow understand that of which I speak in terms of my own experience. I can, of course, grant credit to the experience of others, so long as I have a lifeline back to my own experience of those others and of their probable reliability in relationship to the matter at hand.

Given this understanding of knowing, a skeptical question arises: Does not the knowing claimed for Christian faith elude, defy, and even demean the self's own experience, and so fail to qualify as knowing?

The question is not leveled only against religious belief. It can be directed quite obviously against the so-called ontological argument for God's existence. To suppose that the analysis of a concept—whether the concept is that of perfection, of a "cause of itself," or of something other—can by itself bring us to know the existence of a reality corresponding to the concept analyzed is to defy the test of experience. Of existence we know only through experience—our own or that of others. Even to unfold the concept of God to show that *if* God exists, God exists necessarily is still not to know that God does exist. Here a great gulf remains fixed.[3] At least some proponents of the ontological argument have wanted to argue that no empirical element is involved, even though the argument has been understood as an act of mystical devotion.[4] But as soon as the logic of the argument is distinguished from the motivation of the arguer, it meets what to most moderns seems to be powerful criticism. In the argument no experiential warrant for claims about existence is apparent.

This mention of the ontological argument can move us more fully into the conversation. The plain errors of the argument alert us that less obvious mistakes may be involved in the Christian claim to know. Religion's difficulties, clothed in ceremony, may escape our notice. It may be that in believing anything at all about God, we are wrong to suppose ourselves to possess knowledge, since our belief is never backed by sufficient resources in experience.

This objection can be made with reference to the object or the subject of faith, the propositions or the passion. In the former case we note that we generally refuse to let the past have any automatic authority for us. That folks of time past thought such and such to be the case may be interesting or curious, but in itself it bears no weight with us. We wisely recognize that we must make our own way. We gladly accept the analytic and creative gifts of present human intelligence, gamely whistling our way through whatever graveyard of risk may be part of the bargain. We know we are limited, but we would not go back. But the Christian does go back! Indeed Christianity is stubbornly focused on a particular cluster of events in the first century. What has that fading strand of history to do with our experience? Are we simply dependent upon the multiform layers of tradition that bear something of some original cluster of events to us? Or if what is claimed for that time is able to be experienced somehow even now, have we not thereby dissolved the historical claim's decisiveness? Van Harvey puts the dilemma simply:

> [W]ithout the principle of analogy, it seems impossible to understand the past; if, however, one employs the principle of analogy, it seems impossible to do justice to the alleged uniqueness of Jesus Christ.[5]

The call to faith in such an object must violate the subjectivity of the believer. In what seems to be going on within the believer we cannot recognize anything like what we know as knowing. To speak of knowing by experience is to speak of the tortuous way of trial and error in which the mood of tentativeness fits the experiential nature of our knowing. At least that is true of claims we commend to others as more than a personal opinion.

But religion drinks deeply of certainty. Is not Richard Robinson's grumbling well grounded?

> It seems to me that religion buys its benefits at too high a price, namely at the price of abandoning the ideal of truth and shackling and perverting man's reason. The religious man refuses to be guided by reason and evidence in a certain field, the theory of gods, theology. He does not say, I believe that there is a god, but I am willing to listen to arguments that I am mistaken, and I shall be glad to learn better. He does not seek to find and adopt the more probable of the two contradictories, "there is a god" and "there is no god." On the contrary, he makes his choice between those two propositions once for all. He is determined

never to revise his choice, but to believe that there is a god no matter what the evidence.[6]

It is not a straw theologian Robinson attacks. No less a figure than John Henry Cardinal Newman insists that "assent is in its nature absolute and unconditional."[7] Our century does not come second to Newman's in religious appeals to final truth and unqualified assent.

Persons of Christian faith need to feel the force of this objection. We must reassert that the Christian faith does speak of that which is known through human experience.[8] In saying that, it will be necessary to consider how the documents of the past are not dead, but living, how a commitment can guide rather than impede inquiry, how a commitment can be decisive without claiming irreversibility.

The Christian's understanding of the object of faith will also be affected. The documents are not dead, because the One of whom they speak is not dead. Christian speech about Jesus can be persuasive rather than coercive because it is speech about God. Sense must be made of talk of God with reference to the experience now available to the self. Thus Christians worship no book but hear a living word.[9] Ray Hart is right in suggesting that Christian theologians tend to carry a very heavy inventory.[10] The critical question is how that deposit of faith is handled. One seeks to "merge the horizons" of the text and those of the contemporary audience. Accordingly, it is not appropriate that the work of theology proceed serenely and surely in a deductive mode, for the theologian will need to speak from that which is known in present human experience.[11]

DOES THE KNOWING OF GOD OCCUR
IN THE WORLD?

We have begun with the self, thus reflecting the modern "turn to the subject." But we very well know that the self and its knowing are emphatically in the world. We have not always fully appreciated the intimacy of the connectedness, so that we have tended to let the self-world distinction become a disjunction. But we are clear about this: the self must have recourse beyond itself in order to know and to know that it knows.

Thus our experience may be, in James's telling phrase, a "buzzing multiplicity" of particulars, but we recognize that in our knowing we cannot ride off in all directions at once, simply celebrating the sheer immediacy of the episodes. Rather we say that we know something as the matter finds its place in a framework, a "world" of knowledge, which it also helps to shape. If some claim contradicts what we otherwise suppose we know, we cry foul. We check the claim's credentials, most directly by looking for or even seeking to create its recurrence and less directly by following out corollaries and consequences of the claim and the scheme it suggests. Must . . . can . . . this world be claimed? We may eschew final systems, but we seek to know coherently.

It is precisely we who do so. The self recognizes the right of other selves to contend with itself concerning any claim; indeed it seeks their aid. The world the self seeks in knowledge is not merely one of coherence, but one that includes other selves. It is a populated world. In our communication with each other we are not saying, "You tell me your dream, and I'll tell you mine." We can and will communicate significantly because we not only share knowing capacities, but coexist in what we seek to know. These two worlds work in tandem in our knowing, checking and reinforcing each other. Neither is likely felt to be infallible. Often one yields to the correction of the other and at times the self may cry out that both come together to mislead. But we do not then settle for such an "unworldly" situation. We set about making a new world.

Again I have stated this section's premise very baldly so that faith can hear and consider a basic complaint: the knowing claimed for Christian faith does not occur in our world, for it violates the integrity of both the community of knowers and the consensus of attained knowledge. The problem is not simply that one cannot point to God as an object in the world;[12] it is more that believers try to turn such deficits into capital. God's absence from the world is acknowledged but becomes the first step in a process in which that world itself is attacked and abandoned. Christians seem to believe they can know without the community of knowers and they act against what that community of knowers commonly does know. This cannot be to know!

In a sense the charge is that faith pits the one against the many, the self's singular passion (of knowing or of illusion or delusion) against the world of the knowers and the known. As in the case of the ontological argument, this fault may be more clearly discerned in arguments for God that do not assume faith. The cosmological argument proposes to argue from the universal experience of causality to a first cause sufficient to stop the infinite regress of causality. But is this not precisely to collapse the highly complex unity of the world into the singular, as if the universe itself needed causing like unto the finite effects we know? And is it not actually to appeal to a more sovereign singular against the universal, against the world, in the insinuation that finite being needs "starting" or explaining? Does not the singular thus come to stand above the world, if our teeming plurality can be explained by that one?

Wolfhart Pannenberg shows the difficulty confronting such argumentative tactics by referring to the acceptance of the principle of inertia:

This made the idea of the tireless activity of the first cause of all events no longer necessary to explain the continuance of history or existence in general.[13]

We feel the force of this and we can well understand Carl Sagan's suggesting from our television screens that we "save one step" by saying simply that the universe is endless or, if it is not, that the nothing in which it originates is just that.

Moreover does not the so-called teleological argument, the argument from design, also err in seizing upon a few particulars apart from and even against the universal? If the God for whom we set about to argue from design is supposed to be universally, omnipotently, and beneficently active, how can we appeal to highly selective fragments of purpose to reach such a "whole"?[14] The cosmos in this argument is not the world we know.

These objections to the classical arguments of natural theology may lead us to attend to ways in which the same charge of singularity, of subjectivity, of "unworldliness," may be made against Christian faith. Again the bare bones of philosophical argument may reveal strains and breaks that are well concealed in the rich vestments of religious devotion.

But perhaps the difficulties are not so well concealed after all! We have had friends asking what in the world faith might mean. Some are philosophers. Indeed Anglo-Saxon philosophy in this century has offered to bring this point home to the believer. To pit the singular against the world in religious affirmation is to let meaning die what Antony Flew has called "the death by a thousand qualifications," in which falsifying evidence is turned away from faith's door.[15]

It is as if even religious passion cannot quite deny the world's siren call. To qualify, even a thousand times, is to relate after a fashion. Such nominal courtesy carries faith's indictment, however. Belief has only this desperate tactic available and it must fail! Well, perhaps it is not that simple. After all, to be concerned to construct or connect with a world is not necessarily to capitulate to logical positivism's particular campaign against inwardness. But that campaign did raise the worldly question about the singularity of faith's vision, and can still do so.

Other help with this lesson was offered by students of the human psyche. Freud, for example, declined to recommend that the Christian zealot be accepted by the rest of us, since the passion of the one should not prevail against the critical reflection of the many:

> If the truth of religious doctrines is dependent on an inner experience which bears witness to that truth, what is one to do about the many people who do not have this rare experience? One may require every man to use the gift of reason which he possesses, but one cannot erect, on the basis of a motive that exists only for a very few, an obligation that shall apply to everyone. If one man has

gained an unshakable conviction of the true reality of religious doctrines from a state of ecstasy which has deeply moved him, of what significance is that to others?[16]

These reminders have been necessary for faith; yet, they have proved insufficient. The consideration of claimed Christian knowledge by relating it to the wider world of experience is often discouraged by the Christian, at least implicitly. One may be told that this consideration is fundamentally impossible, for all Christian speech is ultimately about God, who is non-objectifiable.[17] Or the Christian may go gently but firmly on the offensive, observing that in a world where neutral or faithless statements are impossible, the Christian faith is simply one more faith—albeit the true one. The person of faith simply illustrates a truth about all significant human insight and venture: reflection occurs in the light of certain presuppositions. Who can avoid that?

Van Harvey has effectively shown how such an apparently innocuous and common-sensical recognition of the fact that analysis is located in an interested world can be preempted precisely to justify faith's unworldly singularity. Of the slippery use of the term "presupposition" he writes:

> For the Christian apologist uses the term in such a way as to justify the *suspension* of those normal assumptions we use when interpreting our experience. His point is that the alleged events in the New Testament are so unique *that our normal presuppositions do not apply....* It is important to distinguish between these two meanings of the term "presupposition" because only one of them permits some kind of rational assessment within the limits of the perspective.[18]

Finally, the skeptic has to wonder if the objections and questions raised against Christianity are not viewed by the Christian less as undermining than as confirming the faith. All too often the Christian seems less interested in addressing the skeptic's doubts than in simply accepting them as one more demonstration of the narrowness of the way of obedience and of the discriminating freedom of God in enlightening human minds.

What shall we who are Christians say to these things? While matters are more complex than the charge suggests, and thus some argument about the bill of particulars lies ahead, the Christian must say that the concern voiced here is indeed legitimate. Christian knowing does occur in the world. The Christian does accept internal coherence and consistency as criteria that apply in the evaluation of Christian claims. We will return to the matter of this inner world of faith in the next chapter, but meanwhile there are other implications that follow from holding that faith's knowing occurs in the world.

It follows, for example, that faith cannot rest content with the self's singular passion, but will reach out for a community that is in principle unbounded. Christians differ notoriously on how this outreach is to be understood, but I want to argue that recognition of the integrity of the human is essential to it. The recognition of human capacity cannot be a public-relations ploy to be checked at the door of the church on new-member Sunday. This is as much a remark about God as it is a comment on human capacity. At the heart of the Christian message lies the truth that God creates and re-creates freedom. Authoritarian groups in which the members possess and exercise no freedom to criticize, amplify, and appropriate teaching provide no world for a word about or from the God whom Christians worship.

Even if one did not agree that Christian faith in God implies that all persons share knowledge of that God, even if one dropped back to saying that all are to know this God freely, one would still be identifying a world common to faith and unfaith. For if the Christian gospel is to make even one Christian person whole, it cannot extirpate that believer's rootedness in a political, social, and economic world. Moreover, it is not only the Christian who is involved in that world but also—on the Christian's own confession—the God of the Christian. Thus claims about God cannot be extricated from the "nonreligious" experience of the Christian and those others who may not name the same name but surely do tread the same earth. The logical positivists were right in asking the Christian what difference the knowing of God and the knowing of the world make for each other.

Where Christian faith may wish to differ with the procedure of the positivists is not on the positivists' insistence on the worldliness of meaningful words, but on the misleading simplicity of the world put forward by the positivists as standard. Faith need not make this point alone, for there are an increasing number of voices within the broad human community doing so. They include linguistic philosophers who refuse to understand knowing as the passive reception of isolated items of sense experience of an objective world patiently waiting to be perceived.[19] As self and world are increasingly driven together, some surprising alignments are taking shape. Charles Taylor speaks of such surprises when he speaks of how the natural and human sciences

> turn out to be methodologically at one, not for the positivist reason that there is no rational place for hermeneutics; but for the radically opposed reason that all sciences are equally hermeneutic. . . . Old-guard Diltheyans, their shoulders hunched from years-long resistance against the encroaching pressure of positivist natural science, suddenly pitch forward on their faces as all opposition ceases to the reign of universal hermeneutics.[20]

If reality is more complex than we may have supposed it to be, it should not surprise us that our knowing and our speaking will have to take on a like complexity simply in order to be fully worldly. We did not have to come this far in this century in order to learn this lesson. Earlier, poets like Wallace Stevens were speaking of seeking "fact beyond bare fact . . . beyond normal sensibility," while still insisting that "what concerns us in poetry as in everything else, is the belief of credible people in credible things."[21] In many disciplines an interest has arisen in metaphor not as confusion, ornament, or illustration, but as participation in the world and, so, in meaning.[22]

The great danger is that the theologian will find in this complexity a blank check to finance a retreat into monologue. Then matters would go swimmingly for the theologian, still equipped with the serenity of a singular language, even if now lacking a singular experience. The complexity of the world calls instead precisely for conversation between perspectives. Inner coherence is not enough, though it is a worthy goal and a fair test in itself. Correspondence to objective fact is more than any human can seem to have now. But we do have the human world, the social world, the conversation.

IS IT BEYOND THIS SELF-AND-WORLD
TO ACT ON THIS KNOWING?

We have made some progress toward understanding the terms of the question "Can this be to know?" We can recognize that there are both subjective and objective elements in knowing. Knowing has to do with the self's own experience and occurs in our world. Thus one can speak of meaningful use of language with respect either to conveying the intentions of the speaker or to referring to states of affairs outside the speaker.[23] Indeed it seems that neither the subjective nor the objective element should be given a privileged position in understanding what it is to know. Perhaps we have made some progress as well in moving toward a response to the question of this chapter. A direction is clear: faith needs to—and faith does, I believe—locate the knowing of God not in some magical third of God's own self or in faith's unique transport. Faith locates the knowing of God solidly in the reality of self and world.

How solidly? Sufficiently solidly? The question matters because at stake here is whether one will assent to a rather audacious set of propositions and, trusting them, commit one's life to a course of action. Does one know enough in faith to do that? Testimony on that question is divided. Many nontheists would perhaps grant that there are elements in their experience that do seem to support at least certain Christian claims concerning God.[24] Many Christians would grant that there are elements in their experience that conflict with their faith. Perhaps both parties know a very few persons whose piety seems at once sure and yet solidly human and natural. Such neither toil nor spin, and it surely seems that someone must care for them! But while we admire those saints and perhaps even envy them, we others, united in our dividedness, exercise our skeptical faculties toward a third group, those many others who loudly profess to know and love God with a single mind. We know that the human will can attach itself intensely to what is unreal and we do not take lack of self-doubt as a mark of human greatness.[25] There is doubt and disbelief around us and in us.

To recognize that in such a situation of division it is the will of the individual that must decide is not to abandon the opportunity to advise. A strong chorus of modern voices suggests that we know too little to act on our faith. In a famous passage John Locke writes:

> He that would seriously set upon the search of truth ought, in the first place, to prepare his mind with a love of it. For he that lovest it not, will not take much pains to get it; nor be much concerned when he misses it. There is nobody in the commonwealth of learning who does not profess himself a lover of truth; and there is not a rational creature that would not take it amiss to be thought otherwise of. And yet, for all this, one may truly say, there are very few lovers of truth for truth's sake, even amongst those who persuade themselves that they are so. How a man may know whether he be so in earnest, is worth enquiry: and I think there is this one unerring mark of it, viz., the not entertaining any proposition with greater assurance than the proofs it is built upon will warrant. Whoever goes beyond this measure of assent, it is plain, receives not truth in the love of it; loves not truth for truth's sake, but for some other by-end.[26]

The point is that wagers of faith, regardless of their specific outcomes, always tempt the self and others toward credulity. That is why Nietzsche, who knew as well as Pascal that the heart has its reasons the reason knows not of, urged emerging moderns to be "severe against their hearts."[27]

Will not such severity forbid Christian faith? After all, considering the range of the propositions Christian faith comprises and the claims upon life entailed, would not the modicum of assent that fits our divided minds seem insufficient by Christian standards? How can so frail a frame bear so heavy a burden?

Christians may attend to this concern by not claiming to have what we do not have: by not claiming our experience is less ambiguous than it is, by not claiming it is more emphatic than it is, by not claiming that the verdict of humankind is less divided than it is. Honesty on these matters may be rare enough and will amount to a significant response in itself. But the further question is how we should assess whatever we do seem to have. Here there may be a basis for a response other than the modern objection to belief. What is significant, then, is that the difference in response does not represent a different choice rooted only in circular fashion in faith's interiority, but a different reading of our common human situation in the world.

Two steps in this response may be distinguished. The first reaches back to a point suggested in the previous section, that we no longer find convincing the positivist assumption that the test of meaningful statements is the possibility of verification through accumulation of sense data. If self and world are too intimately connected to regard knowing as the correspondence between subjective ideas and objective reality, what does that suggest about how we may be certain that we know enough and confidently enough to act? What standards shall apply as we argue about how we know and about how much we know? Stephen Toulmin has suggested that criteria for argument are "field-dependent" and should not be dominated by the categories available in the luxurious cleanliness of formal syllogisms:

> When we ask how far the authority of the Court of Reason extends, therefore, we must put on one side the question how far in any field it is possible for arguments to be analytic: we must focus our attention instead on the rather different question, to what extent there are already established warrants in science, in ethics or morality, in law, art-criticism, character-judging, or whatever it may be. . . . The absence of entailments in the case of substantial arguments is not a sign of weakness but is a consequence of the problems they have to do with—of course there are differences between fields of argument, and the Court of Reason is able to adjudicate not only in the narrow field of analytic arguments.[28]

So how is argument to proceed in religious matters? Perhaps the difference will only be a matter of degree from the mode actually employed in the natural sciences. One finds in scientific method such elements as creative intuition in the formulating of a hypothesis, deductive testing of that hypothesis by particulars with an inductive direction attained in the movement to larger generalities.[29] Or religious argument may resemble the use of reason in the law, as John Wisdom has suggested:

> In such [courts of law] cases we notice that the process of argument is not a *chain* of demonstrative reasoning. It is a presenting and representing of those features of the case which *severally co-operate* in favour of the conclusion. . . . The reasons are like the legs of a chair, not the links of a chain. Consequently, although the discussion is *a priori* and the steps are not a matter of experience, the procedure resembles scientific argument in that the reason is not *vertically* extensive but *horizontally* extensive—it is a matter of the cumulative effect of several independent premises not of the repeated transformation of one or two.[30]

David Kelsey has shown that such elements of argument as data, backing, and warrant are in fact used very differently, depending on which theologian is "using Scripture."[31] But they are used! The Christian who attends to the reality of self-and-world knows, already before coming to faith's work of reflection, that no single standard or structure of argument applies universally. In this point there is opportunity for the Christian thinker. There still is obligation as well, for it is yet argument of which we speak.

The second step in the response to the modern pitting of prudence against belief is to observe that reality is not only complex, it is incomplete. The sense of temporality is often strong with regard to the subject, as when Newman urges that life is not long enough for a religion of inferences rather than assents,[32] but it needs to be emphasized with respect to much more than the self and its knowing. It is not merely because of how we know but because of what there is to know that Whitehead, for example, remarks that it may be more important that a proposition is interesting than that it is true.[33] If it does interest us it draws us efficaciously ahead into what is coming to be and grants us a role in that becoming as well. It is that role which William James wrote about so passionately in *The Will to Believe*. Given the unfinished character of the universe, there are reasons to defend the right to believe:

> When I look at the religious question as it really puts itself to concrete men, and when I think of all the possibilities which both practically and theoretically it involves, then this command that we shall put a stopper on our heart, instincts and courage and wait—acting of course meanwhile more or less as if religions were not true ... this command, I say, seems to me the queerest idol ever manufactured in the philosophic cave. Were we scholastic absolutists, there might be more excuse. If we had an infallible intellect with its objective certitudes, we might feel ourselves disloyal to such a perfect organ of knowledge in not trusting to it exclusively, in not waiting for its releasing word. But if we are empiricists, if we believe that no bell in us tolls to let us know for certain when truth is in our grasp, then it seems a piece of idle fantasticality to preach so solemnly our duty of waiting for the bell.[34]

There is a danger that we may be swept along uncritically by James's eloquence. It should be recalled that he limited his appeal to options that are "forced, momentous, and living." Moreover, in our choosing to believe, we participate in the becoming of reality, but we do not create that reality out of the nothingness of naked preference.[35] If the reality in whose becoming we participate is ethically a highly mixed affair, we may do well to retain a fair amount of the modernist caution to look before we leap. That being is more basic than nonbeing does not by itself dictate the counsel that assent is more needed than dissent.[36] I cannot therefore follow Newman's heady counsel:

> Of the two, I would rather have to maintain that we ought to begin with believing everything that is offered to our acceptance, than that it is our duty to

doubt of everything. The former, indeed, seems the true way of learning. In that case, we soon discover and discard what is contradictory to itself; and error having always some portion of truth in it, and the truth having a reality which error has not, we may expect, that when there is an honest purpose and fair talents, we shall somehow make our way forward, the error falling off from the mind, and the truth developing and occupying it.[37]

If we are not prepared to appeal to all these "if"s (error's portion of truth, truth's greater reality, honest purpose and fair talents in us), we must still ask, "Do we have as much as we need?" And our answer must be, "That depends." Modern skepticism invites not only modesty about our equipment for the journey of faith, but also about the schedule. My own experience may well lead me to identify with an organism of belief that is in a sense beyond me, one that contains affirmations that lack backing in my own—and perhaps even in all present—experience. But such identification does not close out the possibility that I may subsequently come to understand that this organism on the whole in fact moves against my experience. Indeed the identification requires that recognition. We are not done experiencing and we are not done interpreting experience. Perhaps I cannot specify in advance precisely what would count as a falsifying experience, but the complexity of reality does not keep me from being alive to the possibility of such experience.[38] If reality is not finished, then neither is the venture of faith. I may choose for the future now, but even now I know that in the future I will choose again and again.[39]

I have tried to attend to human concerns about knowing in a way that might commend itself to both theists and atheists. It has thus seemed possible to strike for common ground in a process that lies back before and even within the obviously disparate conclusions reached. But before we employ that process to move toward higher and more contested ground, a final question must be asked.

IS THIS KNOWN GOD SIMPLY SELF
AND WORLD?

In the first and second sections of this chapter we considered charges that Christian knowing of God is not properly selfish and not properly worldly. But of course the nontheist does recognize that self and world are involved in what goes on in Christian faith. What else is there, after all? Surely they are there, but not as they should be. That is, the nontheist believes that Christians misunderstand themselves and their world when they speak of knowing God. The mistake is, according to the critic, so grievous that the believer's relationship to self and world is not genuine knowledge. In faith one loses one's true sense of self and world—that is the double charge we have been examining. But the activity of belief *is* to be understood as a relationship between self and world. Religion's undoubted power can be understood if we recognize that what we meet here is not at all nothing—it is deep aspects of self and world in dramatic dress. So we move to consider the idea that the God known in faith is actually none other than self and/or world. Only such a suggestion can complete the critique of religion in two respects: (1) Here the errors of faith can not only be exposed but actually explained. Thus we move beyond a standoff of charge and countercharge. (2) Here the damage of religion can be undone, as the powers at work in distortion can be redirected for the good of all.

It is quite possible that what goes on in faith is such that it does not fit either how a self knows or how the world is known. And yet self and world might be seen to be the stuff of faith, even if knowing is not its structure. In this last difficulty faith should not suppose that it has dug its own grave by showing in response to the first objections that self and world are involved in the agency and structure of knowing God. For faith to retreat from that response would not be to advance to a God safely known apart from self and world, but to abandon any realistic claim to knowing.

Finally, it will not be helpful to declare triumphantly that the explanations—or more abrasively, the "reductions"—differ among themselves. The explanations of faith could all be correct, illumining different aspects of the Christian phenomenon. Only one need be correct for the faith to be in severe difficulty. Thus Christians need to attend to each of these views and ask about both their pertinence and their sufficiency. "Let us see what you find in faith and ask: Is it that? . . . Is it simply that?" The three approaches we shall consider here provide a pattern that could inform other particular conversations.

John Skorupski provides a useful summary of the "intellectualist" view, which aligns religion with magic as an effort to explain and control the world:

> [T]raditional religion pre-eminently takes the form of a cosmology whose basic explanatory category is that of *agency*: its pantheon of gods and spirits, whose actions have consequences in the perceptible world, can be invoked to explain why this rather than that event; and it affords a means by which men, through influencing the will of gods, can themselves hope to influence the course of events.[40]

The implication would seem to be that the human being who comes to realize there is no magic will soon leave belief in God behind as well. What, then, of the remarkable tenacity of belief? Skorupski notes that appeal can be made to the indefiniteness of religious predictions, the self-fulfilling power of its prophecies, and the fact that apparent successes always make a greater impact than failures do. Moreover, E. B. Tylor identifies other "blocks to falsifiability":

> In the first place, magico-religious rites are often combined with techniques, such as planting seed, which effectively bring about the desired results. Then, on other occasions they are performed to bring about events, e.g. successive stages in nature—cycles, which would have occurred in any case. In the third place, where a detectable failure does occur, it can be ascribed to an improper performance of the rite. And fourthly, it is not supposed by the traditional thinker that results are fully determined by the rite. . . . Other magical forces or spiritual agencies may always intervene.[41]

I pause to agree: the Christian religion does understand itself in such "intellectualist" and "cosmological" terms. So it will not do to claim that the charge fundamentally misidentifies the target. Rather Christians will need to speak clearly about how God acts in the world, about how faithful response to God makes a difference in that world, and about how such talk is not magic. We make a start on that agenda in chapters 5 through 7. There are additional objections. One such objection turns from the cosmos to the self, arguing that the practitioners of magic and/or religion block falsification so tenaciously precisely because they are dealing here with realities fundamental to human selfhood. It is, of course, Feuerbach and Freud who have been most influential in following this approach. While they differ markedly—Feuerbach finding a much more positive dynamic at work in human religion—they come together against Christian belief in a God who is other than the self.

In Freud's analysis of "the remarkable combination in religion of instruction, consolation and requirements" we have his own rather remarkable combination of an apparently historical explanation and a clearly psychological one, and of charges of illusion and delusion as well.[42] To attend to his most influential and most important critique will not require us to consider religion as the remorseful recollection/re-creation of the first father victim of the primal Oedipal horde. But we need to understand that Freud is making the point that the superego with its sense of an absolute origin of good and evil originates in a situation of weakness and dependence. In turn such accusation sets the stage for a message of consolation, as Paul Ricoeur has shown:

> Fundamentally, religion for him is not just an absolute sanction given to the requirements of conscience; . . . it is a compensation for the hardness of life. Religion in that sense has the highest function of culture; its task is to protect man against the superiority of nature and to compensate him for the sacrifices of instinct required by life in society. According to this interpretation the aspect

that religion presents to the individual is one of protection rather than prohibition. It appeals to desire rather than to fear.[43]

Religious belief is an illusion in that wish fulfillment is a prominent factor in its motivation. We recognize that we do not know such belief to contradict reality, as is the case with delusions. But we hardly can justify neutrality about our attitude.

For Feuerbach, not only the origin of faith but even its object is seen to be simply human:

> Religion, at least the Christian, is the relation of man to himself, or more correctly to his own nature. . . . The divine being is nothing else than the human being, or, rather, the human nature purified, freed from the limits of the individual man, made objective—i.e. contemplated and revered as another, a distinct being.[44]

Even in faith's seeming nay-saying it is human interest that is working.

> God acts, that man may be good and happy. Thus man, while he is apparently humiliated to the lowest degree, is in truth exalted to the highest. Thus, in and through God, man has in view himself alone. It is true that man places the aim of his action in God, but God has no other aim of action than the moral and eternal salvation of man: thus man has in fact no other aim than himself.[45]

Hence, Feuerbach can affirm religion insofar as it is a celebration of the splendor of the human:

> [W]e only separate the true from the false—though we grant that the truth thus separated from falsehood is a new truth, essentially different from the old. Religion is the first form of self-consciousness. Religions are sacred because they are the traditions of the primitive self-consciousness.[46]

But even religion is still alienation after a fashion, for while from the vantage point of a particular religion other faiths may be seen as idolatrous, one always "excepts one's own religion—and necessarily so, otherwise it would no longer be religion—from the fate, the common nature of all religions."[47] Thus:

> The necessary turning-point of history is therefore the open confession that the consciousness of God is nothing else than the consciousness of the species . . . that there is no other essence which man can think, dream of, imagine, feel, believe in, wish for, love and adore as the *absolute*, than the essence of human nature itself.[48]

What is it for Christians to attend to these analyses? Three tempting responses need to be resisted.

1. One might seek to point out that the Christian faith declines to identify God as human because that faith declines to identify God at all. Such a

response might get us free from Feuerbach's analysis, but it would do so at the price of freeing us from Christian faith. Feuerbach is right in arguing:

> But that which has no predicates or qualities, has no effect upon me; that which has no effect upon me has no existence for me.... To the truly religious man, God is not a being without qualities, because to him he is a positive, real being.[49]

Those Christians who speak of learned ignorance and the negative way are yet speaking of a God they know: "No person has ever seen God; the only Son who is in the bosom of the Father, he has made him known."

2. One might try to argue that what Feuerbach and Freud fail to recognize is not that we know God, but how we do so. Here the target would be Feuerbach's tendency to let his critique of abstract thought and the Hegel he once followed carry him into an I-Thou-encounter kind of understanding of knowing. In that view the otherness of what is known is easily collapsed into the subjectivity of the knower. But God is not so to be known![50]

This tactic too is to be resisted. Of course one could err by letting everything collapse into the self's cavernous creativity. But it would seem that the pertinent corrective would be not to exorcise God but to expand the human. We have already indicated that Christian faith needs to and does seek a world; indeed, it emerges within a nurturing social world of the church. But such a communal check on subjectivity is still emphatically human, whatever else it may be.

3. One might seek to place a more realistic value on the psychological benefit that plays a prominent role in Feuerbach's notion of projection and Freud's notion of illusion. It is a strange psychological benefit that leaves the self perilously poised before an absolutely free God, whose ways cannot be charted comfortably. Is this really a benefit that self-interest would seek? But such a response would not settle matters, since both Freud and Feuerbach encompass in their analyses Christian themes that appear to negate human worth. More important, for Christians it would hardly help to save God but lose the gospel that God is for us. Paul's confidence in Romans 8, for example, clearly depends on recognizing that nothing outside God or *within* God can separate us from God's love.

In resisting these strategies we are saying that everything the Christian faith claims to know about God is dependent upon a human knowing of a God who is irreversibly committed to the good of humankind. Do the analyses of Feuerbach and Freud then follow relentlessly? Perhaps not. The fact that faith is always human does not prove that it is only human. It does not, that is, unless the human being is some kind of self-contained substance that does not get beyond itself even in its most fundamental knowing.

Feuerbach's hectic eloquence moves from saying that (1) the human self can find the human species to be infinite, to saying that (3) the infinite found for and by the human person must be the human being itself, with a little help from (2) an identification of God as self-contained substance:

1. No being can deny itself, i.e., its own nature; no being is a limited one to itself.[51]
2. How couldst thou perceive the divine by feeling, if feeling were not itself divine in its nature? The divine assuredly is known only by means of the divine—God is known only by himself.[52]
3. Another nature than my own, one different in quality, cannot touch me.[53]

The Christian, I suggest, breaks this chain by contending that beings as decisively and qualitatively different from each other as God and human persons are nonetheless in relationship with each other. That relationship includes knowing.

Once a substance conception (whether of the divine or of the human) is set aside, the reductive analysis of the good news becomes merely one interpretation, not the obvious or privileged one. Our wishes do often mislead us. But so do our fears, not least the fear that news that is good is always also unreal. Moreover, it may well be that the egoistic circle is broken in the Christian understanding, when the self is "surprised by joy," even though the self surely returns in a reconstituted form. The joy itself turns out to entail a surprising suffering with others well beyond the boundary of the self. This seems a strange sort of self-interest, almost as if something other than the self were involved. The strangeness of this good news should not suggest that the believer must be hallucinating. Perhaps the Christian will always find the love of God to be mysterious, but that may witness more to the reality of sin-consciousness than to the inventive character of faith.

Such a response to Freud and Feuerbach does not constitute any kind of knockdown refutation. The decision about the cognitive reference and function of particular beliefs is genuinely open.[54] One brings their critique to bear on particular acts of belief, asking, "Is it that?" and often answers, "Yes." Then one asks, "Is it simply that?" A yes to the first question will not always be followed by a yes to the second.

Finally, we need to consider the suggestion that religious belief simply does not have a cognitive status. Look not, we are told, to the reference of belief, but to its function. Religion is, after all, something that people do. Talcott Parsons thus seeks to redirect our attention:

Ritual actions are not ... simply irrational, or pseudorational, based on pre-scientific erroneous knowledge, but are of a different character altogether and as such not to be measured by the standards of intrinsic rationality at all.[55]

It should be noted that this "symbolist" approach does not deny that the referent for religion is real. In his *Elementary Forms of the Religious Life* Emile Durkheim put this point with particular force:

> Thus religion acquires a meaning and a reasonableness. Its primary object is not to give men a representation of the physical world; for if that were its essential task, we could not understand how it has been able to survive, for, on this side, it is scarcely more than a fabric of errors. Before all, it is a system of ideas with which the individuals represent to themselves the society of which they are members and the obscure but intimate relations which they have with it. This is its primary function; and though metaphorical and symbolic, this representation is not unfaithful . . . for it is an eternal truth that outside of us there exists something greater than us, with which we enter into communion.[56]

Questions occur. Is ritual's role to express the social order, to maintain it, or just to refer to it? Is ritual belief given any independent recognition, or is it simply a rationalization of ritual action? Different answers occur. Yet there is clearly enough unity here to speak of gathered pressure from the approach, and the effect of that pressure is to subordinate the cognitive role of religion. In effect one is saying that religion, far from offering a cosmological map, clearly is doing something else. Must it not, then, seem simpler to eschew cognitive claims for religion, while gladly accepting the cement of religion for social values that need all the help they can get?

Whether it is good that religion exercises a cohesive function in society is a matter to be discussed in chapter 4. What must be said here is that both the Christian and the non-Christian have reason to be dissatisfied with this apparent compromise. The Christian will not deny borrowing *between* the social relations and the faith. Relationships of reinforcement and expression will be discerned. Yet, does not a striking gap remain between the two realities as they present themselves? It does not remove the gap to remark that the connection by which the cosmological manages to represent the anthropocentric or social is unconscious. The nonbeliever may join the believer in wondering whether the claim about the unconscious, which makes apparent deception to be fundamental truth, is not so speculative as to be unable to bear the crucial weight assigned to it.

Or the nonbeliever may wonder whether, on this view, it would not make sense to abjure cognitive pretense in religion. What then can remain? Can we continue in religion without constantly tempting ourselves and others to self-deception? Can faith and science somehow survive together in this smaller world? Durkheim agonizes over this point:

> [I]n so far as religion is action, and in so far as it is a means of making men live, science could not take its place, for even if this expresses life, it does not create

it; it may well seek to explain the faith, but by that very act it presupposes it. Thus there is no conflict except upon one limited point. Of the two functions which religion originally fulfilled, there is one and only one, which tends to escape it more and more: that is its speculative function.[57]

Durkheim recognizes that people "cannot celebrate ceremonies for which they see no reason" and that, hence, religion requires theory. Could religion reconstitute itself, then, in appropriate dependence upon the various sciences? Hardly, for faith must move to action, and the deliverances of the sciences are too slow in coming and too fragmentary in form. Faith will need to continue to make cognitive leaps but with a different set of instructions:

> Thus religions, even the most rational and laicized, cannot and never will be able to dispense with a particular form of speculation which, though having the same subjects as science itself, cannot be really scientific. . . . Ever since the authority of science was established, it must be reckoned with; one can go farther than it under the pressure of necessity, but he must take his direction from it. He can affirm nothing that it denies, deny nothing that it affirms, and establish nothing that is not directly or indirectly founded upon principles taken from it.[58]

The compromise still seems unstable. Apparently the difficulties with the delivery system of science's truth are merely tactical; the direction is sound. But why should one trust the accelerated pace of the pious, if it has nothing more on which to draw than science and yet exceeds what science itself can warrant?

Many writers candidly recognize that the logic of disjunction that controls our thinking must disrupt anguished attempts to arrange an uneasy coexistence for religion and science. Often that disjunction is given historical dress. Perhaps August Comte was simply more flamboyant than most in finding the three acts of the human spirit to be dominated by the increasing ascendancy of science. Religion comes to be seen as a form of, or at best a transition from, magic in the movement toward human maturity. There is something irreversible about history. Things are not going to be the same. Similarly, Don Cupitt finds that as moderns we simply do not think as traditional cultures did. It is time to "take leave of God."[59]

The Christian has reason to agree with such attacks on "business as usual" presumptions. The Christian has no place in the backwaters of religious history and will surely seek to avoid joining those who seem busy returning to where they have never been.[60] The Christian speaks of that which does not change in God, but the Christian also knows that self and world do change. We do not know God in some nonselfish and nonworldly third way, and so, for better or for worse, faith cannot simply remain the same. Indeed the Christian does not say this as a grudging concession, but claims it as a gracious opportunity. The Christian believes that God cannot be excluded from what is coming to be. Faith in God can even make some difference in the dawning of the future. Thus the Christian will be at pains to point out what differences it makes, for self and world, that God is and that we know and worship God.

3 TO ATTEND TO THE QUESTIONS CONCERNING BELIEF

Can This World of Faith Be True?

We must attend to concerns about what Christians claim to know. In doing so we have not, of course, left behind the topic of the knowing self. But we are, as it were, glancing back at the self from the vantage point of the content claimed in its knowing. We set aside for the time being the questions of how the believer gets to these propositions and what the effects of holding them are. Of what lies in between we ask, Can this world of faith be true?

The precise meaning of "true" is not specified in advance. In fact, one may detect more than one sense in which the term is used in the sections that follow. That is not a defensive tactic adopted to give those questioning the faith a moving target. Such plurality of reference rather is required for the human being to speak adequately of what it is to be true—even apart from the claims of faith. So, too, to ask if the world of faith is true turns out to be to ask several questions. The questions raised are serious precisely because the Christian lays claim to no unique theory of truth. To attend to them is complicated because the human conception of the way to the truth is itself manifold.[1]

CAN A WHOLLY OTHER GOD TOUCH ME?

We have already considered the claim that at least some Christian assertions about reality lay themselves open in principle to test by human experience outside and inside the community of faith. If such assertions are false, they can be shown to be false. That claim seems essentially correct, even if the process of checking is softer and more open-ended than some have supposed. Fundamentally, then, the Christian does accept the need to show how the faith fits within human experience, open-textured and ambiguous though that may be.

The first difficulty we face is not some specific instance of apparent noncorrespondence falling within an orderly framework in which believer and nonbeliever may agree that "you win some, you lose some." I refer, instead, to a matter that is first in such a way that nothing further might need to follow. It is the feeling that what the Christian faith talks about is simply so other, so different in kind from what we know as human beings, that it does not—it cannot—engage us. While this difficulty may seldom issue in explicit action against Christian faith, it does condition fundamental attitudes toward the faith. One such attitude seems to be a wistful weekend nostalgia for white-spired countrysides and Bible stories at the mother's knee. There may be a bemused tolerance for those who still seem to live there. One knows that one does not live there—one simply cannot, but one is not particularly angry about those who do. What cannot concern me cannot violate me. On the other hand, there may indeed be anger aroused by the fact that evangelists prey upon the innocent to seek further victims for this message of otherness. In this latter case one is hurrying ahead again to the consequences of the faith.

With respect to the content of faith itself I am seeking to attend here simply to that feeling of stupefaction that is shared by so many over it. Langdon Gilkey has rehabilitated Leibniz's term "compossible" to speak of this:

[I]t is the claim that, because there is a total disrelation of the concept to experienced actuality, the concept and its system are meaningless, or ... "not compossible" with our experienced world.[2]

This is the sort of development to which Peter Berger refers in speaking of a breakdown in the "plausibility structure" of Christian faith in the modern world.[3] The modern person is asking, "Can a wholly other God touch me?"

Take the attributes of God. We have already granted Feuerbach's point that a God without predicates is futile. What does faith, then, say of God? We are asked to begin with the thought of infinity from which other attributes quickly follow: incorporeality, eternality, immutability, impassibility, simplicity, omniscience, omnipotence.[4] What has such a One to do with me? What can I have to do with this One? These questions do not emerge in measured fashion from carefully weighed judgments. They come as the stark and seemingly inevitable recognition of a difference in worlds. While some human beings manage to speak of such a One, their talk for others of us seems simply not to connect with reality as we know it.

The issue here is not that these faith claims are taken to be contradictory. But at a prior stage these claims strike one as so strange, so bizarre, so "out of this world" that they really cannot be considered at all. When the two worlds are put together, one notices that God turns out to be "supreme." And yet human freedom is still defended, almost as if the theologian supposes that what does not touch cannot conflict. Thus Friedrich Schleiermacher writes:

> But the self-consciousness which accompanies all our activity, and therefore, since that is never zero, accompanies our whole existence, and negatives absolute freedom is itself precisely a consciousness of absolute dependence; for it is the consciousness that the whole of our spontaneous activity comes from a source outside of us. . . . But without any feeling of freedom a feeling of absolute dependence would not be possible.[5]

Or consider a theologian thought by others and himself to be dramatically opposed to Schleiermacher. Karl Barth writes of the creature:

> Its activity is still free, contingent, and autonomous. But God controls its activity in freedom no less than in necessity. The control of God is transcendent. Between the sovereignty of God and the freedom of the creature there is no contradiction. The freedom of its activity does not exclude but includes the fact that it is controlled by God.[6]

That supreme world may not touch us, but it does seek to impose itself upon the real world in which we live and die. Indeed, it comes into one's life precisely as an intruder. It fixes itself upon elements of one's living, externally and without touching one's own sense of what it is to be a human being alive in the world. Thus my living is claimed in a concept of ethics that at once dignifies some of my desires as duties, while at the same time divorcing me from others.[7] Alasdair MacIntyre has noted the "conceptual incommensurability" in current ethical debate caused by the taking of rival premises "such that we possess no rational way of weighing the claims of one as against another." We are dealing with mere fragments of conceptual schemes, parts that lack their needed contexts. We should not be surprised that moral argument is in disarray.[8]

Perhaps the sense of the futility of moral argument reflects our gnawing sense of the unreality of any God who could command us. Our harried disagreements bid to disguise, but instead reveal, our dawning sense of dumbfoundedness over any moral discourse that demands reality for itself.

Or our dying is claimed by this other world in an all too generous offer of eternal life. We are inclined to wonder, What could (not, does) eternal life mean for such as we are?[9] Is not "passing on" simply part and parcel of what we are? Yet we do not pass on, we simply pass. The end of life is just that. Wishing it otherwise only hinders a full appreciation of the preciousness of life. Passion, even for the unreal, carries consequences.

What if the person experiencing the "non-compossibility" of faith's world looks at those other people who apparently do not feel the unreality of the Christian faith? Some effort to understand these others is needed. One way is to recognize the beliefs of Christianity as simply the "lagging" of a past culture that is no more despite the presence of several survivors. One could exhort the survivors to "take leave of God" and enter the modern world.[10] Or one could simply shrug and say, Live and let live! I hardly need defend myself energetically against a God so wholly other that I cannot be touched! David Hume knew that and planted his tongue firmly in his cheek:

> We may conclude, that the Christian religion not only was at first attended with miracles, but even at this day cannot be believed by any reasonable person without one. Mere reason is insufficient to convince us of its veracity; and whoever is moved by faith to assent to it, is conscious of a continued miracle in his own person, which subverts all principles of his understanding, and gives him a determination to believe what is most contrary to custom and experience.[11]

As custom and experience continue to convince us that there is no magic, such careful condescension can be replaced by tolerant and amiable indifference.

The initiative for any conversation in this matter may well rest with Christians, since the "other side" is more inclined to let the dead bury their dead. The Christian must resist the tempting idea that the two worlds do not touch. One does not resist if one denies even the relation of opposition, or if one takes over what was thought to be the common ground of human language to say that only God is truly personal or only Jesus is truly human. Nor does one resist if in a final act of triumphal evasion one makes the phenomenon of human bewilderment a witness to the divine magnificence, as Hume's "true believer," Demea, does:

> The essence of that supreme Mind, his attributes, the manner of his existence, the very nature of his duration—these and every particular which regards so divine a Being are mysterious to men. Finite, weak, and blind creatures, we ought to humble ourselves in his august presence, and, conscious of our frailties adore in silence his infinite perfections which eye hath not seen, ear hath not heard, neither hath it entered into the heart of man to conceive.[12]

Today one who appeals to what is not seen, not heard, and not conceived may well be greeted with silence, but hardly with adoration.

But is not God wholly other? There is indeed an ontological difference between God and that which is not God, so that elements of awe, of surprise—of shock even—appropriately appear among the phenomena of the Christian religion. But this is not to speak of something that cannot touch me. I shall argue that in the dawning realization of the relationship to this One who is indeed radically other lies the potentiation of the self, not its immobilization or impoverishment. Faith speaks of a relationship with God. In this faith we do not jettison our ordinary humanity. Any God we can have, and any God worth having, must be in relationship with us as we actually are. Faith confesses a God who is in relationship with every part of us and with every one of us. It will not do to offer for this God a kind of bare coexistence with all, limiting the reality of relationship to the "knowing ones," the Christians. Non-Christians may not know this God, but in their relatedness they can do so. Their experience of non-compossibility cannot be ignored.

I have suggested that many modern persons respond to the brute fact of faith's otherness with mute tact. A conversation becomes difficult when too little is said as well as when too much is claimed. But if Christians attend to this difficulty sufficiently to permit the conversation to continue, and if non-Christians are willing to listen longer to this strange voice in order to hear more fully what is said, then other particular matters for discussion appear soon enough.

DOES THIS GOD'S TOUCH KILL?

Any human being who surmounts the experience of non-compossibility and faces the Christian claims concerning God will encounter this question. Such a person can be touched by the God that faith claims to represent. But what faith says about God and what experience teaches about suffering come together in the question "Does this God's touch kill?"

The question cannot be neatly tucked away in a tidy subsection of a chapter. In some of the tortuous attempts to "justify" God it seems the issue is essentially the one in the section just ahead—that of coherence. But this question also looks ahead to the next chapter in that it brings the claim of God into relationship with an awareness of what is good for humankind. There we ask whether the effects of believing are good. Here we ask whether the God described by Christian belief is good. This question of the good is basic. Even the concern for coherence, while logically prior, reaches ahead to the question of the good. In inquiring about faith's coherence we are asking about God's consistency. We are asking if God is reliable, loyal, steadfast. If faith's claims are true, the word of God is good in both senses.

In this question there is a vestige of the feeling of non-compossibility. At times when we experience evil we cry out, "Why, that's not possible!" or "That simply can't be!" What do we thus express? At least a clinging to our awareness of what the good is; that is not undone by our experience of suffering. There seems to be more: a will or at least a wish to go on with the good, and so a defiant revulsion at the evil we are experiencing.

Well, why "can't it be"? Perhaps our protest is not to be understood merely in terms of our relative innocence and the apparent unfairness of disproportionate suffering.. Perhaps implicit in such reactions is a visceral entertaining of the Christian faith's claim that God works powerfully for the good. The Christian faith, by its witness to the goodness and power of God, invites this sense of outrage and accusation. The unbeliever responds, If your God is real, what do you say about suffering? By the logic of faith one speaks of God as someone who is other, someone "more," someone radically different from the commerce and convention of self and world. Where in reality would such a One, not non-compossible but definitely "other," be apt to be found? Robert Scharlemann speaks for many of us in identifying what in our time seems to occasion such questions:

> No single series of occurrences in the twentieth century has so demanded a second language besides that of human agents, intentions, and actions as has the Holocaust. What happened cannot be adequately told by a narrative whose subjects are human beings, political forces, and national entities. Something "supranormal" occurred. But it is not clear what that second language can be. Some authors (Richard Rubenstein, for example) think it calls for the negation of theological language: that is to say, it does call for saying something about God but what it calls for is that God was not there and perhaps is not at all.[13]

It is not clear. What does the experience of evil say to us of God? How may we pay attention to it? While keeping the focus of this century's experience before us, we may do well to start with a statement of objection that is broader, even if less intense. Suppose we say that evil is what human beings have done. But would not faith find this freedom itself to be, at bottom, God's doing? Given freedom's evil fruit, what shall we say of such a God? Bertrand Russell did not hesitate to answer. His tone seems one more of amusement than of anger:

> Is there not something a trifle absurd in the spectacle of human beings holding a mirror before themselves, and thinking what they behold so excellent as to prove that a cosmic purpose must have been aiming at it all along? ... Would not a world of nightingales and larks and deer do better than our human world of cruelty and injustice and war? ... If I were granted omnipotence, and millions of years to experiment in, I should not think man much to boast of as the final result of all my efforts.[14]

On Russell's view God is not so much malevolent as incompetent. Christians will not recognize their God in such a picture. But Christians surely share the experience of evil and feel its force. The language of lament is theirs. Who is this God against whom theists and atheists alike cry out? The experience of evil is indeed an effective interlocutor. Thus David Hume's Philo tightens the screws to state the alternatives:

> Is he willing to prevent evil, but not able? then is he impotent. Is he able, but not willing? then is he malevolent. Is he both able and willing? whence then is evil?[15]

How does the existential equation end for us? What do God and evil equal?

For some the equation ends in the welling up of the will in revolt. The equation is just that: God equals evil. Dostoyevsky's Ivan makes clear that it is precisely God and the world together, God's world, that must be rejected:

> Yet would you believe it, in the final result I don't accept this world of God's, and although I know that it exists, I don't accept it at all. It's not that I don't accept God, you must understand it's the world created by Him I don't and cannot accept.... It's not God that I don't accept, Alyosha, only I most respectfully return Him the ticket.[16]

Respect aside, this will do well enough for atheism, for here one will not worship God in this world. If it is God who writes this world's story, then surely the tale is a tragic one. The empirical episodes and features of the faith come together to tell us this. The faith tells us that to speak of sin is to speak of what we, tragically, cannot avoid. Do not the outrageous paragraphs of the theologians concerning predestination simply make the fateful implications of the faith explicit? Even the lucky chosen might well reflect on the mechanism of their deliverance. Is not the alleged remedy another tragic instance, if we have here the "hopelessly carnivorous God" who requires his pound of flesh in a very bloody sacrifice?[17] One may not stay to fill out the logic; it is still largely the searing sense of non-compossibility of which we speak here. But one simply knows that while one cannot leave the planet, one will—one must—return faith's entrance ticket to God's world. One will not live here on faith's terms. One cannot leave, but one need not worship God.

Others speak of the shattering of confidence in God. The Jewish novelist Arthur Cohen has spoken of the Holocaust as a "caesura" in which evil "subscends" to shatter any confidence in the eternality of the relationship of the Jew to God.[18] Who can wonder that it is a Jew who leads the way here? But why should not the rest of us follow? This world makes no sense any more. Meaning had been measured on a moral scale. The only truth now seems to be that the impossible, the incredible, has taken place.

It is not strange that people deny that the Holocaust happened, that evil happens. To speak of anyone whose word is good—true, reliable, potent, trustworthy—is this not to deny evil? But we cannot deny evil. If we do not attempt that, perhaps at least we can think evil through to its consequence and recognize that the light of the ancestral faith has gone out.

Jürgen Moltmann observes that in this case one is taking the cosmological or teleological argument at its word. What does one see if one holds up the mirror of evil? The images, he notes, vary:

> [G]od as deceiver, executioner, sadist, despot, player, director of a marionette

theatre—or it introduces the images of the sleeping, erring, bored, helpless and clownish God. "I would not want to be God at the present moment."[19]

Who will want to join the Christian faith in confessing, praising, and worshiping God? How can one do so? Does not this God's touch kill?

What can Christians do to attend to this cry as it rises up around and within the church? Christians cannot deny that evil is real. Redefinition does not get faith beyond the fact of evil. Of course atheist and theist will agree that to speak of evil is to make a human judgment. But it will not do for the theist to make a defense out of this description, muttering something about God's ways not being our ways. Together we experience what we do not doubt to be evil. Many theists have recognized atheists as colleagues in knowing and doing the human good. It is not seemly for the theist to refuse to stand with the atheist in the identification of evil. Faith's perspective must "correspond with" our condition. It must connect with our condition, with our cosmos, even as it creates changes in what we see and what there is to be seen.

The very enormity of the Holocaust at once establishes the indubitable reality of evil and blocks the path to the classical evasions that have tempted the people of faith. Perhaps few were ever fully persuaded by appeals to reduce evil to appearance: evil as contrast or as challenge or as condition for sympathy, and the like. Those who know this century's history cannot even consider such subterfuges. Without denying that good can come *after* evil, that is, in response to evil, one simply must reject the idea of good's coming *out of* evil—as if in the very long view life is proceeding according to divine purpose and by divine providence.

What, then, can faith say of God in the face of evil? It remains for the Christian to take evil the more seriously by granting that the experience of evil is shared not only by atheist and theist alike, but—on faith's reading— even by God. Evil is something that is done to God. It is not only so in special diabolical instances: that would lead to the dramatic trivialization of the experience. This recognition of God's experience of evil must not itself be trivialized by qualification. The faith cannot have it both ways here—as when it is said that evil occurs, even for God, because of God's self-limitation, but that triumph over evil is always possible, since God can annul such self-limitation.[20] The idea of annulment of self-limitation may be incoherent; certainly it is an insult to the victim who cries, "How long?"

In the presence of evil faith struggles to speak by looking back to origin and ahead to outcome. To the degree that we know evil not only as victims but as perpetrators we may manage to speak of its origin "Adamically" in accents of personal responsibility. But as the sense of responsibility blends with that of inevitability we seem drawn to that metaphor which speaks of a primordial struggle.[21] Evil now seems that well established, that full of power and being. In any case it is clear that we can only make sense of life as a fight. We do battle here with evil, even if this requires, often enough, that we do battle with ourselves.

Since battles are won, will we speak of God's victory when we speak of the outcome of evil? After all, an ineffective God would seem to be no God at all. Yes, faith will seek a way to speak of God availing in the experience of evil, but easy talk of triumph will not do. God is to be understood in the battle and nowhere else. God is not withdrawn, waiting to intervene when things get just a little tougher. God is not out ahead, waiting for evil to spend itself or for it to acquire sufficient strength to be an interesting, if yet inevitably ineffective, combatant. The outcome issues from what is here. Thus, faith struggles to speak of a God who is suffering here, but of one who is still God in that suffering. It follows its vision of the one lifted up on a cross as one who can draw all to himself; it speaks of the crucified God as "a God who can help."[22] Insofar as faith finds some such way to speak of God's suffering it finds a way to speak of human suffering. Thus, it seeks to speak of human suffering, including the voluntary suffering of Christians and others, as something more promising than a painfree haze. Yet it does not believe its message to be an invitation to masochism.[23]

I hope here to have heard and stated the charge with sufficient force that my later discussion of faith's commendations cannot ignore it. There are other issues concerning the world of faith that require attention as well. These concerns may be expressed in quieter tones, but they are in their own way as fundamental as those that prompt the questions of theodicy. They go to the issue of the very meaningfulness of faith's claims. They would solve faith's special problem with evil by dissolving the faith itself.

DOES THIS GOD MAKE SENSE?

I wish to distinguish, but not separate, two charges: (1) The individual assertions of faith do not come together to make coherent sense. (2) The individual assertions in themselves offend against common sense, against what we otherwise find to be sensible to say about ourselves and our world. The first charge questions the intelligibility of the faith as a body of propositions, while the second disputes the acceptability of the members of the body even when disconnected from each other.

Instances of incoherence are readily suggested. Is the very word "God" used by Christian theologians in such a confusing variety of ways, exhibiting "radically incompatible logics," that no claim emerges to be considered?[24] Are we done that early? Or does the dramatic form of the query "How can

three be one?" only disguise the fact that Christian speech fails to understand "person" in a sufficiently coherent way that the disputants can agree
that it is three _____s about which they are arguing?[25] Such questions suggest
that faith can hardly begin to talk about its subject, for the subject itself—
God or the triune God—seems to slip from its grasp. But perhaps this is too
severe. After all, many who do not themselves affirm the existence of God
do grant the Christian sufficient conceptual credit to allow the presentation
of, say, the doctrine of God. But perhaps the end is no better than the
beginning, for within and between the sentences of such speaking incoherence rules.

Consider the attributes of this God. The point here is not that God is so
beyond us as to be non-compossible for us. Rather God is not possible for
God; the concept collapses in on itself in contradiction. This difficulty
cannot be dismissed by smoothly saying to the questioner, Your God is too
small. It surely is in praise of the grandeur of God, for example, that one sets
out in faith to say such things as: (1) God is active, indeed does all things,
(2) God knows all things, and (3) God is timeless. All three statements are
made in praise of one God; they are made together. But Nelson Pike is surely
not the only one to wonder how the third statement can stand with the other
two:

> It is not at all obvious that a timeless individual can be consistently charac-
> terized as having *any* creative power, let alone creative power that is unlimited
> or "infinite." We must add that there appears to be no obvious way of under-
> standing the idea that a being existing "outside of time" sustains or preserves
> the temporally extended universe of objects. . . . It may be that the real problem
> is not whether a timeless individual could have foreknowledge of the future, but
> whether a timeless individual could have knowledge of anything at all.[26]

It will not suffice to dismiss the notion of timelessness as something
acquired through the "stylishness" of the Platonic, or as a product of the
association of the helpful notion of substance and the harmful one of
immutability.[27] Other descriptions of God bid to reinstate the contradiction
in his nature. How do we identify God as personal? Have we not come to
understand that persons are known through actions that are publicly discernible?[28] Or, putting the question of knowledge to the side, are we saying
in faith that God as Spirit is a disembodied person? Does God act (however
we come to identify such action) without occupying space and time?[29]

Enough examples are at hand to analyze the nature of the difficulty. Such
talk seems incoherent because it seems to use terms in a way radically
different from the way in which we use them in our ordinary discourse. In
that discourse to say about anything the several things that faith says about
God would be to fall into self-contradiction. Christian faith does not—and

should not, theist and atheist can agree—settle for a schizophrenic coexistence between its assertions and those of the nontheist. It claims to speak of the very reality in which the nontheist lives, and so somehow what it says must be related to the nontheist's description of reality. The relationship between the two descriptions seems to be one of genuine opposition. The faith seems actively to challenge the nontheist's understanding of how things are with us and our world.

To take one of the concrete examples cited earlier, to speak of God's omnipotent action seems to be an alternative way of understanding what goes on in the universe. But is it a more correct understanding? This example illustrates the disjunctive character of faith's logic. Or, if speaking of God's omnipotent action is interpreted as offering an explanation on a different level from explanations in terms of specific causes, in what way does it explain anything at all? What is it to be an explanation, but not an explanation in terms of specific causes? Does saying "God acts omnipotently" merely decorate our drab sense of causality or express our attitudes toward the way things run their relentless course in our lives? We have already said that Christians do not seem prepared to drop back to understanding their talk in such noncognitive ways. In sum, does not the incoherent application of ordinary meanings in religious talk uncover for us the fact that the world of faith contradicts our common sense about reality?

The contradictions are complicated. Christian faith does not seem prepared to speak of God's omnipotent action as a general and presumably nondiscriminating explanation of events we otherwise understand by our ordinary notion of causality. Christians want to hold something back, almost as if faith senses that it would lose in winning the point that God is another—the true—way of speaking of what we all already know. Thus certain special actions are distinctively, especially, claimed for God. To put it rather too baldly, then: the appeal to God's general agency and the appeal to God as special agent both rival our ordinary explanations, though the second appeal may seem to accommodate them in order to gain sufficient support for its own distinction from the first. In any case faith seems to say both things. But the two things do not cohere well, as Don Cupitt has observed in noting the troubled quest of each for the other:

> So here is the paradox! We need the little interventionist God to give personal qualities to the universal God and to stop him from fading into emptiness and vacuity. Conversely, the lawlike cosmic God is needed to give breadth and universality to the little interventionist God and stop *him* from declining into a fantasy guardian spirit. But the two deities, the big one and the little one, are quite different from each other. They presuppose different cultural backgrounds, different overall views of the cosmic order and how it is maintained,

and different views of God's relation to man. Neither view of God will do on its own. They need each other—and yet they do not go well together.[30]

Perhaps one thing the two views have in common is that they set God over against human beings, inviting—alternately—passive acceptance of one's destiny and impassioned pleas for particular providence. For many moderns the strains of these convoluted conceptual maneuvers are too much to bear. It is sensible, in Cupitt's words, to "take leave of God."

The practice of prayer illustrates the tensions we have been considering in the doctrine of God. How is prayer to be understood? In its most aggressive petitionary form does not prayer seek a suspension of the causality by which our world runs? Why does the request for a miracle not undercut the petitioner's confidence in cause and effect?[31] In its mildest form, on the other hand, prayer seeks no special service but still seems to demean human agency by thanking God for what seems to be quite the ordinary run of things. In between these extremes lies all manner of compromise.

The Christian doctrine of the incarnation presents similar difficulties. In talk of "God becoming human," what we say of God and what we say of the human are said problematically of one person.[32] Even the hymn writer declares, "I know not how the Bethlehem babe could in the Godhead be!" Are God and space-time understood in such a way that divine incarnation in a specific spatial-temporal being is possible? Is such even needed, for that matter? Even if Christian faith gets the divine and the human together by declaration, as it were, does it not show its awareness of the difficulty— while also creating another one—by speaking of the human nature of this Jesus as impersonal? It hardly helps to say, for example, that the Chalcedon council was not so much defining a positive formula as determining the boundaries of orthodoxy. To say this seems to imply that a quite splendid range of clear alternatives abides within those boundaries. But what conception at all can dwell coherently there? How can the two natures in this one person at once be "without confusion, without change, without division, without separation?"[33]

And how does the "manger child bring God's life to me"? Is the fact that the church has mustered no particular official dogmatic teaching of "the work of Christ" not of more than historical significance? If we are told that within these changing faces there is still a family identity to be found, we may suppose that candidates for conceptual consideration are coming into view. But difficulties abound and it is not clear that adding views, and so difficulties, really helps. Is God buying off God? Is the One with all power winning a battle over forces whose power remains to be explained? Is God the great teacher giving instruction so persuasive as to be coercive? What of the resurrection? Does faith make available a coherent statement about the resurrected state of Christ, such that one is not talking, for example, of a disembodied soul? Granting that, if the hope is to be for us, how does it not deny our worldly experience of the finality of death? Granting that too, how can the simplicity of heaven (or hell) heed the moral complexity of our tangled lives?[34]

In introducing this section I mentioned concerns spoken in quieter tones. But these last paragraphs seem to be shouting, This God makes no sense! How may Christian faith hear this cry and still speak of knowing God? To begin, the theologian must resist playing as a trump card the nonobjectifiability of God. One must come clean: Are knowledge claims being asserted in the faith? If not, many questions are swept away, of course, but one then wonders what point there is to the educational mission of the churches. Surely God does not become nonobjectifiable only when persons put questions about the sense of the curriculum's claims. If there are knowledge claims being advanced at all, it must be fair to ask how and whether these claims make sense together and for us.

Thus it is appropriate to ask about the internal coherence of the faith. The term "God" is understood and used by Christians not merely as a name but as a concept that can be analyzed. An appeal to revelation cannot answer questions about the meaning or analysis of the concept. Once the truth has been happily revealed to us, the question remains: What does it mean? Instances of direct self-contradiction and instances of the fundamental incoherence of basic notions cannot be ignored by reflective Christians. Part of the complaint in this section has been that the church's teaching precisely contradicts common human experience. The theologian may well be driven back to the originating source of Christian doctrine in the lives of the faithful and inquire whether mistakes have been made either in formulating or in coordinating particular "first order" realities of the life of faith.

I have been arguing that the Christian is committed to the quest for intelligibility. Others do not agree. Consider, for example, Newman's assertion: "It is possible to apprehend without understanding."[35] Does such a distinction permit us to get on with the quest for coherent understanding or does it provide us with an alibi to evade that responsibility?

Similarly, appeals to paradox may serve as an alibi. To be justified such appeals must point beyond themselves to the disclosure of coherent truth rather than leave the human mind divided against itself.[36] Paradox so understood does not rebuff the understanding but engages it and draws it on toward something that has not yet been seen. Kierkegaard, for example, was not reluctant to speak of paradox, but his use of the term looks to the disclosure anticipated:

So the believing Christian not only possesses but uses his understanding, respects the universal human ... but in relation to Christianity he believes against the understanding and in this case also uses understanding ... to make sure that he believes against the understanding. Nonsense therefore he cannot believe against the understanding, for precisely the understanding will discern that it is nonsense and will prevent him from believing it; but he makes so much use of the understanding that he becomes aware of the incomprehensible, and then he holds to this, believing against the understanding.[37]

Faith uses understanding to think the terms of the paradox as clearly as possible and then to think through them to the "incomprehensible," which verily is not nonsense. That it is not nonsense will need to be shown.

Similarly, theological speech in its content must be related to what we commonly take to be sensible speech about ourselves and our world. To relate the two is not to reduce the one to the other, as surely as the identities themselves do not dissolve into a pantheistic, materialistic, or humanistic mush. But God's transcendence does not refer to a being neatly separable from the struggles to understand self and world. Rather, God's transcendence is to be understood not in remoteness but in relationship. If God is in relationship it would seem that God is something and thus not everything or nothing. Thus the theologian will be invited to seek *discriminate* speech about God and God's action, such that the hearer is not faced with the dilemma of considering God-talk in relation to self-and-world talk either as the only real descriptive talk or as only decorative "depth." In this time more than a few are prepared to make a choice, or at least they are unable to manage the splendor of "two track" or "double agent" talk. And Occam's razors are not in short supply.

This is not to suggest that those who object to God-talk on behalf of what they take to be common sense about self and world are in a position to tell Christians what Christ means. I have simply been following out the implications of the Christian claim that the word is for all of us and, moreover, it is about who we are and where we are. If that word of God speaks to us of self and world, faith needs to consider how that speaking is related to other such self and world talk and it cannot presume that the relationship is one of disjunction. To speak of a correspondence between the two may be to claim too much, if that suggests that finality and completeness characterize our knowledge and speaking of self and world. But if correspondence refers instead to the living activity by which we can interact toward the goal of understanding, then that term does call us together.

Will this conversation, in Wittgenstein's phrase, "leave everything as it was"? For that matter, some have said something of that sort of the faith itself. Is it worth knowing or believing?

IS THIS GOD IRRELEVANT?

If Christians are right about God, what difference does such a God make in the universe? What difference does knowing about such a God make? What difference does believing in such a God make? At bottom the question is, What is at stake in the claim that God is?

I do not ask this question of those views that grant that their descriptions of God do not make sense. Such views refuse to reduce reality to anything that could be either relevant or irrelevant. Such a God could hardly be dismissed. God might be a being who, for example, could be in the early stages of totally reconstituting how we think and so, presumably, how we are. Such a God might be accurately described in what we would regard as incoherent descriptions. Such a God might make nonsense of all our ordinary descriptions of reality. Such a God could not be dismissed, but could also not be considered. Our question does not fit such a God.

Such a God does not fit Christian faith any better. Christians speak of God in relationship to that which is not God. In relationship there is distinction, and thus the possibility and the need for discriminate speech about God is given. We have spoken not only of God's acting toward the other but of God's undergoing the other. There can no longer be any doubt that the notion that has been emerging is of a limited God. This God is limited logically so that the law of contradiction applies, yielding the possibility of intelligible talk of God. But this God is limited ontologically as well, so that the possibility is given of correspondence between talk of God and talk of that which is not God. Sensible talk of God and sensible talk of self and world can come together because God, self, and world are together. Self and world are in relationship with God, and as such they are not God. But they do, precisely as such, limit God. Of such a God one may well ask, Is this God religiously irrelevant?

In chapter 5 I will attempt to characterize the kind of being who fits the human capacity for worship. But even here it must be granted that some kind of absoluteness is required. It will take some showing to indicate that a limited absoluteness—a "relative absolute"—is not a contradiction in terms. The heart of the objection may be more religious than logical. Perhaps Hume's "true believer," Demea, puts this point well for us in reacting to Cleanthes' espousal of the finite architect God who emerges from the design argument at Hume's hand:

> It must be a slight fabric, indeed, ... which can be erected on so tottering a foundation. While we are uncertain whether there is one deity or many, whether the deity or deities, to whom we owe our existence, be perfect or imperfect, subordinate or supreme, dead or alive, what trust or confidence can we repose in them? What devotion or worship address to them? What veneration or

obedience pay them? To all the purposes of life the theory of religion becomes altogether useless. . . .[38]

Among the faithful are many who share Demea's worries. Thus in his massive study *God in Exile* Cornelio Fabro comes upon Alfred North Whitehead's finite God and finds here "apodictic proof of the radical despair into which modern thought has fallen" in an effort to avoid a total sellout to Marxist and existentialist historicism.[39]

Not everyone agrees with gloomy pronouncements concerning orthodoxy's insularity and resulting irrelevance. Indeed some have claimed that the high God of Christianity is precisely the only relevant God—that is, the only God before whom it is possible to go on with life in this world. Consider Dostoyevsky's Krillov and his testimony to the bearing of knowledge that a God exists with such a "nonrelational" attribute as self-will:

I can't understand how an atheist could know that there is no God and not kill himself on the spot. To recognize that there is no God and not to recognize at the same instant that one is God oneself is an absurdity, else one would certainly kill oneself. If you recognize it you are sovereign, and then you won't kill yourself, but will live in the greatest glory. But one, the first, must kill himself, for else who will begin and prove it? Now I am only a god against my will and I am unhappy, because I am *bound* to assert my will. . . . I am awfully unhappy, for I'm awfully afraid. Terror is the curse of man. . . . But I will assert my will, I am bound to believe that I don't believe. I will begin and make an end of it and open the door, and will save.That's the only thing that will save mankind and will re-create the next generation physically, for with his present physical nature man can't get on without his former God, I believe. For three years I've been searching for the attribute of my godhead and I've found it: the attribute of my godhead is self-will! That's all I can do to prove in the highest point my independence and my new terrible freedom. For it is very terrible. I am killing myself to prove my independence and my new terrible freedom.[40]

Dostoyevsky finds that knowing precisely the God who is other makes a difference. It is not so much what God does, as who God is, that matters. That there is this God marks a measure for everything else. Very well, but the Christian faith claims that this very God is with us and for us. Does that compromise the otherness of God? Must God withdraw in order to be really God for us? If that is so, why is it so? Is it that when God is understood in relationship—that is, when God is understood—the vacuity of the claims is uncovered? Is it that then God is emptied, so that nothing, or not enough at least, follows from the reality of God? Or is a third way to be found? Can a concept of a God who is truly in relationship with us and truly worthy of worship by us be coherently presented? Later I will attempt to describe such a God, the God—I believe—that the Christian faith commends.

In the meantime it is clear that faith in that God makes a difference.

Whether it simply draws its efficacy from a real God it confesses, or whether it adds its own power to God's, or whether it makes much, for good or ill, out of exactly nothing is not the question in this case. Whichever it is, believers and nonbelievers will agree that believing affects the life of the believer and so the lives of others. What were Krillov's words? Terror, fear, survival, freedom—yes, that is the territory on which the wars of faith are fought.

4 TO ATTEND TO THE QUESTIONS CONCERNING BELIEVING AND BELIEF

Can Faith's Efficacy Be Good?

We would seem to be on at least somewhat solid ground here. At any rate we are on the ground. However one may fathom the self's project as it sets about in faith to know, whatever sense or nonsense one may find in the wondrous world that the believing self claims to know, it is clear to all that such activities make some difference here on earth. They have effects on the believer and beyond the believer. All who are thus affected may well evaluate the effects and so their causes.

I proceed with this chapter with the understanding that such evaluation is natural and pertinent. One might object to the way in which I so quickly link the experience of effect and the possession of capacity to evaluate effect. That link is rejected by two groups.

First, some theologians argue that while human ethical insight applies between human persons, God's ways—and so, apparently, faith in those ways—submit to no such standard. I disagree. I would surely grant that faith finds that the knowledge of God has a kind of independence about it such that it brings its own distinctive weight to bear on our consideration of what is good for humankind. Thus faith will make its own active contribution to the discussion of whether the effects of faith are themselves good. But while faith contributes to the complex process by which we understand the good, it does not control it. Nor can the exercise of evaluation with respect to faith's effects be assigned simply to faith, as if we had here another instance of the police investigating themselves. It will not do to suggest that ordinary human beings can assess governments but not churches. Thus human beings, whether or not they are believers, may appropriately ask and answer the question, Is faith's efficacy good? In chapters 5 and 6 I shall argue that this human capacity ultimately depends upon God's gift and even that there is gain for the activity of evaluation in knowing that. But one can very well know how to proceed in evaluation, and do so, without knowing of such an ultimate grounding.[1]

Second, there are others who look this theological gift horse in the mouth. If ethical judgments are not understood to be fit candidates for evaluation, theological permission for ethical evaluation will not be particularly pertinent. Thus Alasdair MacIntyre traces the collapse not only of Christian moral philosophy but also of the Enlightenment's effort to justify ethics, to the disappearance of the notion of essential human purposes and functions in an emerging "emotivist" culture.[2] What shall the Christian make of this? Does the theologian here have cause to celebrate the fact that at last the reality of finitude and sin is becoming clear? I would rather say that human beings may lack an orienting ground to which they can refer in evaluating ethical judgments. The framework may erode, leaving the ethical judgments stranded. If one must talk about them, one will speak of something like arbitrary choice or equally irrational emotion. But the sense of the good, the experience of good and perhaps especially of evil—the first-order realities upon which ethical judgment depends—last rather longer than our formal understandings of them do. Perhaps that is why MacIntyre can himself proceed with his rather ambitious effort to reconstruct an ethic "after virtue." And that may be why Simone de Beauvoir manages to speak for many other existentialists who insist that judgments may indeed be ambiguous, but they are not absurd.[3]

I have here more asserted than argued the point of human capacity to evaluate the efficacy of faith. I hope theists and nontheists together will find in this chapter and the chapters to follow that the assertion seems reasonable and worthwhile in its results. Before proceeding, I add a caution to this expression of confidence: an evaluation of the efficacy of faith is not enough for a final judgment on faith. This is no last minute retraction on the part of the niggardly theologian who senses that too much ground may have been yielded. In all its speech about God, the Christian faith never leaves the reality of the human. But even on that solidly human ground it needs to be recalled that this chapter is the third of three dealing with human concerns about the faith. Precisely what the relationships and priorities are among the three areas thus considered remains a question. Moreover, that question will take on further complexity when the Christian theologian seeks not only to attend to these human concerns but also to commend a specifically Christian witness, including some self-understanding of faith's bearing on life. Thus, the human evaluation of faith can neither be confined to this chapter nor completed after these three. It will need to be continued as the human being who is Christian speaks. But it can proceed.

DOES THIS FAITH FULFILL THE SELF?

Not everyone thinks so. Erich Fromm found plausible the need for what he called "a framework of orientation and devotion." But while a "humanistic religion" in which God "is the image of man's higher self" could thus be supported, he was sharply critical of Christianity's advancement of "authoritarian religion." Extensive quotation can be justified, since it permits us to feel the bite of his concern:

> God becomes the sole possessor of what was originally man's: of his reason and his love. The more perfect God becomes, the more imperfect becomes man. He projects the best he has onto God and thus impoverishes himself. Now God has all love, all wisdom, all justice—and man is deprived of these qualities, he is empty and poor. He had begun with the feeling of smallness, but he now has become completely powerless and without strength; all his powers have been projected onto God.

And the effect is to deny what is healthy and strong in the self:

> When man has thus projected his own most valuable powers onto God, what of his relationship to his own powers? They have become separated from him and in the process he has become *alienated* from himself. Everything he has is now God's and nothing is left in him. *His only access to himself is through God.* In worshipping God he tries to get in touch with that part of himself which he has lost through projection. After having given God all he has, he begs God to return to him some of what originally was his own. But having lost his own he is completely at God's mercy. He necessarily feels like a "sinner" since he has deprived himself of everything that is good, and it is only through God's mercy or grace that he can regain that which makes him human. And in order to persuade God to give him some of his love, he must prove to him how utterly deprived he is of love; in order to persuade God to guide him by his superior wisdom he must prove to him how deprived he is of wisdom when he is left to himself.

The Christian may be tempted to counterattack quickly, insisting that this century's dark history hardly confirms the supposition that the sense of sin and evil is but the psychic debt incurred in the self's investment in projection. Fair enough, perhaps; but it still remains to ask what the effect is of a Christian's—from whatever motivation—saying things like "I am the chief of sinners" and "Nothing in my hands I bring. . . ." Fromm's point is that to deny worth is to destroy worth in a circle that is indeed vicious:

> But this alienation from his own powers not only makes man feel slavishly dependent on God, it makes him bad too. He becomes a man without faith in his fellow men or in himself, without the experience of his own love, of his own power of reason. As a result the separation between the "holy" and the "secular" occurs. In his worldly activities man acts without love, in that sector of his life which is reserved to religion he feels himself to be a sinner (which he actually is, since to live without love is to live in sin) and tries to recover some of his lost humanity by being in touch with God. Simultaneously, he tries to win forgiveness by emphasizing his own helplessness and worthlessness. Thus the attempt to obtain forgiveness results in the activation of the very attitude from

which his sins stem. He is caught in a painful dilemma. The more he praises God, the emptier he becomes. The emptier he becomes, the more sinful he feels. The more sinful he feels, the more he praises his God—and the less able is he to regain himself.[4]

In chapter 2 we noted the claim that the allegedly cognitive activities of the Christian lack the uncertainty and tentativity we associate with knowing. What is the effect of making knowledge claims in this way? Worse, perhaps, than the probable error about God is the certain deception of the self. Is not the cult's blatant "heavenly deception" of the targeted convert an ironic revelation of its own substantive self-deception? Do not bizarre fringe groups feature only the more dramatically that which is to be found within the core of the religious community? Friedrich Nietzsche did not aim his attack merely at the obvious "crazies" when he observed that authoritarian self-deception is intrinsic to religion:

A kind of intellectual integrity has been alien to all founders of religions and their kind: they have never made their experiences a matter of conscience or knowledge. "What did I really experience? What happened in me and around me? Was my reason bright enough? Was my will turned against all deceptions?"—None of them has raised such questions; all the dear religious people still do not raise such questions even now: rather they have a thirst for things that are *against reason*, and they do not want to make it too hard for themselves to satisfy it. . . .

Accordingly, Nietzsche rejected any effort to classify his activities as religious, even though his paragraphs do read like prophecy:

I want no "believers" . . . I never speak to masses. I have a terrible fear that one day I will be pronounced "holy."[5]

These statements serve to fill out Fromm's analysis. Like a rubber band, religion reaches beyond the earth only to snap back and sting the self. In faith one claims to know something—and to know that one knows—with absolute certainty. Is it any wonder that one's creative capacities to deal with uncertainty, to experiment, to judge, are devalued and in their disuse diminished?

Nietzsche's accusation connects the condition that the act of faith creates in the self with the direct teaching of faith. Consider Christian pity, for example:

[W]e see how man makes himself smaller, how you make him smaller . . . your pity is for the "creature in man," for what must be formed, broken, forged, torn, burnt, made incandescent and purified—that which necessarily must and should suffer.[6]

Nietzsche praises the strong and independent spirit nourished under conditions of "hardness and cunning" and pits such praise against faith's appeal to pity. Moreover, Christianity is doubly mistaken, he thinks, if it links such talk with a notion of human equality. Such a notion represents

a common war on all that is rare, strange, privileged, the higher man, the higher soul, the higher duty, the higher responsibility, and the abundance of creative power and masterfulness—today the concept of greatness entails being noble, wanting to be by oneself, being able to be different, standing alone and having to live independently.[7]

We are on the edge of Nietzsche's hymn to the "order of rank" and the way in which "one's blood decides."[8] One may well pull back from that precipice without losing the question whether Christian faith's egalitarian strain contributes to a leveling out of excellence. From an apparently opposite pole comes the criticism that Christianity diminishes the self by calling for the denial of the richness, the luxuriance, of feeling and the sensual. Actually this criticism is quite consistent with Nietzsche, if one thinks of the self's being paralyzed in both its action and its passion and settling into a barren midpoint fixed by the upward glance, as it were.

Wallace Stevens voices this concern very effectively in many of his poems. Consider a single section of "Sunday Morning," with its critique of the "dominion of the blood and sepulcher":

Why should she give her bounty to the dead?
What is divinity if it can come
Only in silent shadows and in dreams?
Shall she not find comforts of the sun
In pungent fruit and bright, green wings, or else
In any balm or beauty of the earth,
Things to be cherished like the thought of heaven?
Divinity must live within herself:
Passions of rain, or moods in falling snow;
Grievings in loneliness, or unsubdued
Elations when the forest blooms; gusty
Emotions on wet roads on autumn nights;
All pleasures and all pains, remembering
The bough of summer and the winter branch.
These are the measures destined for her soul.[9]

Thus the charges concerning Christian faith's damage to the self accumulate. Faith does have real effects, for it connects with a real self. Consider Stevens's suggestions about the way Christian faith weakens the appreciation of beauty and narrows the imagination. Faith connects with the imagination, perhaps preempts it. The imagination is apt to whip up guilt feelings, leaving people with neurotic compulsions for life.[10] By its admonitions to humility the faith builds a defense against the corrective ministrations of reason. In banishing imaginary problems, reason is free to address our real difficulties, as Fromm notes:

> Indeed, man is dependent; he remains subject to death, age, illness, and even if he were to control nature and to make it wholly serviceable to him, he and his earth remain tiny specks in the universe. But it is one thing to recognize one's dependence and limitations, and it is something entirely different to indulge in this dependence, to worship the forces on which one depends. To understand realistically and soberly how limited our power is is an essential part of wisdom and of maturity; to worship it is masochistic and self-destructive. The one is humility, the other self-humiliation.[11]

On such readings the Christian faith is no simple error, accidentally attached to the self and as easily severed from it. Christian faith is right in recognizing the self's limitations, but it proceeds to do something very wrong with its insight. That analysis of the situation may suggest a direction for the Christian. The Christian shares the unbeliever's commitment to human fulfillment, and does so both as human and as Christian. It is not that concern for human fulfillment is cast in a particularly felicitous form in our time. The "psychobabble" found in the bookshops of the land might well tempt the Christian to reject all talk of fulfillment and to recall with relief that faith sings "soli deo gloria." But this temptation is to be fought. The Christian accepts the call to attend to the concern for human fulfillment.

Belief and unbelief see something in common in the self. The Christian may say to Fromm and Nietzsche, "You are right that the self strives and creates. Indeed you say less than you might about this. According to the Christian faith the self's creativity is more important than you allow, for the self is called into its action by none other than God!" Christian faith underlines the responsibility of the individual, who only mistakenly is reduced to being the passive receptacle of divine determination. If Nietzsche is right that to preach pity is to assume that all suffering is bad, the Christian may well echo his critique of such a religion of comfortableness. One must grant that much of what is touted in the churches as neighbor-love may in fact be "bad love" of oneself, the action of one who flees to the other out of self-hatred.[12]

The alternative awaits description. In chapter 5 I try to show that it is precisely the creative human spirit that is potentiated by hearing and believing the word of Christian faith about God. Carl Jung observes that the faith relationship is a potentiating reality, even in the dynamic of denial:

> Since the idea of God represents an important, even overwhelming, psychical intensity, it is, in a way, safer to believe that such an autonomous intensity is a nonego, perhaps an altogether different or superhuman entity, "totaliter-aliter."

Confronted with such a belief man must needs feel small, just about his own size. But if he declares the "tremendum" to be dead, then he should find out at once where this considerable energy, which was once invested in an existence as great as God, has disappeared to. . . . If it does not appear under the disguise of a new name, then it will most certainly return in the mentality of the one from whom the death declaration has issued. Since it is a matter of a tremendous energy, the result will be an equally important psychological disturbance in the form of a dissociation of personality.[13]

Believers should worry if such description is wielded as psychological intimidation, so that mental illness replaces hellfire as the church's cudgel. But Christian faith agrees that in God the self's restless energy finds for itself a true Other. Indeed the Christian is more ready than Jung to speak of this Other as ontologically real, so that the self's psychological potentiation does not come from itself.

To become itself the self needs and seeks this Other. It needs other selves as well. Christian faith will be critical of the individualistic strand in Nietzsche's criticism and constructions. Alasdair MacIntyre, who is no apologist for Christian faith, can identify the difficulty for us:

Nietzsche jeers at the notion of basing morality on inner moral sentiments, on conscience, on the one hand, or on the Kantian categorical imperative, on universalisability, on the other. . . . But Nietzsche then goes on to confront the problem that this act of destruction has created. . . . [I]f there is nothing to morality but expressions of will, my morality can only be what my will creates. . . . I myself must now bring into existence "new tables of what is good." "We, however, *want to become those we are*—human beings who are new, unique, incomparable, who give themselves laws, who create themselves" (p. 266). . . . The problem then is how to construct in an entirely original way, how to invent a new table of what is good and a law, a problem which arises for each individual.[14]

For Christian faith one can speak appropriately of "each individual's" ethical task only as one recognizes the constitutive character of community. This is not to deny self-relatedness and responsibility. Must the self be alone to be strong? Certainly not! agree a wide range of voices. But among that number are critics who contend that in fact faith in its fascination with the Other fails to care for the others.

DOES THE FAITH WORK FOR GOOD IN THE WORLD?

If a person's beliefs "work" insofar as they result in effective action in the world, how should one assess the working power of the Christian idea of God? Does possessing this idea result in effective action in this world? The "highest" view of God might seem to paralyze the self at the very inception of any activity: "If God exists, all is His will and from His will I cannot escape."[15] Still, it is hard to deny that the Calvinistic tradition with its high God freely predestining has produced very considerable human activity. Thus do believers manifest their election. But can such action be genuinely creative, if it is undertaken as prescribed response to such a controlling Other? Does not such faith tend to specify rigidly the behavior that constitutes correct response? It is as if God's decisive will passes through a self denied creative interplay with its environment. Is not the self thus constricted in its work in the world? Or can it be claimed that the relationship to God precisely expands the self for its work?

It depends, of course, on the particular fabric of the faith involved. For example, Karl Marx does not deny the note of genuine liberation found in Luther:

> Luther, to be sure, overcame bondage based on *devotion* by replacing it with bondage based on *conviction*. He shattered faith in authority by restoring the authority of faith. He turned priests into laymen by turning laymen into priests. He freed man from outward religiosity by making religiosity the inwardness of faith. He emancipated the body from its chains by putting chains on the heart.[16]

The God-relationship here is seen to grant a kind of freedom for the self. But can a body whose heart is chained to its liberator really work effectively in the world where freedom now presumably prevails? Will not at least the intensity of such activity be compromised? Will not the Other relativize the others for the self? How much can the merely human matter any longer, after all? If the one thing needful is in place, how gravely can one regard any other disorder? Must not the relationship to God be the one pearl of great price?

Nietzsche saw the Christian religion "working" in such a becalming way and cried out against it:

> To ordinary human beings . . . religion gives an inestimable contentment with their situation and type, manifold peace of the heart . . . something of a justification for the whole everyday character, the whole lowliness, the whole half-brutish poverty of their souls. Religion and religious significance spread the splendor of the sun over such ever-toiling human beings and make their own sight tolerable to them. . . . Perhaps nothing in Christianity or Buddhism is as venerable as their art of teaching even the lowliest how to place themselves through piety in an illusory higher order of things and thus to maintain their contentment with the real order, in which their life is hard enough—and precisely this hardness is necessary.[17]

When faith in God does not ignore the hardness of life, it justifies it!

One may find this analysis too simple. Karl Marx did. Marx certainly called the half-liberated Lutheran to struggle against precisely that inner priestly nature. But he did not underestimate the difficulty. We are dealing with something that is inner; it is no simple shell to be cast off. Marx found much more than illusion in the reality that is religion:

> *Religious* suffering is the *expression* of real suffering and at the same time the *protest* against real suffering. Religion is the sigh of the oppressed creature, the heart of a heartless world, as it is the spirit of spiritless conditions.[18]

Here faith's passion, if not its propositions, gains respect because of what it expresses. Yet precisely because "*man* is not an abstract being squatting outside the world," religion's heavenly reflection must finally be judged to distract the believer, with the result that a mere semblance of the proper self becomes acceptable—or at least accepted—on earth. Indeed, because beyond Feuerbach the point is not to interpret the world but to change it, such distracting reflection must finally be regarded as an opium of the people, an opium to be forsworn.[19] One does little effective work if one's energy is spent expressing that which distances the self from itself and its responsibility. If to work well in the world is to be effective in changing the world, faith in God does not work very well.

It is not merely that in its passion faith deflects and distracts. The propositions of the faith are in the dock as well. Consider the narcotic effect of some of the central doctrines. Does not the doctrine of original sin mean that we will inevitably fail in our most important human responsibility? Christian faith redefines the human and then reduces it to a meaner state even within that new conception. How much can anything else matter then? With such failure at the center, why sputter away with the nonessential? If the Christian responds, "But we teach more than one Adam," the response in turn may be "More, perhaps, but not different in practical effect." Here the two Adams are together. For does not the faith meet the predetermined human defeat with an equally predetermined divine victory? In that victory is not a single historical particular unnaturally elevated at the cost of squandering the risk and so the challenge of ongoing history?[20] While faith may not claim actually to deliver the victory just yet, it can still deflect human beings from their own proper struggle by offering heavenly recompense borrowed from the future.

Perhaps faith cannot in fact deflect human beings from all worldly work. Rather, faith typically accommodates such work. But what follows for one's understanding of such work, given faith in Christian doctrine? Will not such action as is taken be enervated by the recognition that this worldly kingdom is clearly of the left hand in a right-handed universe? Perhaps Lutheran categories at this point simply reflect the logic of all Christian concentration on the One who has come and who will come again. We live between those times. And in the meantime will not the confidence that the high God ultimately rules over all lend a conservative cast to the believer's action, such as it will be? If the powers that be are ordained by God, will not the burden of proof rest on those who say we must obey God *rather* than human beings? Are not, then, the sociologists of religion right at least about the ordering *effects* of faith, the truth question aside?

The Christian faith may not only have difficulty resisting a government that is totalitarian but orderly; it may even contribute to the momentum of such a regime. People who know with certainty the shape of the future may have the confidence to take action where others who cannot act with divine (self-) righteousness would pause. The passion of faith may reinforce tyranny. Christian faith in God is vulnerable to tyranny because the claim of the others has been relativized and can be canceled out by one who speaks for God. One recalls Camus's bitter comment about capital punishment: only when a state presumes that it acts for God does it suppose that it has the right to reclaim the life that it supposes it has given.[21]

If the self is in fact essentially constituted in relationships, a self's religion will find some work to do in the world, despite the deflecting and distracting to which we have referred. Critics of the faith agree: faith does indeed make a difference in life. In particular, the propositions produced by the passion of faith double back to create vast human suffering. The critic's charge concerns not only the self-deprivation that the masochistic believer may experience—which we looked at in the previous section—but also the immense violence to others done by believers under the impetus of faith. Theological formulations often appear not merely to rationalize prejudice but actually to support it, and perhaps even to instill and incite it. Is Morris Cohen's language really too strong?

> The fierce spirit of war and hatred is not of course entirely due to religion. But religion *has* made a *duty* of hatred. It preached crusades against Mohammedans and forgave atrocious sins to encourage indiscriminate slaughter of Greek Orthodox as well as of Mohammedan populations. It also preached crusades against Albigenses, Waldenses, and Hussite Bohemians. . . . Cruel persecution and intolerance are not accidents, but grow out of the very essence of religion, namely its absolute claims. So long as each religion claims to have absolute, supernaturally revealed truth, all other religions are sinful errors.[22]

Such language is not too strong to cover such late-twentieth-century realities as the religious elements in the strife in Northern Ireland and Lebanon.

These atrocities are not aberrations attaching themselves to the periphery of Christian doctrine. Rather, they connect with fervent faith in central teachings of Christianity. They seem to occur not at some remove from the place of Christ in the faith but in direct relationship to this saving figure. This can be seen in instances where the faith deflects the believer from full human compassion. In *The Myth of God Incarnate* debate, it was persons at least ostensibly within the Christian community who insisted that

> to regard God as having been involved in the sufferings of Jesus in some unique way would detract from the moral and religious value of the myth. For it makes God's presence in the suffering of all men less intimate and less complete than it might be.[23]

Or, to mention something much more overt than the weakening of compassion, think of the connection between Christianity and anti-Semitism. One can hardly counter, What connection? given the long history of anti-Semitic statements by Christians. Consider the golden-mouthed St. John Chrysostom's words to his congregation:

> The Jews have assassinated the Son of God! How dare you take part in their festivals? . . . O Jewish people! A man crucified by your hands has been stronger than you and has destroyed you and scattered you. . . .[24]

Chrysostom's words nicely illustrate how the dramatic power of myth can change the scale of things and so "alter the values," as it were. If one finds in Jesus the focal point of a great cosmic battle between good and evil, will one not readily align oneself with the side of God and find oneself called to scatter the Jews? Jesus himself escapes this charge, for he is not accused of the fatal "high" Christology. The myth reaches beyond this life as well. Thus Nietzsche identifies Christian *ressentiment* in which the weak graciously "create a heaven from which they will behold their masters frying in the flames of hell."[25] But such creativity returns to life with a vengeance. If God's enemies are to suffer in the future, why should they be kept from suffering even now?

Cries of outrage about the effects of Christian faith in the social world can be extended to its effects in the natural world. Christians speak about how their faith "disenchants" nature, so that the physical world becomes a fit object of human inquiry—of science, technology, medicine, and the like.[26] But what if the notion of disenchantment is combined with the idea that the being made in the image of God is qualitatively superior to all things merely natural? Then the Christian myth carries human nature right out of the world. If in one's image of oneself, one belongs more with God than with nature, one may well transform one's inquiry, into manipulation and destruction, in simple response to the command to "subdue the earth." In distinguishing God and those in God's image so dramatically from the earth, does not Christianity put that frail vessel far more in jeopardy than do those religions that stress the continuities between self, world, and God?

Two responses to the critic are inappropriate: (1) The Christian cannot walk away from these objections by denying that the faith makes any claims about God, Jesus, sin, heaven, and the like. We have already argued against such a policy of survival by suicide. (2) Nor can the faith deny the capacity and pertinence of human judgment concerning the worldly effects of faith. On this too we are already agreed.

What shall the Christian say? It must be recognized that both the passion and the propositions of the faith place the Christian in community with all God's creatures. The exigencies of life invite us to act before all the evidence is in, as I have argued in chapter 2. But the recognition of this should make us the more interested in the point of view of those who are affected by our action. In understanding that faith is not complete knowledge, we are not required to renounce all action prompted by our faith. But we will seek to act in concert with what the human calls for in the situation. We will not cleave to a totalitarian certainty in our action, if our faith already knows uncertainty in itself.

What if God is emphatically and inextricably here—where we are? How then can faith in that God deflect the believer from worldly work? How shall the believer retire to some other realm? To speak in this way of God and still to speak of Christian hope beyond this world will not be easy. The reality of this world will not be denied by such Christian hope. God and all else will go together through this world to that one. Together. That is the second point. If the Christian speech about God is irreducibly relational, it will not be talk about a God who is the sole determining reality. It is not only in the "how" of their passionate action that Christians need to recognize their membership in the human community. In "what" the Christian claims to know, the talk must be of a God in unfailing community with humankind. It matters what Christians do in this world, because what they do is done to God. The word is "Inasmuch as you did it to one of the least of these, my brethren, you did it to me." Does this recognition of God as not only the ground of action but also its goal diminish God? Has the Christian here, in what may be regarded as a compensating effort to elevate the reality and responsibility of human beings, simply rejoined the hapless human race? Have we removed the problem of faith by removing the promise of faith? It will remain in chapter 7 to develop the suggestion that to speak of God and of the Christian in relationship to others is not to speak of impotence. It is to speak of how relationships permit power not only to be distributed but to be shared as well. It is to heed the hint of Gregory Bateson who criticizes a "transitive" understanding of power, according to which more powerful is always more powerful.[27] Christians who believe that "a suffering God does help" have reason to join in that criticism.[28]

What help comes from a Christian God who acts and suffers? How may a sense of dependence liberate and a sense of possibility potentiate? And how may those senses be linked, to prevent both inertia and totalitarianism? Perhaps even faith's apparent negations need study at this point. How may the true otherness of God connect with life in such a way as to make the believer suspicious of the divine claims of governments? How may the consciousness of sin inspire the believer to create those self-critical and corrective human structures that make for justice in action, despite the evil that lies in human hearts?

DOES FAITH'S EFFICACY STAND IN THE JUDGMENT OF HISTORY?

It may be the case that there is a determining reality beyond and beneath, and especially before, our reflections on self, world, and God. We do not "start from scratch" in thinking about these things, after all. To speak of a reality that decisively conditions all our conceptualizing is, one could say, to speak of history. I refer not merely to what we write, but to what is written for us in the tides in human affairs. These currents shape the way we approach the world, the way we understand the world to be accessible to us, and what we understand a self to be. To take a pertinent example: perhaps Christian faith at one time was part of the very fabric of western culture and consciousness, so that atheism—"cognitive atheism," at least—was not a living option. In such a historical context, faith would be a matter more of destiny than of decision.

What is Christianity's position today? For many the sheer weight of actuality counts against Christian faith. There are two ways in which this is true.

1. The actual existence and character of the Christian church and of Christians may make the case against Christianity before the defense can begin, and it may do so conclusively. Is that not the likely result if the case of Christianity is that of Christendom? If we are to judge Christianity by the Christians, will it not fail to pass the test of the human?

Of course, one can argue for a distinction between the use and the abuse of any faith. Here one grants the damage done to humankind by Christians, but cuts the connecting link to God. Indeed Christian faith almost seems to depend on the evidence of human failings. One nearly gets the impression that the Christian's wrongs are a witness to the rightness of the Other confessed as God. In the face of the Christian's failings—the implication seems to be—can we fail to realize that the witness we make is not to anything human?

It will not do to seek to convert liabilities to assets in one such daring stroke. For there remains the possibility that the Christian witness is something *less* than fully human. It may be something of our own doing that makes us less good, complete, authentic, human than we otherwise could be. At its best, Christian faith knows this could be the case. It reminds itself that its independently real and eminently good God comes to bless human beings. It grants that there is no reason that God's ways and the conduct of the chosen community must be diametrically opposite in virtue. It accepts the point that it is not strange that the character of confessing Christians comes to bear on the consideration of the God they confess. After all, if on faith's understanding God chooses to work through human vessels, those vessels cannot be jettisoned when the issue of evaluation arises.

We are thus brought back to the matter of the actual efficacy of Christian faith. It is not possible to dismiss the evidence of the actual in its most ordinary aspect. We cannot call up for consideration the cases of Mother Teresa and Martin Luther King, Jr. (or of Jesus of Nazareth) and exempt from consideration the brutal and bumbling behavior of the others who confess the same faith. Why do so few "get it right"? May there even be something in this faith that helps people get it wrong? These questions are not easily silenced. That God recognizes human freedom, that God does not therefore coerce human response—such answers are necessary and perhaps even useful. But they are not sufficient. How many hymns of praise should be sung to a God who wins so few to true worship and obedience? Why should one align oneself with a faith if that faith makes nothing different in life—or at least nothing better? Such questions cannot be silenced. They require a response unless they have already provided their own answer in such a way as actually to preclude a consideration of Christian faith.

2. In the first case the life of faith acts to undercut appeals to faith. Christian works precede Christian witness in such a way that the judgment against the faith is effectively made before the evangelist's words are spoken. But perhaps there is a sense in which the judgment is made apart from either the witness to Christian truth or the witness of Christian life. Perhaps Christian faith does not so much fail as fade in the judgment of history. Perhaps at one time it had a place and made a contribution to human development. But the time of Christian faith may now be past. Thus Auguste Comte could find religion to be beyond magic in the development of what is human, but still short of science.[29] Hegel could endorse the stress on reconciliation in Christian faith but object to the narrowing "positivity" of the Christian concentration on Jesus, which, he thought, holds back independent human and cosmic maturation. More than a few today are prepared to follow Hegel's suggestion and find the divine in themselves. Some do so and still try to speak the language of faith.

What has history taught us, as it has formed us in its womb? Do we know with Marx that all knowledge is itself a product of history? Have we learned with Nietzsche that the God known to one cultural cosmos has died? Perhaps many of us are learning such truths almost involuntarily. At least, these themes seem to structure our givenness much more than the prescriptive visions in Nietzsche's notion of eternal recurrence and Marx's prophecy of a class that is not a class do. Such visionary messages seem at least faintly hallucinatory to us. We wait for the bad news that will surely turn such good news into a joke. Destruction seems more natural, as Nietzsche may have understood in speaking of decadence.

Is this destroying of diverse divinities itself actually positive? Is that what is implied in the judgment that acclaims the pluralistic character of contemporary consciousness? On this view the fault of the Christian faith is less that it has found the wrong meaning in the whole of things than that it has joined the impudent band who proclaim such meaning at all. That seems to be Karl Popper's contention about Christian dogma, if not about the biblical vision itself:

> [I]t is often considered a part of the Christian dogma that God reveals himself in history; that history has meaning; and that its meaning is the purpose of God. . . . I contend that this view is pure idolatry and superstition. . . . To maintain that God reveals himself in what is usually called "history," in the history of international crime and of mass murder, is indeed blasphemy; for what really happens within the realm of human lives is hardly ever touched upon by this cruel and at the same time childish affair.[30]

Popper charges that both Christian and Marxist confidence about "the" meaning of history diminish the sense of the personal responsibility of each individual to make something of life. To have a sense of personal responsibility, one must take upon oneself the task of personally evaluating one's own actions. If this radically personal character of agency and judgment is recognized, history will be seen as a many-splendored thing defying summation and singular judgment. But then it follows that the Christian cannot effectively play off one rival interpretation of the meaning of history against another, as if the God of the ancient creeds might win the hand of an exhausted modernity. The Christian faith has not been granted an exemption from the enervating processes of history. In their very plurality the competing candidates for interpreting meaning illumine the apparent arbitrariness of every attempt to absolutize, if not to choose, a particular vision.

What language about the whole is still possible then? One can attach oneself to this recognition of pluralism and hum a Nietzschean hymn to the protean human will, if one likes. Or one can settle for a softer song concerning the triumph of the therapeutic in which the therapy of therapies is not to attach oneself exclusively to any particular therapy, so that no illusion may survive of some end beyond an intensely private sense of well-being to be generated in the living of life itself.[31]

Or one can proceed with Popper in self-liberation through knowledge:

If the growth of reason is to continue, and human rationality to survive, then the diversity of individuals and their opinions, aims and purposes must never be interfered with (except in extreme cases where political freedom is endangered). Even the emotionally satisfying appeal for a common purpose, however excellent, is an appeal to abandon all rival moral opinions and the cross criticisms and arguments to which they give rise. It is an appeal to abandon rational thought.[32]

What can the Christian do who cannot conscientiously find any of these choices finally satisfactory? What does it mean for Christian thought to attend to these remarks about the judgment of history? It will mean to grant that human history is indeed material reality in whose terms judgment is to be rendered on every faith. Such judgment is not a simple matter. That human history is the arena for judgment does not require that there is no agent of judgment beyond the human. While the Christian will still speak of the judgment of God in and of history, this does not deny that Christian witness, life, and reflection are emphatically human work. In a logic of consequence we do judge ourselves. Self-criticism takes on a special importance. The Christian theologian will recognize the relativity and tentativity of the conscious work of planning and judgment. Indeed the theologian may well learn theologically from Popper's espousal of a "piecemeal" approach against utopian schemes of social engineering. The God of whom we speak may be one, but we are not. And we do not have God apart from us.

Christian faith does face judgment in history. Judgment is possible in principle because the faith speaks of such solidly historical matters as self and world. It can be undertaken in confidence because faith claims that its case is clear, if not complete. While time's story is still being written and much remains unsettled and unclear, the promise of the plot is evident. It is made evident in Jesus of Nazareth—that is the Christian claim. If that claim is compromised—not the least in supposed tactical retreat—the Christian sense of ambiguity erodes into absurdity. Thus the Christian faith offers its judgment of human history and so offers itself for judgment in history. That the first judgment invites the second is itself a sign suggesting that Christian claims about meaning do not move against human freedom and creativity. Kierkegaard put the point with characteristic force:

When God lets himself be born and become man, this is not an idle caprice, some fancy he hits upon just to be doing something, perhaps to put an end to the boredom that has brashly been said must be involved in being God—it is not in order to have an adventure. No, when God does this, then this fact is the earnestness of existence. And, in turn, the earnestness in this earnestness is: that everyone *shall* have an opinion about it.[33]

Thus it is not an honorific act for a Christian to attend to the concerns voiced in these three chapters. Such criticism need not be an idle cursing of the night, if one claims light has been given. That same claim makes it possible to commend the faith. In doing this one is not finished with the task of attending to the questions put to the faith. We shall still speak of self, world, and history. But we shall speak somewhat differently now, for these are no longer seen to be alone. As one hears, one begins to speak.

5 TO COMMEND INTENSIFICATION

On Becoming a Self in Relation to the Other

As a Christian I must attend further to the concerns voiced in the last three chapters. Indeed what has been presented there is merely a program for much more extensive consideration. We have identified objections to and difficulties in Christian belief. We have tried to suggest how Christians might attend to the questions faith in God produces. Much more listening should lie ahead for Christians, as well as the making of such response to the questions as then seems appropriate.

But there is a second movement in the conversation between those who confess the Christian faith and those who do not. Here the Christian speaks from the reality of faith on behalf of that faith. The two movements are related but distinguishable. To attend to the questions of the unbeliever may ultimately drive one to quest after what one has to commend. But such speaking is not merely a responding to the objections attended to, for the Christian has words and reason to speak because of what lives and grows within the community of Christian faith. Nor can the nonbeliever be reduced to a set of questions and objections, for that matter. There is need and readiness to be addressed. Thus there are two dialogues that make up the one conversation we seek. Each participant has two roles to play.

In this book the Christian role that appears first is the more receptive but also responsive one of attending to unbelief's questions. The burden of proof may rest with the Christian, as I have suggested, but one who will bear that burden begins best by listening. But at some point the Christian takes the initiative by inviting the non-Christian to share the quest that is Christian faith. Now the unbeliever may hear and consider the Christian commendation and, in turn, find new questions to which the Christian must attend. So runs the course of this single conversation.

In both dialogues, moreover, there is something in common not only in the talkers, but in the talk. Consider the topics for these dialogues. In chapters 2 through 4 the Christian was called to self-examination in the light of attending to how a self knows, to what world there is to be known, and to what follows in fact (we could say, in history) from faith. Now in chapters 5 through 7 Christian faith will speak from its store in relation to self, world, and history. The fit is not as fine as my brief statements might suggest, for the first speakers in each dialogue do not approach self, world, and history with exactly the same questions in mind and indeed the terms "self," "world," and "history" must not be taken to refer to realities about whose identity both participants in the conversation fully agree in advance. Yet the two dialogues do intersect to constitute one conversation, because their content is ordered by converging choices of topics.

The convergence seems more than formal. In chapters 2 and 3 we considered human knowing and human knowledge. With this Christians and non-Christians alike are concerned. Chapter 4 cast the net more widely to speak of what one might call human flourishing or human diminishment—again a matter of common concern. Now as Christian faith sets about to start the second dialogue it does so in relation to similar realities of common concern. They surely intersect with knowing and flourishing, but I name the realities intensification, comprehension, and reconciliation. All three—and not least the last, despite its religious ring—are matters of common concern. The Christian speaks thus: "Since you esteem this ____, will you not consider the faith in that connection, will you not confess it?"

How shall this second movement begin? We start here with the notion of the self, for four guarded reasons:

1. While the self may be an abstraction, it suggests means and end for our speaking. We speak with, we commend to, persons who do not cease being persons when the subject of religion arises.[1] There may be a gain in realism for the dialogue in recognizing and remembering this personal involvement.

2. The difficulties to which we have been called to attend find forceful expression in the notion of the self. Does Christian knowing fit the ways an authentic self knows? Does the effect of faith fulfill the self? If we seek to continue a single conversation as we begin this second movement, the presence of common concerns so close at hand may assist us.

3. A sense of that other abstraction, world, may be less available today as a connecting point, if those observers are right who speak of a contemporary sense of pretheoretical uncertainty about all frameworks. If worldlike structures seem to fade with "the end of ideology," to seek to connect there in order to commend might be to try to move to the positive through the negative. Of course there is the risk in our choice that in striking for a connection with the contemporary consciousness of self, we may settle for what is shallow and sick, simply sinking into the swamp of subjectivity. Clearly, after all, even the protean self will not create a real world without

also finding one.[2] We must not forget the world, but we may be wise to begin with the self.

4. Most fundamentally, the Christian faith materially engages the quest to become a self. Niebuhr was right to say that "to have a self is to have a God."[3] If we can understand this, we will have commended Christian faith. This is not to say that our second dialogue must begin here, but it is to assert that it can occur here.

STARTING POINT: THE PRECARIOUS PROJECT OF THE SELF

To what do we refer when we speak of the self? Whitehead remarks that no one ever says, "Here I am, and I have brought my body with me."[4] Anglo-Saxon empiricism has convincingly emphasized that we depend upon the physical expressions of others to identify their intentions.[5] Biologists have argued effectively for the classification of human beings as members of the animal kingdom within which their evolution occurs.[6] Thus, to speak of a human body is not to speak of a springboard to selfhood, but of something of abiding and essential significance to it. Arthur Peacocke summarizes the evidence that blocks any effort to identify selfhood with disembodied mind:

> [L]et us recall the strength of the evidence for the intimate relation between mental activity and the physico-chemical state of the brain. It includes *inter alia*: the dependence of personality on hormone balance; the genetic determination of the human body, mental attributes and defects (and so their basis in DNA structure); the effects of drugs on mental states, and of mental states on the effects drugs can produce; personality changes in patients who have undergone frontal leucotomy or temporal lobectomy, i.e., separation of the frontal or temporal lobes, respectively, of the brain from the remainder; the studies of Sperry and his colleagues on the states of consciousness and the control abilities of patients whose two cerebral hemispheres have been severed at the *corpus callosum* and the problems these raise concerning the unity of their consciousness and of their personality; evidence that the threshold of consciousness of sensations is passed only when there has been an elaboration of the spatio-temporal patterns of impulse discharged across as many as 200 synaptic linkages between nerves, each impulse activating the huge number ($\sim$ 10,000) of nerves with which it is in contact over an unimaginably complex network.[7]

In the face of all this it is not surprising to be told that "modern psychology takes completely for granted that behavior and neural function are perfectly correlated, that one is completely caused by the other" so that

> "Mind" can only be regarded, for scientific purposes, as the activity of the brain, and this should be mystery enough for anyone . . . the appalling number of cells . . . and even more appalling number of possible connections between them. . . . The mystic might well concentrate on the electron and let behavior alone.[8]

If even such a humanistic psychologist as Carl Rogers can state approvingly that determinism "is the very foundation stone of science," it will not be surprising to find behaviorist schools taking the biological and social given-ness of the human to be an exhaustive account of the self's reality.[9]

Yet the fact that matters are not that simple is suggested not so much by the presence of several general psychological schools as by the current tendency toward the collapse of all such grand views under the sheer volume and variety of research results. Students of the self settle for working with specific miniature systems such as learning, sensation, perception, intel-ligence, and—still hankering, however divisively, for wholeness—person-ality theory.[10] We seem to move toward saying that biological determinism is a qualified (in both senses, competent *and* limited) contributor to the dialogue concerning the human. We have not ceased speaking of the phys-ical, but we seem required to speak of it in increasingly complex ways. Perhaps we may be learning that to speak of the human is to speak of something that is happening. Something is under way here that defies final capture in a formula. The self seems as much project as product.

A biological account of the novel complexity encountered in the human project can be given. Peacocke summarizes the consensus of the scientific community concerning the continuities and discontinuities between human and other living creatures:

> Any such list would include the following and no doubt more besides: the exceptional level of man's intelligence, which is manifested in his capacity for abstract thought—itself related to an exceptional ability to use both verbal and visual symbols for communication, to his exceptionally avid curiosity in the exploration of his environment, to his unusual flexibility and adaptability, and to this capacity for handling and storing wide ranges of information; man's self-consciousness, which includes the ability to transcend the environment in thought and to survey it as subject; the use of "I" which seems thereby to constitute a new kind of entity, a "person," which makes each one a bearer of rights and unique, so that we can imagine ourselves changing places; the ability to act rationally, to make moral choices and set long-term ends; man's aesthetic sense and creativity in the arts, literature, science, and in play; the ability to worship and pray, that is, man's openness to God. . . . What is clear is that, even though the various distinctive components that constitute the human often have some correlate in other biological life, they are intensified and enhanced, often to the point of qualitative difference, and combined in a distinctive and unique unity.[11]

The remarkable range in such a list of irreducible human characteristics suggests that the project of the human is not finished. In the human organism evolution has become strangely conscious of itself, so that the continuing course of evolution is itself able to be deliberately affected by this product that is project. Empirical evidence seems to exist that would differentiate the human species on the basis of symbolic thought.[12] As the stimulus-response connection is "rounded" by the movement from signals to symbols, the unpredictable character of the human project is constituted.[13]

To what are we coming? Considerable caution is called for on the part of the theologian surveying studies of the human with which Christian speech is supposed to connect. The unpredictable and nonreductive character of the human project may prove tempting for the eager advocate of spiritual freedom. I should not want to imply that this surely hurried and perhaps even scattered survey of opinion constitutes some kind of untroubled consensus from which theological flights can take off into the thinner air of dogmatic speculation. If one does take off, one needs to understand that one cannot leave one's body behind. Thus D. C. Phillips suggests that to grant that "the whole is more than the sum of its parts" and even that "the whole determines the nature of its parts" is not to grant that a whole cannot be explained, retrospectively, in terms of its parts.[14] Or as A. N. Whitehead has said of the many that make up the human whole:

> It is obvious that we must not demand another mentality presiding over these other actualities (a kind of Uncle Sam over and above all the U.S. citizens). All the life in the body is the life of the individual cells.[15]

Perhaps it is not quite obvious. Such explanation "from below" is clearly possible and surely necessary. Is it sufficient? Still, there are difficulties in asking for anything more than this.

In any case we can say—whether from "above" or from "below"—that whatever is human is not inert deposit but living development. We may put it in different terms by speaking of a rejection of a psychology of identity. To speak of what is most important in the human is to speak of something, some*one*, who is coming to be in an unpredictable fashion.[16] Or if we wish to reclaim the notion of the identity of the self, we may speak with Kierkegaard of a relationship that "relates itself to itself." The self is not a substance, but an activity—a relating.[17] It is in the making—by others and by itself.

What may be said of that project? We are not silenced by the intrusion of temporality into our talk. I am wise enough not to aspire to some global synthesis of the rival views of the human. Such major views as the existentialist evocation of authenticity, the Marxist insistence on social relatedness, and the psycho-therapeutic exploration of inner rootedness are not parts that can be put together to make a tidy structured whole. What may be possible is the more modest task of identifying some of the elements that need to be incorporated in any concept of the self's project. That may in fact be the more useful task to attempt, if what the theologian seeks is to explore the connection of Christian speech not with *theories* of the self but directly with the reality that the theories seek to describe. We do not suppose we can evade the theoretical, but we may hope to avoid being entangled in the internal disputes of particular theories, if we can elicit our pretheoretical conception of what it is to become a self.

It is clear that the project of the self occurs in relation to the other. On the one hand, there is the matter of relating to the nonhuman environment, as the human realities of work, science, and technology show. On the other hand, there is the sociality of the self. We become human together, as the neo-Freudians stress in shifting the emphasis in personality theory from Freud's biological orientation to an orientation toward interpersonal relationships.[18] Whether one sees this sociality as the good news that assent is basic to our being or recoils in the conviction that hell is other people, one has to agree about the givenness of the other(s).[19] Out of this relatedness to the other arises the concern for identity, which often takes the form of a quest for coherence in the multiple relationships that make up a human life.[20]

The others do not hold still, nor do we. In the self's project of becoming a self in relation to the other, the constitutive reality of temporality bears on the self in several ways. There is the dawning of a sense of immediacy, which will carry as well a sense of radical novelty. This moment is now and, as such, it is new. Whether the novelty is greeted with anticipation and hope, or with revulsion and terror, the naked sense of possibility is there. In this the self can hear the inward call of its own burgeoning potentiality. Or the self's temporality may speak less of freedom and more of fatedness. It is not clear. The self is becoming. Something can happen through it, to it. Something will happen.

In knowing our temporality in the moment of becoming, we sense that our life stretches out ahead and back. We do not only become in this moment, and then in the next ones indefinitely. In this very moment we intend beyond this moment and we remember what came before it. Thus the concern for coherent identity in relationship to the others now becomes the quest for consistent character within one's own story. Friedrich Nietzsche voices this call to continuity:

> What is essential (in heaven and on earth) seems to be, to say it once more, that there should be *obedience* over a long period of time and in a *single* direction: given that, something always develops, and has developed, for whose sake it is worthwhile to live on earth; for example virtue, art, music, dance, reason, spirituality—something Transfiguring, subtle, mad, and divine.[21]

Finally of the self's becoming one must say that it comes to an end. With the sense of temporality the awareness of finitude, of limitedness already known in the experience of the others, is heightened qualitatively. We come to an end now in relation to—relatively, therefore—the others and we will do so "then" absolutely. That this is so is clear, but our responses seem to evaluate the truth differently. But whether we deny our dying in heroic flights of ambition or claim it as the conclusion of our story that even now can bestow a unity on our living, that sense of finitude continues to teach its lesson of the radical contingency of the self's becoming. We might not have been what we are; we might not have been at all—for we will not be any longer.

Any listing of the elements in the concept of the self's becoming itself must include another: complexity. When one considers the variety of features jostling for position within any moment of the self's life—physical locatedness, symbolic possibility, self-affecting efficacy—when one realizes as well that this one here and now is inextricably caught up in the there and then, one begins to sense the dizzying complexity of the self's project. The self may quite naturally seek to steady itself, to gain some equilibrium by finding some stable point. But such balance seems itself a precarious virtue. Unity is understandably sought in the midst of the dispersedness of one's life, but life's reality seems to warn against a fascination with some single or all-unifying ideal.[22] Fanaticism orders by destroying. One seeks continuity, but not that of a living death immune to spontaneity, novelty, and change.

If we ask what it is to be a self, we can surely say at least this. We have been trying to outline an understanding of human life without employing theological categories. Christian faith claims that the self is created by God and so is called to "attain to fullness of being, the fullness of God himself" (Eph. 3:19). The goal is not the given. Between given and goal lies the drama of the self's becoming, with its uncertainty, its risk. This unstable mixture that is the self is potent and accessible. It is amenable to what we may yet loosely call "intensification," but it bears no guarantees. Its project is precarious.

We must consider the Christian claim to intensification. All our non-theological reflection on the human is pertinent to this as a description of the very stuff of a self called to know and love God. In faith's view, if one speaks at all accurately of the self's project, one speaks of what it is to be caught up in God: it is to be corrected, fulfilled, consummated. Moreover, to assess faith's claims one must speak of something that is not faith but is rather more than the definitional given of the self's project. For along its way the self may undergo experiences that do not speak directly of God, yet do seem to constitute qualitative intensifications of the human.

AESTHETIC COMPLETENESS AND MORAL COMMITMENT: SELF-TRANSCENDENCE AND SELF-TRANSFORMATION

The self may spend its time, its self, in the chaotic whirl constituted by its sociality, its temporality, and its complexity. There may be nothing other than that to say about many moments, many lives. But with others there is more. Within the whirl the self undergoes experiences that seem to involve a qualitative alteration of the self. It is notoriously difficult to compass this variety in a definition. Whether by compression, by contrast, by extension— somehow, experience occurs that is still that of the self but within which the self becomes more. Becoming more seems to entail becoming other, as a difference of degree bids to become a difference of kind. Aesthetic and moral experience seem to entail such intensifications. But how is the Christian religion related to these other experiences of intensification? Are they alternatives to it, preparations for it, allies to it?

There is eloquent testimony that it is art that can elevate the beleaguered reality of human life. In the nineteenth century Walter Pater put it so:

> We are all under the sentence of death but with a sort of indefinite reprieve . . . we have an interval, and then our place knows us no more. Some spend this interval in listlessness, some in high passions, the wisest—at least among "the children of this world"—in art and song. For our one chance lies in expanding that interval, in getting as many pulsations as possible into the given time. . . . Of this wisdom, the poetic passion, the desire of beauty, the love of art for art's sake, has most; for art comes to you professing frankly to give nothing but highest quality to your moments as they pass, and simply for those moments' sake.[23]

Here is talk of intensification—that is clear. But how shall one describe what occurs in aesthetic experience? Perhaps one may speak here of a kind of self-transcendence in which the becoming self is caught up in something radically other than itself. What is that other? It surely has to do with order, as Plato knew:

> The artist disposes all things in order, and compels the one part to harmonize and accord with the other part, until he has constructed a regular and systematic whole.[24]

Near at hand lies the Platonic preference for form, for that which is perfect because it is not caught up in the change and corruptibility of matter. Perhaps, then, the radical otherness of aesthetic intensification has to do with the timelessness of art, which surely would call us away from the radically temporal character of our existence. John Maynard Keynes spoke of the emphasis on timelessness to be found in the Bloomsbury Circle of writers and artists, which included such figures as Roger Fry, Duncan Grant, Lytton Strachey, and Virginia Woolf:

> Nothing mattered except states of mind, our own and other people's, of course, but chiefly our own. These states of mind were not associated with action or achievement or with consequences. They consisted in timeless passionate states of contemplation and communion, largely unattached to "before" and "after." . . .[25]

Or consider Schiller's commentary:

> It is neither charm, nor is it dignity, which speaks from the glorious face of Juno Ludovici; it is neither of these, for it is both at once. While the female god challenges our veneration, the godlike woman at the same time kindles our love. But while in ecstasy we give ourselves up to the heavenly beauty, the heavenly self-repose awes us back. *The whole form rests and dwells in itself—a fully complete creation in itself*—and as if she were out of space, without advance or resistance; it shows no force contending with force, *no opening through which time could break in.*[26]

Of course the artist employs the material of this temporal world: objects, shapes, fabrics, words, figures. But what is produced with them is something other than the present passing world. Thus Wallace Stevens pleads that poetry must resist the Freudian "surrender to reality" and—admittedly risking sentimentality—permit the imagination to point us toward what reality may become.[27] It would seem, though, to do this pointing rather suddenly, as if to help us leap ahead. It does not work overmuch on the pedestrian task of getting us from here to there. Or is the leap back? Matthew Arnold, stricken with despair and skepticism, reaches for the time of the beginning, of the ideal, in his "Memorial Verses" on the death of Wordsworth:

> He too upon a wintry clime
> Had fallen—on this iron time
> Of doubts, disputes, distractions, fears.
> He found us when the age had bound
> Our souls in its benumbing round;
> He spoke, and loosed our heart in tears
> He laid us *as we lay at birth*
> On the cool flowery lap of earth,
> Smiles broke from us and we had ease;
> The hills were round us, and the breeze
> Went o'er the sun-lit fields again;
> Our foreheads felt the wind and rain,
> Our youth return'd; for there was shed
> On spirits that had long been dead,
> Spirits dried up and closely furl'd
> *The freshness of the early world.*[28]

Aesthetic experience does not seem to involve a selective and discriminating engagement with the reality of this temporal world. In the words of one analysis, "everything in our perceptual environment is available for aesthetic experience" as surely as everything can be seen as "possibly interesting—something with its own unique quality, which can be suffered or attacked, on the one hand, or savored and enjoyed on the other."[29]

The subjective side of aesthetic experience is often characterized as particularly "integral," with the person being drawn into the unity of the object of art. There is surely intensification here, but it is not clear that the experience quite belongs to the ongoing stream of ordinary life. Thus, the experience need not "teach," for it has its own integrity, and does not seek an end beyond itself.[30] Indeed, in some understandings of the experience this "nonfunctional" aspect is viewed as itself contributing to the intensification, so that one may say that "a good work of art carries a person who is capable of appreciating it out of life into ecstasy."[31]

It is dangerously easy to overstate the nontemporal character of the self-transcendence known in aesthetic intensification. One might be led to overstate it if one concentrated on, say, painting and sculpture instead of music and literature. Perhaps more than the spatial artist the poet seeks to know a livingly human nature, to look for our resemblance in the other.[32] Even the painter may struggle to find the continuity in the change from the child to the adult, for example. Thus consider this comment on the work of the contemporary British artist Peter Blake:

> I think Blake has a particular feeling of affection for people whose faces show the signs, even the damage, of experience. But here there is a piquancy in the combination of innocence or naivety with knowingness, sometimes sexiness. . . . Certainly our culture's concept of the fairy or elf combines elements of childhood and smallness, but also of great age or agelessness, unconventional beauty or ugliness and so on. . . . Clearly one of the recurrent themes of Blake's work is the continuity of childhood in maturity.[33]

Blake is, after all, the artist who dedicated his 1983 retrospective at London's Tate Gallery to "everybody who is less, but better, than perfect."

Yet we may not be quite content to exempt this intensifying self-transcendence from criticism. If Albert Hofstadter is right that the self's "fundamental impulse is towards freedom . . . to be with other as own,"[34] one may wonder if the self's project does not need to be engaged intensely precisely within the ambit of its ordinary relations. One thus seeks self-transformation in commitment as well as self-transcendence in completeness. In that case one will be critical of the indifference of pure form to moral considerations. Thus D. H. Lawrence denounced the "Holy Ghost of Significant Form":

> Oh, purify yourselves, ye who would know the aesthetic ecstasy and be lifted up
> to the white peaks of artistic inspiration. Purify yourself of all base hankering
> for a tale that is told, and of all low lust for likenesses. Purify yourselves, and
> know the one supreme way, the way of Significant Form. I am the revelation and
> the way! . . . Lo, I am Form and I am Pure, behold, I am Pure Form.[35]

I believe Lawrence is right. Form may be pure, but we are not, and in our
temporality we seek a tale that is told—one sufficiently like us that we will
be able to recognize ourselves in the intensification. Of course, to eschew
pure form is not to accept formlessness. The power of aesthetic form is not
easily resisted even in the sphere of the moral. Shelley wrote:

> A man to be greatly good, must imagine intensely and comprehensively; he
> must put himself in the place of another and of many others; the pains and
> pleasures of his species must become his own. The great instrument of moral
> good is the imagination; and poetry administers to the effect by acting upon the
> cause. . . . Poetry strengthens the faculty which is the organ of the moral nature
> of man.[36]

Nonetheless, the otherness known in moral experience seems sufficiently
different from that known in aesthetic experience to require separate treatment.

Moral experience satisfies knowledge's need for specificity; in this it is
distinguished from the broader sweep that characterizes aesthetic experience. Particular selves are not so clearly transcended in moral experience.
The knowing that comes of moral experience occurs "naturally" and lies
emphatically within the human. To argue that moral consciousness depends
on religious consciousness, for example, would seem to demean the person
twice over; in any case, such an argument runs afoul of the substantial
evidence that the self's project undergoes moral intensification without
benefit of religion.[37] Indeed, there are not many now who would speak of
the other in this relationship even as some kind of law or principle that can
be separated from human beings. Rather, one recognizes that any laws that
legislate do so naturally, because they have to do with the broad constraints
of human nature and survival.[38]

The moral not only *discloses* a world of space and time and human
relationships, the moral *originates* in this world. One may speak of the duty
we discern as simply a segment of the desires we naturally develop.[39]
Somehow we manage to derive "ought" from "is." Perhaps our moral sense
originates in certain social conventions—as, say, that of promising.[40] Or
perhaps certain activities in which we want to participate simply presuppose
that we consider the intentions of others.[41] Some students of the moral grant
that such a simplifying naturalism still must face further questions.[42] What
is one to say if asked why—why promise, why discourse publicly, why act,

even? Such questions deserve responses, but they do not, it seems, require one to leave the world of the self and its relationships. One responds to such questions by talking about what it is to be human. To be a free and creative self is to resist the injustice, immorality, and amorality that threaten the self's project.[43]

In whatever way one understands the basis of moral intensification, what are its substance and structure? Through very considerable variety there seems to sound the theme of the self's sociality. The self is not transcended here, nor are its relationships. One may say the moral involves the other(s) in that all are understood to face the same challenge, as the moral reaches for that which can be universalized. Or the other is recognized as the end of action, as in an emphasis on the making and keeping of promises. Or the other enters the very agency of the ethical act in a conception of collegial conduct. Thus, Alasdair MacIntyre has written about how after the decline of the classical virtues we need to resist the false alternatives of egoism and altruism by recognizing that human life is a conversation, a story with more than one author. In that story our identity is not that of a psyche set off against the others, but that of a constant character in a tale told in common.[44] Of course, this does not happen without the individual self's willing to have it be so. But in the self's commitment to the other in constancy there is a transformation of the self that constitutes genuine intensification.

Aesthetic and moral intensifications seem to feature different elements in the self's becoming in relation to the other. Perhaps they complement each other; perhaps they do so by correcting each other's onesidedness. In the aesthetic the self is so caught up in the Other as to transcend the others and so itself. In the moral the self is so committed to life with the others that there may be little sense of being borne up by anything or anyone Other than us all. The possibility—yes, even the tendency—of such onesidedness again underlines the precariousness of the self's project, also in its intensifications. Nervously, one may wonder if there is more. May there be something available to the self that is not a shuttling back and forth between intensifying experiences that resist settling into some stable synthesis that might risk compromising precisely the splendor of their respective ecstasies?

To ask about this is not to label these realities inauthentic intensifications that should be set aside. In morality, virtue has long been its own reward. And Eugene O'Neill speaks well for the aesthetic in refusing to be dismayed by the tragic character of art:

Sure I'll write about happiness if I can happen to meet up with that luxury, and find it sufficiently dramatic and in harmony with any deep rhythm in life. But happiness is a word. What does it mean? Exaltation; an intensified feeling of the significant worth of man's being and becoming? Well, if it means that—and not a mere smirking content with one's lot—I know there is more of it in one real tragedy than in all the happy-ending plays ever written. It's mere present-day judgment to think of tragedy as unhappy! The Greeks and the Elizabethans knew better. They felt the tremendous lift of it. It roused them spiritually to a deeper understanding of life. Through it they found release from the petty considerations of everyday existence. They saw their lives ennobled by it. . . . I don't love life because it's pretty. Prettiness is only clothes deep. I am a truer lover than that. I love it naked. There is beauty to me even in ugliness.[45]

Amen! I accept O'Neill's criteria and his criticism. But one may still ask whether in and beyond the aesthetic and the moral there is a hymn of joy that is dramatic precisely because it catches up the deepest rhythm of life.

THE RELIGIOUS AND THE CHRISTIAN: THE UNCONDITIONAL AND THE INCARNATE

On religion's reading of reality there is certainly something Other. Already in the first chapter I spoke of how at the very root of the Christian consciousness lies the conviction that God is different from us, and of how this difference must be regarded as categorical, a difference in kind. This emphasis is not the private property of the Christian religion. Indeed, perhaps it is not limited to the religious, for the otherness experienced in aesthetic intensification seems similarly radical. Moreover, there are other aspects of human existence that suggest such transcendence, even if they do not assert it.[46] Among the most striking of these is humor, which seems to depend on the suspicion that life is caught up in a contradiction such that the self's passionate project may be placed in a perspective in which its drama—its delights and its dilemmas alike—are dwarfed by something Other.[47] Believing that—or bemused by it at least—the comedian is wise enough not to argue about it.

Religion does argue and assert, for its life depends on the reality of the Other. The arguments and assertions are variously formulated. It would be quite possible to assemble historical examples wherein that Otherness is juxtaposed to that which we attribute to the self: temporality, sociality, complexity. Running through all such descriptions would be found the note of the unconditional. God is other than we are, for God is not conditioned. This is conveyed in the notion of God's eternality, for example. Most important, as such God is free from internal conditions. If God is eternal, one need not ask of God's current condition, as if God could change.

Nor does God undergo change caused by external conditions, for God's existence is *a se*, "from itself." The existence of God does not depend on anything that is not God; surely here lies the undeniable religious appeal of the ontological argument. Religious experience seems deeply linked with the awareness of the conditioned character of our existence—with our sense of being limited and contingent. It is as if the awareness that—beyond our choosing and doing—we might not be, that we might not have been at all, and that one day we will not be any longer occasions a sense of that which knows no such conditions.

Tolstoy's Ivan Ilyitch reveals how the experience of contingency compresses the accidental and the certain into a question. Climbing a pair of steps to demonstrate how a drapery should be arranged, Ivan falls, "but, being a strong, dexterous man, he saved himself. He only hit his side on the edge of the frame. He received a bruise, but it quickly passed away." But of course it did not, and as the illness that follows deepens, Ivan asks, "And is it true that here I have lost my life on that curtain as in a charge! It is possible? How horrible and how ridiculous! It cannot be! It cannot be! but it is." His experience of contingency seeks the stability of purpose, even if it be that of punishment. Along with many others, Ivan is attracted even by the possibility that he is the object of divine punishment.[48]

It is important to avoid the temptations of overstatement at this point. That the idea of the unconditioned occurs in connection with the experience of ontological contingency of course does not show that the person entertaining the idea is experiencing a reality corresponding to that idea.[49] Of course it seems clear that for many persons religious experience includes two realities: our contingency and God's unconditionedness, the latter seeming at the very least no less real than the former. But it must be granted that for others it is not so. For some the sense of terror, or of absurdity, is the end of it. For others this presumably most radical experience of contingency does not provoke particularly powerful passions either positive or negative. Thus Ronald Hepburn speaks for more than himself when he counsels us to conclude from our finitude not that human life is ultimately valueless, but that it is penultimately valued and valuable. Indeed the "best viewing distance" for the art of life may be precisely the finite span our days provide.[50] His point is well taken and it helps to remind us that we are conducting a dialogue here, not clinching an argument.

We are commending Christian faith, in this instance in terms of the intensification of the self's project. To that end the connections made between the experience of contingency and religious experience—whether rare, universal, or more probably, ranging between these extremes—do serve to introduce the subject of what happens, according to Christian faith, to and for the self in relation to an unconditioned God. It is clear that it is not only Christians who have opinions about this. Nietzsche and many others contend that belief in the Unconditioned, however illusory, has the real effect of diminishing the self in its striving. Are those mystics who say that in knowing this God we know that we do not know, and that our best speaking is a keeping silent, granting credibility to the Nietzschean charge that living with this God is really a dying? To the contrary, the Christian claim is that in relation to God human life is intensified; indeed that this intensification complements aesthetic and moral experience.

We become selves in relation to the other. That is inevitably so. It is intensely so in aesthetic experience of the Other and moral concourse with the others. In religion the human person becomes in relation to an Other characterized by the completeness of the beautiful and the collegiality of the good. These are together in such a way as to evoke intensification. This claim may be amplified as follows:

1. To know God promises to identify the self formally, since the other, the unconditioned, never comes into being or ceases to be. This eternal one conditions all the self's conditions. In all its becoming the self knows itself as in relation to this God. Thus the psalmist asks and answers:

> Whither shall I go from thy Spirit?
>   Or whither shall I flee from thy presence?
> If I ascend to heaven, thou art there!
>   If I make my bed in Sheol, thou art there!
>   (Ps. 139:7–8)

2. To know God promises to unify the self materially, for the unconditioned is the constant one, the one whose reliability does not know change. In all its complexity the self has this constant, affording the possibility of equilibrium. The psalmist was able to go on to say:

> If I take the wings of the morning
>   and dwell in the uttermost parts of the sea,
> even there thy hand shall lead me,
>   and thy right hand shall hold me.
>   (Ps. 139:9–10)

Are these aesthetic-like intensifications "good" for the self? Surely they will be so only if they contribute to what is changing, that is, to the self's own becoming. The unconditioned, the constant, must engage the conditioned, the changing.

3. To know God promises to potentiate the self, for we speak here of a relationship to One who actually exists. In knowing this One the self will not be unaffected. Kierkegaard puts it so:

> But this self takes on a new quality and qualification by being a self directly before God. This self is no longer the merely human self but is what I, hoping not to be misinterpreted, would call the theological self, the self directly before

God. And what an infinite reality the self gains by being conscious of existing before God, by becoming a human self whose criterion is God.[51]

Thus, for the psalmist staring up at the heavens the human person may be a mere dwarf, but because the maker is "mindful" of and "cares" for this one, the dwarf is but "little less than God" and crowned with glory and honor (Ps. 8:3–4).

4. To know God promises to direct the self, for we speak of an unconditioned will for the world. The prophets knew what God required (Micah 6) and called out for a river of righteousness (Amos 5:24). To know this Other is to be connected with all the others in responsibility.[52]

Are these moral-like intensifications fit for the self? Surely they will be so only if they do not compromise completeness in order to connect with becoming.

5. To know this God promises judgment for the self, for the unconditioned has the scope to assess and the fixity of stance to settle the anxious actions and shifting opinions that make up our lives. The writer of the psalm cited above may be questioned about his desire that God slay the wicked, but he knows what a God is for:

> Search me, O God, and know my heart!
>   Try me and know my thoughts!
> And see if there be any wicked way in me,
>   and lead me in the way everlasting!
>   (Ps. 139:24)

Judgment requires a word that is at once comprehensive and decisive. We leave to chapter 7 the question whether the judgment identified by Christians may gladden human hearts. But T. S. Eliot may be right that, caught up as we are with muddling through, we want such a word to be spoken:

> [T]he possibility of damnation is so immense a relief in a world of electoral reform, plebiscites, sex reform and dress reform that damnation itself is an immediate form of salvation.[53]

Well, perhaps not quite. But—electoral reforms aside—we can recognize the intensification that would occur were a unifying and decisive judgment to be given, a word about us that is not by us.

One finds this structure of intensification in the reality of religion. Consider, for example, the five points above as they appear in the Shema of Deuteronomy 6:

> Hear, O Israel: The Lord our God is one Lord; (1 and 2)

> and you shall love the Lord your God with all your heart, and with all your soul, and with all your might. (3)

> And these words which I command you this day shall be upon your heart. . . . (4)

You shall not go after other gods, . . . for the Lord your God in the midst of you is a jealous God; lest the anger of the Lord your God be kindled against you, and he destroy you from off the face of the earth. (5)

I believe the Christian stands with other faiths in this formal analysis of religion. But if we inquire about how Christian faith specifically intensifies human becoming, we will have to speak of one actual human existence, that of Jesus of Nazareth. Christians, after all, are those who gather around the manger.

Jesus is seen as humankind's way to God only because he was God's way to humankind, as Pannenberg recognizes:

Faith in God's becoming man and his taking flesh in Jesus . . . represents the real intention of the nativity story.[54]

Here something like the singular completeness of the aesthetic sets the Christian apart from the ethicist's sense of the universal, as Kierkegaard notes:

[T]he believer is . . . different from an ethicist in that he is infinitely interested in the reality of another (for example, in the fact that God has really existed).[55]

Yet the interest is in the actual existence of the singularly complete and so set apart from beauty's intensifying ideality. Indeed what is special about this singular one has to do with what is most ordinary about him, his sheer existence. Thus Kierkegaard builds on the "example" just cited to criticize orthodoxy's confusing embellishments:

[A] childish orthodoxy has also gotten the decisive attention directed to the fact that Christ at his birth was swaddled in rags and laid in a manger, in short, to the humiliation involved in his coming in the lowly form of a servant, and it believes that this is the paradox in contrast to coming in glory. Confusion. The paradox lies chiefly in that God, the eternal, has come into existence in time as an individual man.

Whether this individual man is a servant or an emperor is neither here nor there; it is not more adequate for God to be king than to be beggar; it is not a greater humiliation for God to become a beggar, than to become an emperor.[56]

Here, then, the unconditioned is related to human existence because it is one with human existence! Surely this will intensify every person in existence who confronts this claim seriously. Kierkegaard has his eyes on each such individual in speaking of the one individual said to be God in time:

[A] self directly before Christ is a self intensified by the inordinate concession from God, intensified by the inordinate accent that falls upon it because God allowed himself to be born, become man, suffer, and die, also for the sake of this self. . . . Qualitatively a self is what its criterion is. That Christ is the criterion is the expression, attested by God, for the staggering reality that a self has, for only in Christ is it true that God is man's goal and criterion or the criterion and goal.[57]

So Kierkegaard knew that Christianity is in principle a passionate affair, whatever one must make of the practice in Christendom. He was right in that, for in this faith we have the intensifying components twice over: divine completeness constituting a thoroughly temporal Christ, and human responsibility facing an unconditional issue. A self bent on intensification would be more than a little interested in this claim.

But passion seems too simple a test. There are questions that must be considered before this faith can win a fully human affirmation. We identify these questions at the end of this chapter in order to address them in the chapters that follow.

CAN THIS WORD BE TRUE?

Hans Küng asks our question "Why should one be a Christian?" We share his answer "In order to be truly human." This is his brief summary of what that means:

> By following Jesus Christ man in the world of today can truly humanly live, act, suffer and die: in happiness and unhappiness, life and death, sustained by God and helpful to men.[58]

Well, that is worth talking about at least. We may agree—theist, agnostic, atheist alike—that even the brief statement of claims made in the last section does "raise the bid" in the game of human life. This is not an idle tale, this gospel. But as the dialogue continues there are a number of questions to consider before we can be done with this issue of faith's intensification of human becoming. They amount to asking, Can this word be true?

The self asks, Is it true for me? At least part of that question is this one: Is it true *to* me? That is, granting—if only for the moment—the claim about the reality of this God, is this word good, does it bless? We may not be prepared to accept with Eliot decisive damnation as a satisfactory salvation. Contemporary representatives of the world of religion should not wonder that this question is asked. Decades ago Rudolf Otto's highly influential analysis spoke of the holy as the *mysterium tremendum et fascinans*.[59] To what we have said of God thus far, both terror and fascination seem possible responses. This God is not dull, and any religion having to do with this God is not boring. But is the word good, sweet? Is it true to me in my need?

This question does not disappear when we consider the specifically Christian claims centering on the existence of Jesus of Nazareth. That God is one with the human in this one—is this good news?[60] For that matter, is it even news at all *for me*? That in this incarnation of the unconditioned there is an intensification of existence may be true, but what has that to do with *my* existence?

How, for example, does the action of God in a first-century figure named Jesus accommodate my reality? Does it in any sense need me? Or, to soften the chronological difficulties somewhat, how does the God who acts in Jesus need me, if that action is—as we are told—truly decisive? Which way is it? Shall we say that the message of incarnation directs us to the sheer decisiveness of this one birth? Very well, that birth is done. But is that its strength or its weakness? How is the word of that birth true to me? Can it welcome my becoming somehow? Does it somehow fit me? What, for example, does it have to do with what is past in my own self's project? As I am called to believe in this saving birth, the invitation seems to pull me way back behind and before my becoming. Does not the dramatic singularity of Jesus' birth sever me from my own history?

Is this disconnection-with-self-become-connection-with-Jesus itself held forth as good news, so that one is to celebrate the chasm and give up trying to find human identity in lived continuity? We have been following Kierkegaard's trenchant statement of the Christian call to intensification. He sometimes seems to find connection precisely in the discontinuities. Thus he ponders together incarnation and original sin:

> From eternity the individual is not a sinner; so when the being who is planned on the scale of eternity comes into the world by birth, he becomes a sinner at birth or is born a sinner, and then it is that existence, by surrounding this being at all sides so that every communication with the eternal by way of recollection is cut off, and the predicate "sinner" which is then first applied but applied at once at the moment of coming into the world—then it is that existence acquires such overwhelming power that the act of coming into the world makes this being another. This is the consequence of the Deity's presence in time, which prevents the individual from relating himself backwards to the eternal, since now he comes forwards into being in order to become eternal by relationship to the Deity in time.[61]

Such candor may be commendable, but does the content carried by these audacious sentences commend the gospel? If the self is to find this strange world of two births to be true, three tasks must be addressed by the representatives of Christian faith:

1. It must be shown that the crucial connecting condition, the ineluctable reality of sin, is truly mine. To do that one must show that the responsibility that is intrinsic to humanity is not replaced in this understanding by fatedness. Ironically, only if I can be shown that this life of sin is truly my life,

will I be willing to give it up to claim the decisively new word as salvation for me.

2. Some connection needs to be established between faith in the decisive Jesus and all that in human life which is truly mine but is not sin or at least not simply sin. What of the elements of the human project, for example— one's physical locatedness, one's entertaining of possibility, one's sociality, and so on? And what of those experiences we have called aesthetic and moral intensifications of human becoming? Are participation in beauty and in human affection and commitment to be renounced in order to buy the decisiveness of the Christian's new birth?

3. Granted that a new life is needed and that we wrongly cling to much that counts against fuller humanity, is the new actually permitted in the Christian understanding of things? As compared with the first century is it not I who am the new? Can, for that matter, *anything* future for Jesus be accommodated, be enhanced? Is history in effect closed off in the knife-edge thinness of one person's life in the first century?[62] The self asks this question about more than itself, but it does ask it of its own self. I am told new birth awaits me. But how effectively new can I be, if I cannot matter in the course of history? Does it help to say that the particularity of the incarnation dramatizes the contingency of all human becoming?[63] Will Christian faith settle for the decisiveness of a paradigmatic illustration? Is it useful to say that the movements of new birth begin in the very becoming of the human self that is such, even setting the Christian particularity aside, as must defy any "substance" view of human identity?[64] Must not some statement of the connectedness, however "dynamic," be forthcoming?

These questions need to be addressed and in the chapters that follow I will take them up in probing the connection between Christian faith and human striving. But it is at least clear that Christianity regards its objective word to connect with the subjectivity of the hearers in one respect: it is to be believed. Can I, then, believe this word? Well, for that to occur it must be a word. Here one asks not of the word's fit with human becoming but of the word itself. Does it fit with itself? Is it coherent? We may note that this question of coherence arises with any religious appeal to the unconditioned. In chapter 3 we raised the issue by asking whether a wholly other God can be believed to touch human life. Can the unconditional character of God be formulated in relation to human life in some intelligible way? Some traditional ways seem closed to us today. Thus, it is doubtful that we can make much of a great chain of being linking us to the unconditional God. We doubt that being comes in such degrees at all. Perhaps it is just as well that this way is closed, for such an approach seems to let a difference of degree present itself as a difference in kind. But to see through one formulation is not to discern a better one. The difficulty must be addressed.

This difficulty is reflected in the notion of incarnation, in which we are told that the two realities, seemingly non-compossible, have in fact become one. How can this be? The game is up if we say we are actually talking about a God who only appeared to be a man or about a man who once was God (though that in itself would be hard enough for most of us to conceive). In this one are united two radically different realities—that remains the claim even when the sermon is ended. But if this is the game, how is anyone concerned with coherence able to play it? I doubt it will do to appeal to paradox, unless one can show that this paradox is better than a logical contradiction. We will likely not be satisfied with the assertion that this reality is nonobjectifiable in speech, unless we hear convincing nonecstatic talk about the status of such a category and the appropriateness of its employment in this instance.

These are questions about the relationship of God to the world. They arise because that is where the self is—in the world. If the questions are not faced, the promise of God bids in effect to pry the self out of its constitutive sociality, to lift the believer out of the world. The history of religion includes more than a few instances of world-denying faith. For that matter one may wonder if there is something mistaken about the way the question is put— the question to which faith holds the answer. Does the preoccupation with unity and identity itself run counter to our realistic sense that life must be lived out in the many?[65] One may hope that human beings inside and outside the churches will be little tempted by a call to become solitary knights of faith walking with the Lord in inwardness. Perhaps we understand with new clarity today that for a self to leave its world to be with any God would be for the self to leave itself. The subtle totalitarianism of such a faith is surely no less an evil than the overt totalitarianism of the state.[66] But again, to recognize a path as wrong is not to find a new way forward. We will not find such a way without thinking very carefully about God and the self-in-world apart from the figure of Jesus.

Enough has been said for our conversation concerning the Christian gospel to continue. We must ask, In what world would that word of God be true? In our world? Christian faith does not find that question alien at all, for it believes that God is precisely the one who creates a world for the self.

6 TO COMMEND COMPREHENSION

Toward Having a World by Reason of Word

Does faith make sense? Is its intoxicating intensification that of fantasy, or does it stand on solid ground? The question matters. Faith promises to make a fulfilling difference to the becoming self, but it can do this only if it truly connects with that self. Faith does not connect by merely confirming that which is there apart from faith. Intensifying differences do not come about by duplication. Instead faith might identify with life precisely by identifying life: its status, its significance, its upshot. Such a connecting would count as making sense of life. But faith cannot make sense of life without life. The central Christian claim about Jesus of Nazareth suggests as much: the one who is qualitatively other comes into our world so that we who live out our days here may now do so differently. We are to become in relation to this Other. That is the claim concerning intensification considered in the previous chapter. But that claim's connectedness with this world cannot be taken for granted.

It is a world for which we are looking. In seeking to understand its God, faith is seeking a world—that is, a kind of connectedness in the truth it claims to bear. But Christians can only understand their God when at the same time they understand how the word about God connects with their world. This word is not its own world.

Our world does not have itself on its own either—that is the witness of faith. This world is a gift; it is being given. This claim matters enough to interest us, to irritate and intrigue us. For we are looking for a world. That quest is not limited to Christians. Simply as humans we want to know how things hang together. What is a world for? The person who travels to other places and the historian who studies other times quest for the sustaining structure by which reality becomes accessible.[1] Two interests, to live creatively and to understand coherently, persist. These two often stand in reciprocal service. Thus physicists hunt for subatomic particles that would permit them to unite their understanding of the natural world in a single framework. That seems a speculative dream, but it is clearly one that depends upon a nuts-and-bolts technology to which it would in turn pay dividends.[2]

Particularly in our time the question of how we can live well together worries politicians and political scientists, psychologists and sociologists. Richard Sennett has told us of the fall of public man; Christopher Lasch has told us what the culture of narcissism looks like.[3] The details of such analyses will require debate, but we are not in doubt that the inward turn could encounter merely the stagnation of our own solitariness. Or what is more than inwardness may become as dangerous as insularity. Thus, today those who sense such danger call for a movement beyond balance of power or national individualism, in the search for world security.[4]

Such a quest for a world in which to live and understand may be seen no less in those who seem to specialize in intensifying particularities: the musicians, the film-makers, the poets. Or does the quest in fact concern them especially, since they know creativity requires some kind of order to nourish its children, yea, even to bear them?

Christian faith offers itself to those seeking a world. Other religions do so as well.[5] But we will be well occupied in considering the Christian claim about God as creator. In that claim the world sought and found even independently of faith may itself be comprehended. Thus the Christian gain in intensification is consolidated and complemented.

CLAIM AND CONSEQUENCE: THE WORLD IS CREATED BY AND SO COMPREHENDED IN GOD

The Christian faith speaks of God as the world's creator. In the many words that bear this witness there is such diversity that it is not completely clear how the claim is to be understood. Yet there is a broad consensus regarding some aspects of the claim.[6] First, to speak of one's creatureliness is not to speak of how one thinks but of how one is. The self and its consciousness do not dominate this speaking. Rather, in speaking of creation one speaks of the self as a part of the cosmos. The earth is full of God's creatures who praise God by simply being what they are (Ps. 148) and who look to God, from whose hand they receive their food (Ps. 104). God's continuing creative work is not conditional upon the moral performance of its recipients, for the sun and the rain do not so distribute themselves (Matt. 5:45). Christians emphasize the sheer gratuity of God's work of creation: its unconditional and universal character.

Yet, secondly, there is a kind of contingency that characterizes this work. The comings and goings of the gifts of creation at times appear arbitrary; at least they are beyond calculating. Wisdom settles for saying, The Lord gives

... the Lord takes away (Job 1:21). We speak, then, not of metaphysical givens, but of creative gifts. In any case, to speak of creation is to speak of will. As the fruit of will, creation may be contingent, but it is celebrated in its constancy. That is a matter of special comfort to God's people:

> The Lord is the everlasting God, the creator of the ends of the earth. He does not faint or grow weary. . . . He gives power to the faint. . . . (Isaiah 40)

Such constant action is gift; it does bless. Moreover, it is blessing that is to become a blessing. In the first three chapters of Genesis humankind is given the commission to subject the earth to dominion, as well as the commission to cultivate and take care of the garden. With the gift the task is given as well. God intends that something will come from this work of creation. Here one bids to identify a world. Here is a stable structure freely given to nourish the self's becoming. If the God of whom we speak when we speak of Jesus is the creator of this structure, then surely the Bethlehem story is a matter of "coming to one's own." To become a self before such a creative and constant One could hardly be to jettison the human. Any newness would be that of intensification.

Is this claim that connects the availability of a world with the creative action of God credible? The stakes are high enough at least to make clear that this is not an idle tale. It is worth considering how the experience of faith may be fit for humankind. We attempt to do that in the next section. First we seek to fill out the connection claimed. God gives to all persons a world so that they may create and understand. Christian faith declares that this world itself is created by and so understood in God. Thus, human "worldly" acts of comprehension and creation are fortified and extended.

Perhaps such a contemporary Christian approach to creation parallels a pattern discernible in biblical speech. We began Christian commendation with talk of the conscious intensification of human existence. Similarly, the God that Israel would confess is often portrayed not as a God of nature but as a God of a people (the Fear of Isaac, the Shield of Abraham, the Mighty One of Isaac). This is not a God of place but a "leader" God. Over against the "Elim" of Canaan and the fertility religions, Yahweh is a nomadic God who leads the people through the desert to the promised land. Whatever else is unclear, it is clear that this chosen people is on the move. We are speaking here of power, of potentiation. But more needs to be clear. The intensifying word cannot be fruitfully possessed without a world, and the biblical writers do subsequently speak of creation. On the plains of Jericho the people of Israel ate of the produce of the land: "And the manna ceased on the morrow, when they ate of the produce of the land; and the people of Israel had manna no more, but ate of the fruit of the land of Canaan" (Josh.

5:12). Israel needs to know that it is Yahweh who gives such produce (Hosea 2:5, 8), and fertility is to be recognized as Yahweh's blessing. Thus David can bring the nomadic ark of God to the holy city Jerusalem in order that the Lord of hosts may be worshiped there (2 Samuel 6).[7]

Perhaps it is, then, because of a very particular redemptive word that God's people come to ponder the world and its beginning. Yet that is not the only way to get there. Indeed as one comes to that matter one will meet others who have something at stake here as well, if not that particular word. Thus Westermann writes:

> The Creation myths . . . had the function of preserving the world and of giving security to life. . . . It was not the philosopher inquiring about his origins that spoke in the Creation narratives; it was man threatened by his surroundings. The background was an existential, not an intellectual problem.[8]

One may agree with this description of the motivation of at least some creation talk and go on to observe the consequences of such talk. Such talk provides a foundation for more than a redemptive word. There arises the possibility of interest in and trust in the "wisdom" of the world in itself, and thus in human responsibility in living creatively in that world.[9] The person of faith accounts for such human flourishing by recalling the gracious constancy of the Creator. The story of the flood vividly reminds the faithful of the contingent or gift character of the cosmos (cf. Jer. 31:35–37; 33:20–26), but the story's ending rehearses the reliability of the cosmos for all:

> I will never again curse the ground because of man . . . neither will I ever again destroy every living creature as I have done. While the earth remains, seedtime and harvest, cold and heat, summer and winter, day and night, shall not cease. (Gen. 8:21–22)

Thus, to speak of God is not to demean and deny the world but to compliment and comprehend it. Because of this God the world makes sense. Anyone who makes sense does so *through* the world; people of faith make sense *of* it. People of faith make this connection in a number of ways. A brief consideration of several approaches will shed light on the Christian claim to comprehend. The claim appears most aggressively in the classic theological proofs; it is still present in a softer form in the "approaches" that parallel the proofs.

The cosmological approach to God indeed seeks to "comprehend," that is, to "contain or hold within a total scope" *(O.E.D.)*. It is precisely the cosmos, the ordering and ordered whole, that is here affirmed to bear witness to its creator. The affirmation is not an uncomplicated one. A fundamental formulation has been that of an original creation of the world out of nothing.[10] In the next section I will offer a reformulation of what I take to be the intent of this notion. Here, though, some comment is in order. The notion of an origin that is absolute (hence from nothing) seems to be a "limiting" conception that stands at the edge of our thinking. Or is it in fact beyond our thinking? Is it too difficult to think? Is it unthinkable? To speak of such a reality as absolutely unique seems to reidentify the difficulty rather than to remove it.

Someone considering these conceptual difficulties will not be much aided by attempts to explain, or even defend, the notion empirically. Theologians may be interested in the ascendancy of the "big bang" cosmology, but it remains unclear how something—however volatile—might bear witness to nothing. (If that did become clear, would we then understand how that nothing reveals Someone else?)[11]

Mortimer Adler finds it useful to turn to the fact that our contingent cosmos continues, and to draw from this fact the reasonable conclusion that there is a "preserving Cause." But Adler speaks here of persuasion, not conviction: "[T]he proposition that the cosmos is radically contingent and needs an efficient cause of its continuing existence . . . cannot be affirmed with certitude but only beyond a reasonable doubt."[12]

One might applaud the candid modesty of this assertion, but what is worrisome about the cosmological "proof" is precisely its failure to take the contingency of the cosmos radically enough. Would we not take the universe's contingency truly radically if we simply said nothing to explain it? Or if we insist on saying something, could it not be that something like the principle of inertia, which helps to explain change within the universe, applies as well to the system as a whole?[13] Is something else, something analogous to the efficient causes that team with inertia within the system, some super efficient cause, needed to explain the system? Why? What counts as sufficient explanatory reason? What does it mean to say that every event has a cause? Indeed a strong form of the principle of sufficient reason threatens to explain too well, undercutting precisely the free-flowering finite efficient causes with the claim that every state of affairs requires an explanation outside itself.

Perhaps, then, we are not dealing with a matter of proof and self-evidence.[14] Proofs aside, the cosmological approach still claims the world is comprehended in God. The first meaning of "comprehend" is, after all, "to see the nature, significance, or meaning of." In faith's move, the ordering function of the world is grasped and understood the more fully. Thus, to speak of a cause of the system of causes is to confirm availability of that cosmic system in its role of supporting action and understanding. That this reference to the creator contributes to comprehension is indicated by its consequences. Given God the creator, one comes to expect to make sense of things. Thus, to know what faith knows about the whole is in principle to know something about every particular, or at the very least to expect to learn something about every particular. One is following out the coordinating move of the act of understanding to its logical conclusion. If to understand is to employ a world, will it not help to have that world guaranteed and gathered in its givenness?

Still, one must move delicately. It is possible that the reference to God yields a "clarity" that in fact undercuts the creativity of that which one is trying to understand. Thus the imagined meaning of the whole may cause us to miss the true mystery of the parts. If the contingent creatures are not to be compromised somehow, the description of God's creative and preserving causality must contain considerable "play" for the parts.[15] If, for example, we say that the adventure of creaturely freedom is "grounded" in God, do we thereby really support or actually stifle the splendor of existence? Ground is support; existence is thus affirmed, and perhaps there is as well a hint of the goodness of being in this metaphor. Yet one may understand either too much or too little. Too little in that, since we are talking about the cause of the whole of things, we seem to discover in the knowledge of this cause no guidance for the particular choices that must be made if life is to be fostered rather than suppressed. Or too much in that, without a correction by some other elements in the believer's understanding, the cosmological move may in fact curve back away from our creative present, whether toward philosophical determinism or toward popular piety's appeals to "old time religion" and the golden age of Eden.

There are other approaches. The person of faith knows something new about the cosmos, for faith declares what it is: the creation of God. Perhaps the Christian here has moved from saying, "What a wonder that there is a world!" to saying, "No wonder there is a world, for God is." But if that change is not to be stultifying, a wonder-removing piety that actually explains away contingent creativity, another question needs to be asked: What is the world for? The teleological approach, the approach from design, takes up that query.

As with the cosmological approach, here too the theist and the atheist see something in common. The theologian F. R. Tennant sees such things as (1) the adaptation of thought to things, (2) the internal adaptation of organic being, (3) the fitness of the inorganic for the organic, (4) the aesthetic value of nature, (5) the world's instrumentality in the realization of moral ends, and (6) progress in evolution.[16] The philosopher of science Errol Harris constructs his list around the notion of a "nisus to integration immanent in things from the beginning":

So in terrestrial conditions there is the potentiality of life, in primitive organisms the potentiality of elaboration, in auturgic self-maintenance of biotic activity the potentiality of consciousness and conceptual thinking.[17]

There does seem to be something to talk about. How shall we understand the nearly undoubted presence of purposing phenomena, particularly in those instances where purpose is neither immanent to its agent nor imposed by an earthly designer? How shall we understand, for example, not the evolution of one species from another but the origin of species as such?

Faith comprehends this by speaking of a God who not only creates but who in creating intends and so designs. God acts and in acting aims at a further state of affairs. Once again, faith does not prove this. The connection between purpose and design is too weak; faith will not try to counter that by capitalizing on the incoherences in alternative explanations of the existence of unconscious purpose. Moreover, faith feels the force of charges that the appeal to design denies the reality of genuine innovation in nature. It understands that one can miss the meaning of life's spontaneity either by fixing too firmly on life's beginning or its end.

Faith will find better those teleological explanations that concentrate on particularity and novelty in the churning middle of life. Here design is less apt to be defined and discerned at the expense of the other, the designed. For example, Whitehead's appeal to the whence of ever-new forms of relevant order within ongoing universal creativity attracts faith's interest.[18] One seeks to avoid conceiving order in static or deterministic terms. Static explanations in effect explain away, and with the aim so ambitiously defined, always risk resorting to an appeal that converts apparent counterinstances into capital. "This suffering is so pointless that it must reflect God's purpose"—as if absurdity were the incognito of divine intentionality. Appeal to God's plan, even God's purpose, is a dangerous thing. But it could not be dangerous if it were not powerful. It does, that is, understand something. It understands that this life is for something. It is, faith says, for some*one*, even. It is thus the case not merely that life has a basic goodness to it in that it reflects God's choice to create. Something is to happen here, something specific.

We are on the brink of moral talk, and the third approach I want to discuss. Design does involve a conception of the good. Consider, for example, quite nonreligious talk of adaptation for survival:

The modification must have "value" as an *improvement* of the system in the environmental conditions, as increasing its efficiency and operation. Otherwise survival will be jeopardized. But when we speak of "improvement" and "efficiency" we are using teleological language, and there must be some criterion of value by reference to which improvement and efficiency are measured.[19]

In being good *for* something, created life is called to turn *against* something. Some at least of life's functions seem to depend on the freedom of the living. The reality of moral choice confirms this emerging hunch.

Also in this third approach there is indubitably a world to be understood. One need not speak as forthrightly as those do who experience the moral intensification of which we spoke in the last chapter. Indeed one may try to cloak the particular "bite" of the normative. Thus, one may try to define abnormality as deviation from an average without specifying appropriateness.[20] But there remains, more pointedly, the stark experience of the ought to which human beings continue to bear witness. Indeed what has withered in our time is not the experience of moral conviction but a structure of understanding in which such experience makes sense. That structure would need to recognize the distinctions between the moral, the immoral, and the amoral.[21]

Faith comprehends this. Or, once more in the dictionary's phrasing, it "sees the nature and the significance" of the moral. It understands that an Other who is the creator of life would have the needed moral "leverage." Such leverage is rooted in the very "is-ness" of what is created. But faith understands as well that if the creation is genuinely other than its Maker, there will be ambiguity in discernment and difficulty in the realization of the direction. It knows that the moral carries the particularity of will so that while all life may be good, some choices are not good but evil.

Faith comprehends morality; it does not create it. It makes no effort to exorcise moral consciousness, as if one were to be told there can be no morality without religion. Fortunately that is not so; fortunately the world of the moral is more firmly given by God than that. But to one who would understand moral experience in its origin and status, faith bears a witness that the good, the right, is God's will for the world. One does not need to know that in order to perform good acts—again, fortunately. But knowing it may alleviate suspicions about the mere subjectivity of moral consciousness, even as the personal relationship to this Other may provide intensifying incentives for moral action.[22]

The world is created by and therefore comprehended in God. We have traced three approaches by which this claim can be developed. The claim speaks about two realities: this world and God. Here two into one will not go. Neither one will suffice alone. It may be particularly tempting to the person of faith to give unqualified priority to God. God alone is to be worshipped—faith believes that. But one must work from both ends to understand the sentence "The world is created by and therefore comprehended in God." God may in some sense be one in perfect simplicity, and so, unchanging, but the world is neither, and does not become so by being mentioned in the same sentence with God. If one speaks of creation, and so comprehension, without speaking of contingency, of change and plurality, it is not this world one is describing.

Recent work in science supports this. The ordering of movement seems to have alteration and novelty at its very core. David Bohm's experiments suggesting instantaneous "action at a distance" seem to support Niels Bohr's quantum theory against Einstein's preference for a relativity theory in which "God does not play dice."[23] Similarly, to speak of evolution seems to be to speak of alternating advances and stabilizations rather than of a steady and predictable progress.[24] Or if the physicist teaches us that "the observer is inescapably promoted to participator," should not the philosopher forgo the fantasy of holding an objective mirror to an independent reality?[25] Still, the lesson of uncertainty, of indeterminacy, may be hard to learn. If science stresses continuities in its method, will it not be "catastrophic" to have to acknowledge the discontinuities?[26]

The lesson seems no easier for theologians. Perhaps, though, it should be and would be if faith's own witness were heard. For faith knows that it was by will that God created us, and there are therefore in life the regularities that befit the constancy of will. A real world is offered here, as Daniel O'Connor makes clear over against, "at the one end, the Greek view of intelligibility through participation in archetypal forms and, at the other, such an emphasis on the inscrutable omnipotence of God as to eliminate all intelligibility."[27]

The Christian word about the creator God and the nonreligious description of the dynamic character of the world seem to cohere very well. That fit will be still more impressive once it is recognized that there is a true reciprocity between the realities described. Then it will be harder for the witness of faith to explain the data by explaining them away. Rather, the appeal to faith will aid in the understanding of our world precisely because what is there to be understood, "that" world, is itself caught up in God. Is God changed by that world? Can faith not only claim that the world reflects the character of its maker but grant as well that the world contributes to that character? To suppose so is actually only to follow out faith's own logic. If in creating, God intends, indeed wills, something bearing on that which is created, then surely this is a matter of consequence for God. If the world is to be comprehended in God, it will find in God not only its ground, but its goal as well. In its coming and its going the world puts the question of its whence and whither. The world is understood in God and it is realized in

God. All things come from God and they go to God. This life matters because it is lived in relation to God; to believe that intensifies life. The moments of time acquire a new measure of momentousness. Faith knows that the God before whom life is lived is the beginning and the end. But alpha and omega are not the same, unless what is between them is only illusory.[28]

The faithful say that the world is comprehended in God. Faith sees what those without faith see when they set about to explain experience, and it "accounts" for that, completes that. Nonreligious explanation orders contingent particularity and arranges the order hierarchically. Faith accounts for the ordering as it completes it, by finding the world's explanation to be ultimately singular: God.[29] May, then, theology find its place within a company of systems, ranging from the subnuclear structure of physics to ensembles of ecosystems and beyond? Given the field-dependent character of reasoning, can we say of the attempt to comprehend the whole world, that its arguments have a rigor appropriate to their scope?[30] Is the case for Christianity, as it presents itself in the effort to comprehend the world in God, not about what we should expect if reality is a plurality-in-relation of free entities—only one of whom is God?

Here is an invitation to affirm Christian claims. But at least two major questions remain before such an affirmation is warranted. First, how can the serenity and confidence implied in faith's understanding of this world as God's creation be reconciled with the reality of absurdity and evil? And second, is not faith's message actually double talk? Is there not a fatal incoherence in speaking of God as ontologically truly other and yet as intimately connected with this world? Can a God who is truly ground (a matter hard enough in itself) be a goal as well? If God as goal awaits the world's efficacy anxiously, how can such a God provide the sure ground sought for the world? Can faith have it both ways?

CONNECTION AND CONDITION: THE WORD IS IN THE WORLD AND IS ITSELF WORLDLY

Faith tries to comprehend the world by speaking of One who is other than the world, God. Faith fulfills our desire and effort to have a world, by fortifying the givenness, the directedness, and the momentousness of life. We can accept that benefit. But we wonder about its basis. How does faith manage to speak of that which is more or other than this world? However it does, will that speaking not rob the rest of our speaking of full significance? May it not be better to muddle along without the peace that the "explanations" of a bad faith can bring?[31]

Christians need to make clear—to themselves and to others—that the call is not to cancel the world but to comprehend it. Once again the dictionary instructs us: to comprehend is "to take in or include by construction or implication." Faith looks to God, but it looks at the world and takes it into itself. It need not deny the world—that by and in which we create and understand as human beings. Indeed, it must not, for its Word is in the world and this word is itself worldly. The Word has come to be among us with unconditional decisiveness and as such may be properly described as worldly. Three senses of this worldly Christian word may be distinguished.

1. There is the external or objective word that evokes the Christian's response. The externality of this word to the Christian is most dramatically evident in speaking of Jesus, the Word made flesh. "Flesh" should not leave this Word's worldliness much in doubt, and it was not left in doubt at Chalcedon, where Jesus was spoken of as "consubstantial with us in manhood, like us in all things except sin."[32] One may question speaking of the human nature of Jesus as "impersonal," as well as the other efforts at Chalcedon to deny the reality of Jesus' relativity.[33] These efforts fail before both the biblical witness to Jesus and the contemporary witness to what it is to be human.[34]

2. Christians know that their own responding word of confession is no less worldly. Christians share the struggle of this earth when they turn to claim the word of promise as their own. Who, after all, are the leaders of this company? A Paul who saw through a glass darkly, a Luther who struggled with temptation mightily, and in our century an Eliot who wrote that, unlike the tenets of the Marxists, "my own beliefs are held with a skepticism I never even hope to be quite rid of."[35]

3. The Christian should surely recognize that the reflective word that proceeds from and ponders the evocative and responsive words is itself emphatically worldly. In speaking this third word Christians strive for understanding, but always with a sense of incompleteness. Theologians increasingly recognize that even such central, "given," dogmas as Chalcedon's christological formulation of Jesus as one person with two natures give the church a task. In Karl Rahner's words:

> Work by the theologians and teachers of the Church bearing on a reality and a truth revealed by God always ends in an exact formulation. That is natural and necessary. For only in this way is it possible to draw a line of demarcation, excluding heresy and misunderstanding of the divine truth, which can be observed in everyday religious practice. But if the formula is thus an end, the result and the victory which bring about simplicity, clarity, the possibility of teaching and doctrinal certainty, then in this victory everything depends on the end also being seen as a beginning.[36]

To speak of the worldliness of the word is to acknowledge incompleteness, tentativity. But it is also to contend for understanding, for clarity. If Christian faith is worldly in this last sense, it must speak its words coherently. Christian faith says that God is here. That is hardly superfluous, for it could certainly occur to a religious zealot that the best way to have a God would be precisely to leave this worrisome world. To the contrary, God is here and indeed the specific manifestations of God's presence in theophany and tabernacle stand out, but do not exhaust God's presence. The psalmist can exclaim in praise: "Whither shall I go from thy Spirit?" (Ps. 139:7). Psalm 139 was cited in the last chapter, but its beautiful and pertinent witness may be repeated:

> Whither shall I go from thy Spirit?
> Or whither shall I flee from thy presence?

Moreover, people of faith know that God is not only in their world. God is in the world *with* them, interacting with them, moving into a future that is open. Thus God suffers because of the suffering of the people—weeping (Isa. 16:9; Jer. 9:10; 48:32), wailing (Jer. 48:31), crying out (Isa. 15:5; Jer. 48:31), moaning (Isa. 16:11; Jer. 31:20). And God suffers because those people have rejected the one who bore them. God is described as grieving (Gen. 6:6; Ps. 78:40), burdened (Isa. 43:24), and wearied (Isa. 43:24; Mal. 2:17; Jer. 45:3).[37]

To cite so many passages is to the point because the reality of the divine suffering is so seldom taken seriously. Perhaps those looking the other way, as it were, have worried that such a God—so emphatically with us—might seem to lack the otherness needed to make a true difference. But that we are still dealing with one who is qualitatively other may be suggested by looking at another remarkable group of passages that speak of another mode of interaction, the divine repentance. While these passages vary significantly, an important theme in several of them is precisely that God's will is clear and reliable. Abraham pleads for the righteous in Sodom: "Shall not the Judge of all the earth do right?" (Genesis 18). Moses rehearses to God the names of Abraham, Isaac, and Israel, "to whom thou didst swear by thine own self . . ." (Exodus 32).

God is here, with us. Thus it turns out that if Christian theologians are to speak coherently of their God, they will have to speak of a God in relationship to the world. How does that go? As theologians seek to formulate their reflective word, they will do well to consider a theme that lies within the more immediate responsive words of faith concerning the suffering and repentance of God: the will of God. It is by God's will that the relationship about which and within which we speak exists. It is to God's will that the people of God repair in confidence. Christian faith in God as creator is faith that we have this world because of God's will.

Indeed, the conception of a creation *by* will but *out of* nothing may well recognize the integrity of that which is not God in a way unavailable to more pantheistic outlooks. In those outlooks a depreciation has been seen to follow from the idea

> that the reality and value of finite things consist in the degree to which they are identical to or united with God. What is not God, then, is neither real nor good.[38]

If, on the other hand, God's reality need not be pitted against that which is not God, if the not-God can be recognized as real and good, then a way is opened to those who cannot doubt the reality of the world to look for and to God. That fits the fabric of biblical speech. God does not have to be the only being or have to be alone in order to be the only God. Rather God is "the holy one in your midst" (Isa. 12:6; Hos. 11:9; cf. Ezek. 20:41; 28:22). Holiness is loosely thought of as entailing a transcending distance or even an absence, but for Isaiah the Holy One is "great in your midst." The creative will that the other be is thus a will to be in the midst of the others, to be affected by those others.

We can recognize this divine reality as will; it traffics in possibility, choice, and consequence, as does our own willing. But in two respects the divine will is distinctive because of its unconditional character: (1) It is self-determining in origin. (2) It is decisive as it meets that which is not itself. There is thus an absoluteness about this will. In this, God is surely ontologically different from us, and it is little wonder that metaphysical categories in their perceived givenness have often functioned as a divine incognito. Neither of these distinguishing characteristics is in contradiction with the give-and-take of God's relationships with that which is not God. Rather it is here that God's will is working itself out. Thus it is that faith believes God wills to be God. We in faith do not speak of a relationship with one who once was God. God has not stopped being God by being God for us.

If this much is clear to Christian faith as it seeks to speak its reflective word, more may become clear as well. It will be important to think about the attributes of God as descriptions of the God who has willed to be for us. One will avoid carrying virtually unchallenged inventories of attributes and seek to move out from the "category proper" that cuts across the length and breadth of Scripture:

> The Lord, the Lord, a God merciful and gracious, slow to anger, and abounding

in steadfast love and faithfulness, keeping steadfast love for thousands, forgiving iniquity and transgression and sin . . . (Exod. 34:6–7)

It will be helpful to seek to describe the "formal" attributes in dependence upon this material description. Consider such a classic attribute as eternality; Robert Jenson points the way toward reformulation:

> As to how, positively, Yahweh is eternal, Israel's interpretation is that he is faithful. Where other ancient religions said that God is beyond time, Israel said: "For ever, thy word is firmly fixed in the heavens. Thy faithfulness endures to all generations; thou hast established the earth, and it stands fast." (Ps. 119:89–90)[39]

As temporality is taken within God the formal basis is in place for faith's sense that we matter to God, indeed that we can affect God. That will not diminish God if the theologians who focus on the future are right in criticizing "the spurious freedom of unaffectedness": "Genuine freedom is the reality of possibility, is openness to the future. . . ."[40] Indeed one might find this genuine freedom anchored in such a supposedly arcane formula as the "begetting" of the Son. The Son may not be created, but temporality is not denied:

> Nobody claimed to know exactly what "begotten" meant in this connection, and yet a tremendous assertion is made: there is a way of being *begun*, or receiving one's being which is proper to Godhead itself. To be God is not only to give being, it is also to receive being. And there went the rest of Plato.[41]

How, then, does God act? May God correctly be understood as the sole and direct cause of specific events? May God appropriately be called upon to do certain things in behalf of the faithful? What good is a will for us if that will or the one willing never does anything? Perhaps we do well to consider how the church's confession of the "ex nihilo" quality of God's creating coexists with recognizing a wide range of passages in which God creates (acts) through that which is not God, as in fashioning from material (Gen. 2:7—no less a case than the human person formed "from the ground") and even through conflict (Ps. 74:13–17; 89:9–10; 93; Isa. 27:1; 30:7; 51:9–10; Hab. 3:8). Perhaps the clue to understanding how God works now is to recall that God continues to be the world's creator.[42] Perhaps, then, faith means to say something like this: God works in an unconditioned way through means. The means do matter; it is through them that God works. But God will not fail to work, whatever the means—that is faith's confidence.[43] God always works with such self-determination and decisiveness that one may well say God always works "first," whether that be "before" or "within" that which is not first.

We are, I realize, some way yet from a clear conception of how this creative work "works." Fairly complex distinctions may be needed in formulating what is necessary for such an understanding. Eugene TeSelle, for example, focuses on the ex nihilo emergence of levels of complexity within the evolutionary process and describes three different ways of asking the question of divine action in relation to that which is not divine:

> It may be asked in terms of the sheer "thatness" of these radically contingent levels of activity. . . . Or it may be refined and phrased more analytically in terms of the *order* they evince—not their physical structure as such, but the functioning of all the parts and especially the complex interaction of these functions. . . . The question may be asked, finally, in terms of the quasi-voluntaristic *unification* of these many inter-relationships into focused acts. Here there will be an emphasis, above all, upon God as will, sustaining the activities of each being from within itself. . . .[44]

In one way or another God's action enters the being of that which is not God. That being's uncoerced responsive action in turn affects God. How do God's working and God's suffering our works in joy and sorrow come together? Faith confesses that God's act is always at once prior and pertinent. In reflecting on this confession it is possible to focus chiefly on the unity and priority of God's will so that one speaks somehow of history as a single act of God.[45] But such a focus fails to catch adequately the livingness of God's action in relation to the world. In attending to the interactions between God and the world, one is led to speak of God's actions as also reactions and, perhaps, to recognize that immutability, far from denoting a static remoteness of God, is rather an "attribute of the attributes" of God.[46]

Clearly we are not far from what has been called "the paradox of two agents."[47] It may be helpful to speak of different language strata, as one does in the determination of guilt or innocence in a court of law when one distinguishes but does not separate the action of personal intention and the action of molecules. But is it also a paradox to speak of more than one agent acting in every event that occurs in our lives? Are not the multiple actions of which we so speak not only distinct in their origin but different as well formally, in the way they come together to yield a particular single event? There is work for theologians in such a question. Perhaps Aristotle's four causes may still serve to point us toward a sufficiently subtle set of distinctions. To speak of God as creator, in any case, is to recognize the fundamental or internal character of God's action. Given that character, God's action may not "come up" in certain strata of language attending to other aspects of an event, even though that divine action is nonetheless toward and so even with the other action in the event.[48]

Christians claim that both the action and the passion of God are eminently realized in Jesus of Nazareth. The direction of Christian reflection concerning Jesus rightly follows the clues already given concerning God and the world. God and the human are together here. Faith will surely resist efforts to compromise God's presence and commitment. Historically the doctrine of the Trinity derives from the Christian desire to assert the full presence of God in Jesus. Therefore in Jesus we understand who God is. Thus even Tertullian, wary of Athens, could speculate:

> So in a sort of way you have in you a second discourse by means of which you speak by thinking and by means of which you think by speaking; discourse *(sermo)* itself is an other. How much more completely therefore does this action take place in God whose image and similitude you are authoritatively declared to be, that even while silent he has in himself reason, and in that reason discourse. So I have been able without rashness to conclude that even then, before the establishment of the universe, God *was not alone*, seeing he continually had in himself reason, and in reason discourse, which he made another beside himself by activity within himself.[49]

For God to know real relationships within the world does not go against the very life of God. Nonetheless, much current Christian reflection on the Trinity finds the distinction between the economic and the immanent Trinity to incur some compromise of the fullness of the divine commitment in Jesus.[50]

It is clear that faith wants to say that when we have to do with Jesus we have to do with all of God—that too is the point to speaking in the classical mode of "the external indivisibility of the works of the Trinity." But it is not in Jesus that we first have to do with this God. Indeed one must resist the temptation to defend the uniqueness of Christ by evacuating the rest of reality of God's presence. Such a Christ would be not decisive but demonic—having nothing to do with the structure of our personhood, as Tillich nicely put the distinction between the divine and the demonic.[51] The decisiveness of the divine will reaches back behind Jesus (Hosea 11:8–9).

Thus E. Schillebeeckx develops his massive works *Jesus* and *Christ* in accordance with the theological and anthropological principle that God had guaranteed that human life would have a positive significance, that he had himself staked his honor on it, and that that honor was his identification with the outcast, with the exploited, with the enslaved, above all with the sinner.[52] Even the formal mode of God's working this material will is not without preparation in the Old Testament theophanies, which can lead Eichrodt to speak of God as one who "can temporarily incarnate himself."[53]

The recognition that it is not in the human Jesus that God first has to do with what is human can help even in the effort to understand how the human and the divine are together in this Jesus.[54] Jesus, simply as human, is

God's creation, made in God's image, fit for God. Wolfhart Pannenberg stresses the connection:

> The openness to God that characterizes Jesus' humanity in his dedication to the Father and shows him to be the Son constitutes his personal identity with the Son. This is not alien to the humanity of man as such. It is in Jesus' Sonship that the destiny which has stood over man and which is intended from all eternity to become his future is fulfilled. Openness to God is the radical meaning of that human "openness in relation to the world" that constitutes man's specific nature in distinction from all animals.[55]

Does it also help to try to build upon that openness a new reality by appeal to a Hegelian dialectic? Pannenberg seems to offer such a construction:

> [I]t is the essence of the person itself to exist in dedication. . . . Thus the divinity of Jesus as Son is mediated, established through his dedication to the Father. . . . The mutual dedication of Father and Son to one another, which constitutes the Trinitarian unity of God, also established thereby first of all the true divinity of the Son.[56]

Questions remain. Are those of us who do not exist in such dedication not persons then? Are there none such? If all are such, or if any others are such, what is special about this Jesus? In trying to speak at once coherently and faithfully of God we have found we must try to speak coherently of God with us, as the case of Jesus dramatically demonstrates. A fuller response to remaining questions awaits chapter 7's account of a "decisive advance" in Jesus. But it is time to begin to evaluate this effort. Does the word make good sense? We ask: (1) Is this word sufficiently coherent to make sense? Is this word worldly in the sense that it holds together as free from internal division? Does it thus belong with candidates for making sense that need to be tested in the actual struggle of life, or does it stand with expressions numbing and blocking thought? (2) Does this word make convincing sense in the actual struggles of existence? Is this word in and of what we know as the world in such a way as to win our assent as a word that molds us as it fits us?

How shall these two questions be answered?

1. The notion of a will unconditionally committed to and in relationships conveys coherently both the sense of qualitative difference and that of existential involvement. That this is so does not clarify how such a will could or did create out of nothing. A. N. Whitehead may illuminate this question when he speaks of a divine primordial decision that at once "establishes and exemplifies the categoreal conditions" that characterize this world and action in it.[57] In reflecting on the character of such a divine decision, we get

a sense of a work of creation that is indeed not merely *in* but actually *of* the world.

Such an approach to the conception of God is not exclusive to the tradition of Whitehead. It belongs to all Christians who speak of God as one who wills radically. To speak of willing radically is to invite further discussion of the consequences of God's decisions. Thus Kierkegaard clearly speaks both of the "in-and-of-oneself" and the "for the other" that are together in the willing of God that issues in Jesus:

> God's servant-form is . . . not a disguise, but is actual; not a parastatic body, but an actual body; and from the hour when he with the omnipotent resolve of his omnipotent love became a servant God has so to speak imprisoned himself in his resolve, and now must go on (to speak foolishly) whether he wills to or not. He cannot then betray himself; he does not have the possibility which is open to the noble king [who tries to appear as a humble servant in order to win a maiden's love], suddenly to show that he is after all the king—which, however, is no perfection with the king (to have this possibility), but shows merely his impotence and the impotence of his resolve, that he does not actually have the power to become what he wills.[58]

Kierkegaard is known for his emphasis on the "infinite qualitative difference" between the divine and the human, and God's commitment to the human demonstrates rather than denies that difference, as surely as "purity of heart is to will one thing."

2. With this degree of clarification of faith's claim to commend a coherent word comprehending creation, does it make sense to accept the claim? It may be difficult to fathom fully this word, but it does not seem to be essentially unintelligible. It does not cancel out our other claims about meaning in a principled challenge perhaps, but is it to be trusted? This seems a more empirical question than the first question about coherence. To consider it we must move back and ahead from the sheerly particular redemptive word concerning Jesus to the claims concerning the world's ongoing relationship to its creator. The contention that faith's understanding supports and so fulfills the logic of our experience of life—its givenness, its directedness, its momentousness as aspects of its worldliness—this is perhaps more an appeal to rational completeness or to elegance than it is an empirical argument as such. But there are other elements of experience that offer themselves to persons caught up in the truth-seeking conversation of humankind. In the last chapter we spoke of experiences of joy, meaning, awe, and mystery. Of course these occur in this world, indeed often in relation to this world's coming and going for us. But that does not disallow the faith claim, for such experiences seem to witness to that which is other than the world.[59] It is to such experiences that specifically religious experi-

ence attaches itself in bidding to be authentically in the world by way of the broader human realities that connect with and carry it.

Of course these experiences—both the broader supporting suggestions of the numinous and specific religious experiences—can be variously explained. But among those explanations the one that does make a God-claim deserves a full hearing. The very variety of roads to "truth" encourages us to take seriously the inevitably distinctive claims of faith to account for such experiences. This is not to relativize the quest for truth in the sense of splitting the human community into miscellaneous special-interest groups. Such a babble does not serve God any more than the spurious simplicity of Babel did. It is rather to argue for a complex human conversation in which faith's commendations are taken seriously along with accounts that do not credit God-claims. Here our words, our conversation, reflect our world again. This method makes sense if reality is actually happening so that it will not hold still for static analysis and, moreover, if we who converse are ourselves caught up in that happening and so cannot afford the illusion of analytic transcendence. Thus Richard Rorty, giving up the deceptive lure of a neutral matrix for method, but questing still for "the largest possible story to tell about the history of the race," finds that

> to look for commensuration rather than simply continued conversation— to look for a way of making further redescription unnecessary by finding a way of reducing all *possible* descriptions to one—is to attempt to escape from humanity.[60]

Is the Christian faith a fitting description of reality? Can it contribute convincingly to this human conversation? How shall one decide on criteria for settling that question? If large-scale theories are never easily falsified, what combination of interest and suspicion should guide us as we consider faith's claims?[61] We will return to that question in our last chapter. But we can delay no longer the consideration of realities that seem to fly in the face of faith's claim about a good and powerful creator.

GOD AND FREEDOM'S FAULT: THE WORLD AND THE WORD ARE AT RISK

The directedness, momentousness, and givenness of the world available to all point to their ground and goal in faith's God. Where does evil fit within this conception? Or, rather, what does it do to the conception? William James describes the data well and draws the consequence:

> Beauty and hideousness, love and cruelty, life and death keep house together in indissoluble partnership; and there gradually stands over us, instead of the old warm notion of a man-loving Deity, that of an awful power that neither hates nor loves, but rolls all things together meaninglessly to a common doom.[62]

The world is at risk in this respect and so, surely, is the word. With no stable directional structure ready to support and receive my deeds, does not the claim that my choices matter ultimately, by mattering to God who grounds them—does not that seem incredible? What is given to us in the course of life seems a very mixed blessing, and so one that makes us anticipate that the ending so surely awaiting us is hardly apt to be happy. What can faith say to this? Is the game of coherence over?

Faith's word is an anguished one, since it does not deny the data or fail to feel the challenge of the argument based on the data. What can a faithful Jew make of the Holocaust, for example? Arthur Cohen stands aghast before "the singularity of a machinery conceived and constructed to destroy a whole people," but manages to stammer the word "caesura":

> The death camps cannot be transcended. There is no way of obliterating their historicity by overleaping them. Quite the contrary. If there is no transcendence beyond the abyss, the abyss must be inspected further. The descent deeper into the abyss must take place; in a word, the abyss must be *sub-scended*, penetrated to its perceivable depths. The task of excavating the demonic is not metaphor. How can we regard the atomic bomb, or Vietnam, or the revelations of Solzhenitsyn's *Gulag*, if not as modalities of the abyss, excavations and elaborations of the human penchant to self-infinity, to the ultimate *hubris* which brings not only Jews but all creatures to the borderlands from which there is return for none.[63]

Certainly Christians, involved, if differently, are in no better position to put the Holocaust tidily in its place. Christians will agree with Cohen that "it begins with the Jews and it may end with the habitable world." Christians know that as the world dissolves, the word withers. Christian faith will not be created out of nothing or by negation, as if the enormity of human evil enhanced the grandeur of an answering God. The evil in a theistic universe does not demonstrate the utter blindness of humans without also making an accusation against their creator. Such "escapes from evil" may tempt any of us, but the Christian call is not to them.[64]

Faith's word remains anguished. But it knows where to begin. It cannot cancel out what has been its confession: that God is here, unconditionally present with us and committed to us. What has that to do with evil? If God is inextricably committed to the reality of the other and thus to the other's freedom, then even a God ontologically superior in will cannot prevent the exercise of the freedom to produce evil. Consider the evil of unbelief. Kierkegaard states the point most directly: God does everything possible to win the creature's free response but cannot prevent the possibility of offense:

> [I]n Christianity God makes himself man (the God-man). But in this infinite

love of his merciful grace he nevertheless makes one condition: he cannot do otherwise. Precisely this is Christ's grief, that "he cannot do otherwise"; he can debase himself, take the form of a servant, suffer, die for men, invite all to come to him, offer up every day of his life, every hour of the day, and offer up his life—but he cannot remove the possibility of offense. What a rare act of love, what unfathomable grief of love, that even God cannot remove the possibility that this act of love reverses itself for a person and becomes the most extreme misery—something that in another sense God does not want to do, cannot want to do.[65]

Even the call to faith only "raises the bid" since God is committed to the creative venture of freedom.[66]

Thus the first thing Christian faith wants to say about evil has to do with the freedom of that which is not God. This is true freedom and not a cloaked form of divine causality. Sin illustrates that point with utter clarity. That which is against God, unfaith, is not itself from God. However strongly the Christian may want to stress the priority of God's creative action, it is crucial to make clear that such action "before" and "within" is also always "toward" the other(s). Whatever one may say of original creation ex nihilo, freedom is not now nothing. Statements about God, such as those concerning God's knowledge, must be adjusted accordingly. That will ease the difficulty in facing the question whether freedom was "worth it," that is, in considering the moral quality of the divine choice. In freedom there is uncertainty, given in freedom's complexity. We are an unstable mixture, a volatile synthesis. Freedom will happen here—that is freedom's power. Evil can happen here—that is freedom's "fault."[67]

In his magisterial study of *The Symbolism of Evil* Paul Ricoeur affirms the "pre-eminence" of the Adamic myth with its focus on human freedom, in part because this is "the place where one can best listen to, hear, and understand what all the myths together have to teach us."[68] The Christian begins here because this myth's exoneration of God fits well with the experience of guilt and the sense of responsibility. But there are other aspects of the experience of evil that seem to elude the Adamic treatment and indeed turn back against God, or at least reach beyond individual human beings. Even if we think only of moral evil—of that evil having to do with human volition—there seems to be a continuity, a persistence, indeed a givenness, that defies the individualistic emphasis of the Adamic myth. Moreover, this seems just the sort of thing that a moment ago we were calling a world pointing to its God. Is it not, then, God's doing, that freely wrought evil finds such hospitality in the conditioning that cradles choice? Should not the sinner be the object of compassion rather than blame?[69] And should not the accused be none other than God?

The "free will" defense we have been discussing may be applicable in some cases, for often we do harm ourselves and one another. But it seems fanciful to extend this defense to cover suffering outside human causality. Why, indeed, do "bad things happen to good people"?[70] Yet the believer who speaks of freedom is not done speaking even now. C. S. Lewis thus spoke of what freedom needs, to be freedom—before and beyond itself:

> What we need for human society is exactly what we have—a neutral something, neither you nor I, which we can both manipulate so as to make signs to each other. I can talk to you because we can both set up sound-waves in the common air between us. Matter, which keeps souls apart, also brings them together.[71]

Perhaps Lewis's point is more plausible if separated from his Platonism. God creates freedom and gives it what it needs to be freedom. If to be free is to create consequences by one's choices, one must have access to the structures of continuity. That helps in thinking about the continuity in sin of which we spoke. And those structures that serve human freedom's efficacy carry their own efficacy for good and ill, the more surely since we have no selves apart from the radical materiality of our being situated in this particular time-and-space world. "Natural evil" may come about precisely because we do have a reliable world.

Well, then, perhaps there is a sort of world here, after all. Perhaps we have a world that makes sense, given freedom's risk. This world may not be the worst one we can imagine. With Dorothee Soelle one might prefer this actual world, even with its suffering, to what would incontestably be a more comfortable way of life:

> The consequence of this suffering-free state of well-being is that people's lives become frozen solid. Nothing threatens any longer, nothing grows any longer, with the characteristic pains that all growth involves, nothing changes. The painless satisfaction of many needs guarantees the attainment of a quiet stagnation.[72]

It was in this way that William James took courage despite the "buzzing multiplicity" of good and evil. Cordell Strug comments:

> Of course one could see in Darwin the bleakness, the struggle, the materialism; but what James saw was change, movement, freedom, nature in motion, creation unended and unending, and the appearance of "spontaneous variations" which brought new qualities into existence. Darwin had distinguished between the production of an organism, its appearance, and its maintenance of survival and the theory of natural selection was formed to explain the latter. James, however, fastened on the mere fact of the former, the appearance of variations, as nature's great offering of novelty, a living sign of creation and possibility, the gift of a future.[73]

Is not this clearly a pluralistic universe, as James argued? It may be that we have not lost a world but found that the one we have is "in the making." We may prize the awesome gift of freedom and accept, mostly gladly, the regularities of nature, insofar as they serve freedom, but we notice that there seems to be a dizzying randomness about how all this is together. Thus the world is not simply God's world: God and all the rest of us and all the rest of it seem to be at work making whatever is to be.

But have we not saved God's goodness—especially if one prizes the awful gift of freedom—only to lose God's power? That God is goal, the world's ultimate destination, may seem to reassert God's qualitative otherness. But does that not simply make God the ultimate victim? It may help to know that we do not ever suffer alone, but is that enough? Indeed does not God actually finally suffer alone, if the "third face" of evil, finitude and death, prevails over us all? That death serves to make room for freedom in an evolving world seems true but unsatisfyingly incomplete. Is that what it will all come to in the end? If our world is so radically at risk, does it really help simply to register such dividedness and volatility by speaking the word "God"?

Norman Malcolm recounts:

> Wittgenstein was often struck by the feeling "How extraordinary that anything should exist!" and should testify it was always accompanied by the experience of feeling absolutely safe.[74]

Faith's claim about God as creator does so link the reality of the world with a redemptive word. The God who creates a world and comes to that world does more than raise the bid. God wills intensification and comprehension. But even in these experiences the human person looks for something more. Indeed, without something more it is not clear how the alleged gifts of intensification and comprehension are themselves available any longer. But it is not yet clear how more can be had, if God's superiority still exists in relation.

7 TO COMMEND RECONCILIATION

Toward Telling Time's Story in Actual Advance

THE RHYTHM OF RECONCILIATION:
A THIRD IS NEEDED

Something is needed. There seems to be difficulty between these two. In chapter 1, I spoke of a volatility or instability in the structure such that each term in the relationship bids to center reality independently and even exclusively. I suggested that the tugging in one direction or the other and the grudging accommodation of the other side could be seen in the rivalry between rationalist and empiricist theories of knowledge. I have further suggested that in the contemporary world we still employ the self-world structure, though with an ever-softer hyphen.

Perhaps a dawning sense of the artificiality of the separation of self and world should point toward a single unified understanding. There are indications, however, that instead the rivalry of perspectives has accommodated the convergence and risen to new forms and new levels of opposition. Do not, for example, many contemporary scientists propose to explain the self by understanding the world? Thus the gaps locating human uniqueness seem to shrink. Only a few decades ago proteins were thought to be hopelessly complex mixtures that could never be described like other molecules. But the 1982 Nobel prize awarded to Aaron Klug seems to celebrate the Cambridge "nuts and bolts" approach, which says that if you understand chemical structure, biological function will become self-evident. Persons who were shocked by Darwin's theory that they were descended from apes will not have an easier time acknowledging clay-crystal particles as the antecedents that possessed the ability to grow, reproduce, and pass on meaningful information and thus to evolve into "higher" forms according to natural selection.[1]

One does not expect such developments to pass without comment by those interested in the self. A characteristic form of response is to accept cosmological exploration but to deplore the associated tendency to deflect and even damage the understanding of the self. In his aggressively titled *Lost in the Cosmos: The Last Self-Help Book*, the novelist Walker Percy wonders why "it is possible to learn more in ten minutes about the Crab Nebula in Taurus, which is 6,000 light-years away, than you presently know about yourself, even though you've been stuck with yourself all your life." His response is at one level an answer and at another a second putting of the question:

> Every advance in an objective understanding of the Cosmos and in its technological control further distances the self from the Cosmos precisely in the degree of the advance—so that in the end the self becomes a space-bound ghost which roams the very Cosmos it understands perfectly.[2]

One could pause to observe assorted manifestations of this rivalry between self and world. From the vantage point of the self, for example, other selves may themselves come together to represent an alien world. Is that world or this self to be accorded explanatory preeminence? For example, do we learn to think and learn to speak by virtue of the social world's conditioning, or is there an inner resource simply waiting to grow, as it were?[3] Or, more prescriptively, the individual may find in the social world a threat to fundamental rights or a reality that promotes eros only by inflicting death in the form of guilt on its members.[4]

Happily, there are indications of a recognition that our life is not to be understood or advanced by juxtaposing self and world. Students of human relationships, for instance, remark that self-identity, while not an illusion, is an abstraction from the constituting relational matrix of life and so serves poorly as a guiding ideal. To speak of the self is to speak of the world—not merely because the self is in the world but because the world is in the self. The *world* is there, so that it is not surprising that manipulation of the brain hormones or neuropeptides will affect memory, mood, perception of pain, and the like.[5] But the world is *there*, in the self, so that a "romantic medicine" can be practiced in which play and music are the great liberators of the sick.[6]

As self and world are increasingly seen together, it may be better to employ another distinction, that between possibility and necessity. In chapter 5, I cited Kierkegaard's conception of the self as a synthesis in freedom of possibility and necessity. There is a givenness about the self—a locatedness, a structure of stability. But there is also a dawning sense of possibility, of burgeoning novelty. Perhaps one may speak of the givenness of the self as "body," suggesting something solid, fixed, and earthly. Then one may speak of the yet-to-be-realized goal or becoming of the self as "mind," suggesting something inquiring, imagining, and interested. These two are together in the human. Kierkegaard's suggestion is that the two are together in such a way that a third is given:

> In the relation between the two, the relation is the third as a negative unity, and the two relate to the relation and in the relation to the relation; thus under the qualification of the psychical the relation between the psychical and the physical is a relation. If, however, the relation relates itself to itself, this relation is the positive third, and this is the self.[7]

One easily oversimplifies the human predicament, as when one sees the problem to lie directly between the two in that a healthy part is infected by its sickly partner. The problem is not that thought is dependent on the sensuous, or that the sensuous self loses itself in abstract thought. Nor will it do simply to celebrate the third of will as if here we reached some untroubled new ground for the human. The trouble is in the "parts" and it is in their synthesis. Thus Arthur Cohen in reflecting on the Holocaust calls for reason to "mark and contain" the otherwise destructive energies of freedom.[8] The survivors of this century will agree about the risk and portent of freedom. But there seems to be insufficient ground for any confidence that reason will not be usurped for evil ends.

Our discussion, at the end of the last chapter, of the several faces of evil should itself make clear that human hope needs more than what is gained in advancing to human freedom or doubling back to the clarity of either one's physical givenness or reason's sweep of possible projects for the self. Will I speak of freedom? Then I will speak of how I know my own responsibility in the evil I do and in the good that I do not do. That is the keen "Adamic" grasp of moral evil. But in this use of freedom there seems to be something more than the choice of evil possibility. There seems a kind of givenness even within this use of freedom, such that evil acquires an almost natural necessity. Thus one speaks of a sense of being driven: Am I captive to my will? Is my will itself captive? Moreover, that the very structure of being is involved in the territorial disputes of necessity and possibility seems to suggest that the problem is actually metaphysical. Moral reform of the will does not fit the scale of the difficulty.

That the trouble is metaphysical—that we are not satisfied with "the way things are"—is evident when we inquire about how necessity and possibility are together beyond the human self. We do ask on the largest scale how self and world or, more evenly formulated, possibility and necessity are together. To speak of this seems to be to speak of the third of temporality. So we ask of the temporal: What will be the outcome of the being-in-becoming that is temporality? Will there be an outcome? An outcome would presumably carry continuity and yet bring something new. We may not be satisfied with how things are, but we do seek the continuity with our condition that the word "outcome" conveys. We hope reality is adding up to something or at least contributing to something—to something different and better. We want that something to be such that it will then be clear that reality was telling some story, moving toward some consummation. Thus Dante traces Pilgrim's journey from hell to heaven and Proust traces Marcel's reverse trip. And Marx seeks the coincidence of appearance and reality in an irreversible revolution.[9]

It seems clear that such an outcome cannot be given necessarily. If reality were strictly a matter of necessity, if temporality were a mechanism governed by machinelike law, then it would seem hyperbolic to seize upon the dynamic language of plot to speak of some story here. Indeed what seems necessary to us—death—hardly qualifies as a creative conclusion, however decisive it may be. Is the truth simply that we live in a neutron-bomb universe in which all that lives is destroyed?[10] We sense that our dying accommodates the living of others. But such a circle does not seem to constitute a conclusion. Similarly, even if current physical theory discourages strictly mechanistic conceptions of the universe, it hardly helps us if its more dynamic understanding curves the end back to the beginning, as matter decays once again into energy.[11] Little wonder that we come to speak of future life in terms of bare possibility become sheer fantasy—whether that of science fiction or religious vision.[12]

It appears that if possibility and necessity are to come together happily on the largest scale in temporality a third is needed. Robert Jenson characterizes that need in this way:

> [O]ur acts threaten to fall between past and future, to become boring or fantastic or both, and all life threatens to become an unplotted sequence of merely causally joined events that happen to befall an actually impersonal entity, "me." Human life is possible only if past and future are somehow bracketed, only if their disconnection is somehow transcended, only if our lives somehow cohere to make a story. Life in time is possible only, that is, if there is "eternity," if no-more, still, and not-yet do not exhaust the structure of reality. Thus, in all we do we seek eternity.[13]

Jenson goes on to note that our explicit seeking, religion, tends to take the form either of refuge from time or confidence in it.

There certainly are reasons to be less than confident. It is not clear that such a third is given. At least evil seems to suggest that God is "an impossible requirement," that reality is no divine comedy. Even if history does come to something, it is not clear that such a third of "universal history" would be good. We have already noted that the human third of freedom is a frail venture indeed. Who would take any more confidence from a survey of the very mixed bag of "third Ages" announced by Joachim of Fiora, Norman O. Brown, William Reich, and—in his way—Adolf Hitler?[14] Why should we be any more sure of God?

The Christian commendations developed up to this point do not reveal a God such that one could confidently say a third is given and good. Why, after all, is not faith's intensifying activity not simply the frenzy of possibility run amok? In chapter 5 we spoke of a God who could promise a judgment possessing universal scope and unconditioned stance. But a promise is just that. In chapter 6 we outlined a God-conception by which faith could comprehend the givenness, the directedness, and the momentousness of life. But to speak of God as a ground supporting rather than suppressing life, it seemed necessary to speak of God as a goal as well. But it was not clear how we could find the goal—now named God. We asked and ask: Why is not a worldly God who always acts toward us not simply caught with us in the grim necessity of life's failing struggle? So the questions pile up:

Can God do anything decisive?

If God can and does do something decisive, will that work and word be for or against me?

Would not a decisive work and word have to be against me? That is, would they not subjectively deflect me from the duties that make up my days, even if they did not objectively close off the history holding those days?

It is tempting to turn away from the quest for such a third. Perhaps Hegel was right over against Kant in insisting that to be aware of a limit is already to be beyond it.[15] Perhaps Jung's word is wisdom telling us to look nowhere beyond the conjunction of the opposites.[16] Perhaps we need to understand that life, if not a divine comedy, is not necessarily a human tragedy. Perhaps it is part of growing up to know this, to settle for finitude as the right "viewing distance" for the picture of life and so to go forward in courage.[17] Perhaps, indeed, and yet perhaps not. At least the Christian faith submits that the third we need is in fact given.

THE REALITY OF RECONCILIATION:
AN ACTUAL ABSOLUTE IS GIVEN

The hymn that is Christian faith is cast in sentences that carry the rhythm of reconciliation. Christians confess a God through whom healing is given for self and world rent asunder, and health is glimpsed beyond the territorial disputes of necessity and possibility.

It should already be apparent that Christian belief in God holds promise for persons questing after a third. This God is indeed third in one sense: not self or world surely, and not simply necessity or possibility either. Nor is

God understood by Christians to be a dependent third, a whole composed of two, or however many, parts. Rather Christians speak of God as truly independent and indeed prior. God is absolute. To compress this into a sentence: God can be genuinely third because God is truly first.

The Christian faith holds interest insofar as it speaks of an absolute God. But the faith does more: it speaks of something happening to and through this God. What this God does and undergoes is actual. That is, it occurs nowhere else than in that very temporality of which we have just spoken in characterizing most broadly the togetherness of necessity and possibility. And within that temporality it happens nowhere else than in a human self. In speaking of this Jesus, Christian faith declares that an actual absolute is given. The claim is that in this actual absolute we have the third we need.

Christians have not had an easy time formulating the logic of their faith. Indeed the lines may even be nearly indiscernible, clothed as they are in ecstatic vision and ecclesiastical dispute. But of the reality found in Jesus, Christians want to say three things:

1. This has to do with God. As such it has an absoluteness about it—an independence, an unconditionedness. If God is at work here, God is at work here because of God. Gerhard Forde notes that this sense of absolute origin has made the "objective" view of the atonement attractive as against its rivals:

> Ultimately, God must answer for the cross. No doubt, that is what gives the "objective" views their right and strength. Neither the persuasiveness of the example nor the defeat of demons—nothing exterior to God himself—provides sufficient reason for abandoning Jesus to his cruel fate.[18]

Yet, as if to make this point the more surely, some theologians have placed the entire reality of the event within God. They may not have done that formally by denying the humanity of Jesus, though we have noted a tendency even toward that. But they have understood the event as something done by God to God.[19] Ironically, however, then the very unity of God seems to be put in jeopardy so that it is not clear that we really do have God involved, or that the one involved is any longer God.[20] If we lose the human, we lose the divine as well.

2. To avoid or correct such distortion faith must remember a second thing about the reality found in Jesus: it has to do with us. As such it traffics in the contingency, the novelty, the change that make up our condition. The event may indeed originate in God, but it passes through one who is fully human. Indeed even in its origin the event is for the rest of us, because of us. Moreover, it reaches us. It may of course change us, but it does not do that without reaching us, without fitting us, without being right for us.

As one emphasizes this point, however, there is a tendency to confuse our status, so that we become the event's agency rather than representing its efficacy. The lines of the Jesus-event then spread and soften. One can less easily speak about something truly decisive having happened. We, after all, are very much still under way. And yet one tries for such talk. Thus one may say, "Here is the revelation of God and so the offer of God." But it is not clear what good an offer is, if it is not accepted. Ironically, one may tend to retain the language of decisiveness in a countermove and end up speaking of God's revelation as irresistible. Then, though, it seems that the responsibility of the human is put in jeopardy, so that it is not clear that we really do have the human involved, or that the one involved is any longer human. If we lose the divine, we seem strangely to lose the human as well.

3. To avoid or correct such distortion, faith must remember a third thing about the reality found in Jesus: it has to do with Jesus. As such, it speaks of a particular historical person. Faith seeks to understand that the reality of which faith speaks actually happened here—in this particular one, this figure who always threatens to disappear from us in the sands of history. Faith needs to remember that even that quite unacceptable development, the disappearance of Jesus in our memory and understanding, would not rob the event of Jesus of all significance. The reality of historical events is not equivalent to their recognition. For something was done there, something was settled there.

To make this point more emphatically, faith may speak of this event as a great battle between good and evil. There is much that seems right about that. But such an emphasis can tempt one to think of the decisiveness as something remote from us who are the alleged beneficiaries of the victory. As the human thus fades, so does the one who here acts to be our God. Ironically, when thus separated from such constituting conditions, the figure of Jesus itself is altered. The talk of war and battle becomes fanciful and fantastic. If one loses the human and the divine, one loses Jesus as well.

Faith is not alone in finding it difficult to formulate the logic of an actual absolute. Perhaps it is that the actual and the absolute inevitably tend to separate. No single historical particular seems then able to hold them together. Thus Hegel would speak of the absolute as actual, and could herald such an event as Jesus as "unique in its kind; it can occur only once." But the absolute seems to control this convergence in that "once is always in the Idea." All that is not God and so also this human being is held fast in the dialectic of the Idea. So, to speak of an actual absolute is to speak of God as self-moving, so that self-reconciliation follows surely upon self-diremption.[21] The sense of actual advance fades back into the eternal. This metaphysical compliment seems a very mixed blessing. That which always happens seems to happen never. The unity of the absolute never comes to be decisively one with the unity of a single historical particular. Does it happen once if it does not happen once for all?

The same tension appears when one asks Hegel whether a final "closure" to history may be expected or whether the process of the dialectic is itself the final truth about reality.[22] Marx may have stood Hegel on his head in other respects, but he did not avoid this difficulty about the actuality of the absolute. For both Hegel and Marx, "once is always" seems to turn out to be suspiciously like "once is never." Thus with Marx it does not appear that we should actually expect that for which we hope. Consider this comment by Maurice Merleau-Ponty:

> Marxism does not offer us a Utopia, a future known ahead of time, not any philosophy of history. However, it deciphers events, discovers in them a common meaning and thereby grasps a leading thread which, without dispensing us from fresh analysis at every stage, allows us to orient ourselves towards events. Marxism is as foreign to a dogmatic philosophy of history which seeks to impose by fire and sword a visionary future of mankind as it is to a terrorism lacking all perspective. It seeks, rather, to offer men a perception of history which would continuously clarify the lines of force and vectors of the present.[23]

In speaking of God, of us, and of Jesus, in the event of Jesus, faith seeks to understand the absolute and the actual together. How is that to be done? The components compete to control the conception. Thus one may speak of the absolute as an idea or an ideal and so as eternal and necessary. Such a notion seems to emphasize the absolute at the outset. One then goes on to say that the event of Jesus in and almost in spite of its actuality is that which aligns us again with the eternal. But the actuality of Jesus remains a puzzling and potentially embarrassing vehicle for the eternal. On the other hand, when faith starts out by speaking of the event of Jesus as actual, it is quickly caught up in the sense of the novel and the contingent. But it is not clear how such an event trafficking with possibility can have the certainty of the absolute, especially if that is understood as necessity.

Frederick Dillistone has traced these two emphases in his magisterial study of the atonement:

> [T]here are *two* basic shapes or patterns. . . . The first assumes that there is a *determinative cosmic idea* in the very constitution of ultimate reality. Being itself is a constant pulsation of life and death, a going forth into life counterposed by a retraction into death. . . . The soul of the universe, it is imagined, breathes out and breathes in. . . .

If life runs to death, does death also issue in new life? That question might arise and will be asked by human beings at once intent on self-preservation and sensing that such clinging to life runs counter to the rhythm of the universe. Thus arises, argues Dillistone, the idea of being reintegrated into the original, the creative, the constitutive pattern of all existence through sacrifice:

> In all its many forms sacrifice has involved some kind of deliberate offering which appears to deprive the original owner of some valued possession. In this sense it is a deliberate acceptance of a symbolic death. It is a renunciation, a surrender, a conscious recognition through a sacramental action that the ultimate principle of existence, the highest that we can conceive, is *through-death-to-life*.

Here the eternal has accommodated the historical, taking possession of the very dynamic of life. Dillistone notes the difficulty that arises, however, when one tries to identify a particular historical instance as special and crucial, as absolute:

> If the very nature of His being is in fact life-through-death, how could we conceive of something which might be deemed an *extra*, an addition to what is eternal in its expression?

But history's claim about the deliverance is rooted in a sensitivity to the actuality of the disease, which points to a second emphasis:

> The second pattern, then, reflects a state of affairs which lies at the heart of the world's *historical* development. Life is constantly threatened by death, is engaged in a ceaseless struggle with death. . . . Must it not be that man's guardian deity is himself forever engaged in a struggle with the forces of evil and subject to their vicious intents?

Will life triumph over death in one's own life and death? That question might arise and will surely be asked by human beings who know that they themselves often choose death over life. Thus also in this second framework there arises a fitting candidate for our recourse:

> The answer which alone faces the situation realistically is expressed in terms of a critical confrontation between good and evil on the plane of history, when the good having been wounded, seemingly defeated and even killed still emerges victorious and all-powerful. . . . The critical event is most conveniently described as an act of *Redemption*.

Here the historical gathers itself to ask of the eternal, but again not without difficulty, as Dillistone notes:

> But is it thinkable that such an adventure is part of the activity of the living God Himself? How is it possible to imagine Him as One Who, in the vivid word of the Epistle to the Hebrews *tastes* death for everyone?

How can the vanishing point of the particular reach beyond and behind itself to compass the universal? Thus we come to Dillistone's summary:

> The Idea and the Event, Being and Action. We cannot, I have urged, rest in one pole *or* the other. We cannot express what we feel bound to say about the Christian Interpretation of Atonement by means of words or categories or images drawn from one pattern or the other. Both are essential.[24]

Both are essential, I submit, because it is essential that they be *together*. We need the absolute and the actual together, not to check each other in the perpetuity of the pendulum, but to create the reconciling third we need. Jesus was not simply two natures, but one historical person.

But how can the two be together? The theological task before us is not to appeal to a paradox constituted in trying to conceive the coming together, while gladly banking the benefits that the two independent themes deliver. Dillistone has nicely demonstrated that the long shadow of paradox cannot be dismissed as a second-order reality residing in the togetherness of the two emphases, but reaches back independently into both primary orientations as surely as each seeks to accommodate the other. Similarly, if we see the togetherness of the absolute and the actual to be an equally primary conviction, we should be able to see as well that some statement of the how of that togetherness must surely be attempted.

I have spoken of the otherness of God as revealed precisely in the radicality of God's commitment to us. In this notion of God's sure will for humankind there already lies an anticipation of the full togetherness of the absolute and the actual. The rhythm is right. This commitment is God's choice and as such is actual. But it yields a reality that is fully as unconditional as any idea or ideal. To begin, thus, with God's eternal resolve not only gets the components of the actual and the absolute before us quickly, but by doing so encourages us to keep them there throughout our thinking about "the work of Christ." Beginning here we should be less tempted, for example, to let God be divided in actuality. If we yield to that temptation we can only go wrong, for whether we choose the good God of Jesus or the at least less good God of the Old Testament, we in fact end up with no real God at all.

To speak of God's eternal resolve for humankind is, materially, to speak of God's love for and affirmation of the human. But what more can one say than this? Christian faith struggles to say that in the reality of the event of Jesus there is added to the note of the Creator's affirmation the recognition that here God's full identification with humankind becomes a final identification in humankind. God comes to be with us so decisively that we come to be in God. The absolute and the actual co-constitute each other. In this one this is clear. In this one an actual absolute is at hand. This is the vision of Christian faith, even if we may not be very clear about how this can be said.

Contemporary Christians should be ready to develop the vision. Perhaps our current sense of the thoroughgoing temporality of reality can be more help than hindrance. That sense may have helped us break the associative connection between the absolute and the timeless. While that sense can linger even in the break so that we find ourselves simply bereft of any sense of the reality of an absolute, that need not be the case. We can instead be freed to inquire further into temporality in quest of a renewed and reconstructed sense of the absolute. Perhaps the existentialist and process traditions in contemporary thought can combine to further such inquiry. Thus one could add to the voluntarist emphasis on God's commitment to humankind the theme of the willed suffering of God.

To speak of God's identification with such as we are will surely be to speak of suffering. This is the theme that has been variously developed by Abraham Heschel, Kazoh Kitamouri, Jürgen Moltmann, and Dorothee Soelle, among others. A single statement by Moltmann will set the tone of such speech for us:

> The justifiable denial that God is capable of suffering because of a deficiency in his being may not lead to a denial that he is incapable of suffering out of the fullness of his being, i.e., his love.[25]

But despite the wide acceptance of the theme of divine suffering, rather little seems to be done theologically with the theme. It sits in the systems as an isolated, if not an awkward, insight. Our own experience of what suffering does to us, along with the idea that God acts in suffering, should point the way toward a more integrated treatment.

God's identification with us yields God's identification in us. We have been close to saying that. A God who can suffer with us can suffer because of us. But God's suffering because of us has been held apart from the center of God's being, as it were. Surely, however, part of the point of making the statement that God suffers because of us is not to talk about us, but to talk about God. The point here is not to say how terrible our sin is that it makes even God suffer. The point is to talk about the wonder of this God who is so emphatically for us that because of us something, suffering, comes to be in God. God is different because of us. Because God comes to be with us, we come to be in God. If the absolute is not the timeless, an absolute God can actually—yes, precisely, *actually*—advance to a new identity in the other.

Are we left then with the indefiniteness of actuality in our hope for the future? Have we simply replaced the splendor of the sovereign with a God who can do no other than suffer in this one and so presumably in all the others indefinitely? How much would that help? As surely as God is one we may be sure that within the reality that is God this suffering does not lurch about in uncontrolled abandon or throb on in inconclusive perpetuity. In freedom and love God chooses to be for us, to come to be with us, and so to suffer all that such identification entails.[26] We spoke of willed suffering: here is will—not only to suffer, but in suffering. Thus there is here an actual advance in the life of God who undergoes—in an undergoing that is an undertaking—all that finitude and sin hold for us. As surely as God is one, no more than this is needed. It is enough; it is finished. God's will prevails. That is, God still wills to love, and the will that thus emerges from the event of Jesus is the eternal will that has worn the flesh of creation and crucifix-ion—once and so forever.

It is currently rather fashionable to say something like this:

> The incarnation means quite simply that the narrative identity of Jesus Christ, as given in Scripture, is also the disclosure of the identity of God.[27]

What needs to be understood is that in so speaking we do not make an epistemological point merely, but more fundamentally an ontological one. The event of Jesus reveals God because that event constitutes God. Here the absolute and the actual are one.

We have tried to articulate this in some halting formulations. Moltmann has emphasized the "within Godness" of the cross, as is dramatically sug-gested by the notion of the father abandoning the son. Such talk reflects the radical experience of rejection that God, freely committed to humankind, undergoes. If we had a way to speak effectively of the divine feelings, such talk of abandonment would not have to crowd its way into the one will of God, threatening thereby once again to divide God and so to lose any real God at all.[28] But at least such talk makes clear that in this actual moment the absolute God is involved. Talk of this event as God's self-justification also emphasizes God's involvement. Karl Barth was good at such talk:

> But did God need to justify Himself? . . . It is clear that He did not need to do so. He does not need anything. God is completely free. . . . But as the living God . . . is He not free and able to justify Himself? . . . Certainly God is—and was and will be—righteous without having to prove Himself righteous. But seeing He willed to and did prove Himself righteous, it is only right to count on it that He did not do so in vain.[29]

To put it so does protect the continuity of the divine will, though it may fail to say strongly enough that the one willing becomes one with that which is not itself, and undergoes rejection, suffering, and death. In that actual other the one divine will can actually attain an advance. Thus, one is not left trying to expunge the feel of defensiveness that a more self-contained sort of self-justification carries. This Jesus is not an instance of divine self-protec-tion, but of divine self-projection in the other.

What must we say about Jesus' person, if we are to say that his work is the advance to an actual absolute? Clearly, the connection between these topics is not arbitrary. In a sense his person is his work. Or what may be conventionally spoken of as his work came about and claims special significance because of his person. Clearly, therefore, we must have God here constitutively; indeed, not merely must we have God in the event that is Jesus, but we must thereby have Jesus in the event that is God. But if it is "here" that God is to be so emphatically present, this Jesus must be fully human as well.

To protect that full humanity theologians have at times tried to reconceive the divine. Thus a kenosis theologian like Gottfried Thomasius spoke of a divine self-divesting of such "relative" attributes as omnipotence, omnipresence, and omniscience that presumably would contradict full union with finite humanity. But Thomasius strove to retain another class of attributes that refer to God's own self-relatedness:

> [B]y the incarnation the Son did not surrender these divine essential determinations, which as such are inseparable from the essence of God, and no more does he, as the incarnate one, withhold their use.[30]

It is not clear how these "immanent" attributes—of absolute power, truth, holiness, and love—do not get caught in difficulties when the God possessing them is related to the world. But this effort points in the right direction in emphasizing that the very essence of God precisely as absolute is joined with full and finite humanity.

In our time we will need to find our own way to formulate faith's conception of an actual absolute. We may not choose to carry along the question of the status of divested attributes, sensing there not only an awkward concept but also possibly a dangerous equivocating as concerns the divine commitment and presence in Jesus. And we may not be as quick as earlier thinkers to speak of attributes and natures and so of their communication.[31] But it is clear that Christians in our time will seek somehow to formulate afresh the logic of the event of Jesus.

One such effort is John Cobb's employment of the logos tradition and contemporary process categories. Cobb does not find Jesus to be special simply because God is present. The God present in Jesus is the God present elsewhere. In every moment of reality, indeed, God is present acting inwardly or toward the other, as I suggested in the last chapter. When that action is perceived by its recipient, it is usually understood as precisely other:

> "I," or the organizing center of human existence, is usually constituted by conformal continuity with the "I" of preceding moments of the same personal

life. . . . Similarly in ordinary Christian existence the call to conformation to Christ . . . is experienced as coming to the self from without.

But this is not the only possible structure of existence:

In another possible structure of existence the presence of the Logos would share in constituting selfhood; that is, it would be identical with the center or principle in terms of which other elements in experience are ordered. In that structure the appropriation of one's personal past would be just that ideal appropriation made possible by the lure . . . that is the immanent Logos. If this occurred, the usual tension between the human sin and the ideal possibility of self-actualization that is the Logos would not occur.[32]

Even such a bare sketch of a particular formulation can serve to illustrate a broader point: what is special about Jesus rests in the divine choice. In this one God chooses to bring to decisive form an eternal commitment. That choice is particular, for it is now actual. But it is not capricious, for it is for all. That is why one can speak of the mission of Jesus as that of proclaiming the kingdom of God. It is indeed fitting that Jesus was first understood to be an eschatological prophet. If the quest for a third is a question about how "it all adds up," that quest can only find its answer in this event if Jesus is "the eschatological face of all" or "the climax of the human race."[33] If "parousia Christology is the mother of all Christianity," we should not be surprised to find much variety among the family. Such variety fits our condition, for the third was seen to be needed for reasons moral, natural, and metaphysical. Presumably the response will be no less variegated.[34]

All this may indeed be about a God who is for me; but is it about me? How does an actual absolute become the third needed? Simply necessarily? Merely possibly? Both? Neither? Does this Jesus replace me, represent me, substitute for me? Christian faith accepts these questions and endeavors to make a response, for it believes that the reconciliation that is real in Jesus is yet to be realized by us.

THE REALIZATION OF RECONCILIATION:
FREEDOM IS FULFILLED

Necessity and possibility are together in the human third of freedom, but we are hardly satisfied with the fruit of that freedom. Self and world are together in the more-than-human third of history, but we hesitate even to hope for a happy outcome. If in the event of Jesus an actual absolute has been given, how does that help? What difference does it make for my freedom and for all history?

Through this one all that which is not God is identified. Each of us and all of us are identified, for God's judgment abides as surely as does God. We spoke in the previous section of God's identification with that which is not God, and so of God's own identification in the event of Jesus. To speak of that which is not God is to include us; this is about us. The commitment of God has advanced to flesh and has been embodied even in death. Now God is for us forever. God's decisive identification does not speak only of God. It speaks of selves struggling with the volatile synthesis of necessity and possibility that is human freedom. We are God's beloved. For persons whose travail with the third of freedom yields a knowing of their guilt in the misuse of freedom, the word spoken is one of forgiveness. The question of how this "works" has much occupied the church's theologians and hardly can be said yet to be a tidy and settled matter. But some suggestions can be made concerning "the work of Christ."

In thinking of this Jesus one is thinking of a victim of a sacral tyranny who himself becomes sacred, cutting the link between the sacred and the oppressive in human life. But faith holds that in this death much more happens for us than that we get "back to zero" in our perception of the sacral. Something happens in our relationship to the real. Thus Rowan Williams writes:

> The pivotal point is this: death is normally a drastic severing of relations, death isolates. But for Jesus, it is through death that a new and potentially infinite network of relations is opened up. The effect of his death is the opposite of isolation.[35]

How does that which seems so surely and tragically to close come to open so richly?

God's will prevails. Thus one may well speak here of victory, as God's identity is not shattered by the suffering and death undergone. Or one may speak of sacrifice, as God willingly undergoes the consequences of human rejection and death.[36] In any case, one is speaking of something that is so willed as to be decided. One is speaking of God's decisive identification with and in the actual. Paul knew that judgment belonged to God and therefore he could say that nothing could separate him from the love of God in Christ Jesus (Romans 8). God will not be divided. God's will prevails. Perhaps that is not so clear in those aspects of the event of Jesus where what we see seems to be controlled by that which is not God, indeed by that which is against God. But it is with God's will—God's living willing—that the rejection, suffering, and death are received. Here, then, is no unwitting victim. The death of Jesus is no suicide, but he did set his face steadfastly toward Jerusalem. He came to do the will of the one who sent him and that will was done even through the doings of evil against him.

Because God's will prevails this event is decisive. We do not know such decisiveness otherwise. Human rejection seems never to be at an end; there is at least no decisive affirmation evident in the course of our comings and goings. We remain quite unsure how to live with each other, how much to trust, how to receive, what to initiate. But with the suffering and death of Jesus there is finished the forming of that in God which began before the foundation of the world" (Eph. 1:4). God's suffering will not end until suffering ends, but Jesus died once for all. Thus was forgiveness made fast and so does it abide. God wills to forgive, and that forgiving will shall surely prevail.

If this scope and significance of the work of Christ was not clear to faith in the crucifixion, it should be clear in the resurrection. It is God who does this, who raises up Jesus, and it is done. The resurrection, moreover, may more clearly suggest to us that no less than all of history is thus identified by the event of Jesus. I shall say more of this in a moment, but I want to point out here that in this we deal not merely with moral evil, which in its contingency may seem to attach itself only accidentally to our human condition. Rather the resurrection addresses life in its constitutional fragility, in our finitude. As such it speaks to that which holds us necessarily. God's reconciling work in Jesus is more than forgiveness, then. It reaches out to receive all that which is not God, as Williams understands:

> The resurrection as a symbol declares precisely our incapacity for apocalyptic destruction.... God's act is faithful to his character as creator, and he will destroy no part of this world: his apocalyptic act is one of restoration, the opening of the book which contains all history.[37]

The human self and the whole of history can be identified as the objects of the eternal love of God, which advances to decisive actuality in Jesus. This identification abides. Whatever we are, whatever comes, what was done in Jesus remains true.

That final truth about us and our universe reaches back to make a difference in who we are and what we do now in the time before the end. It matters now that we are so identified. Thus we may speak of the bearing of Christian faith on the actual lives of Christians. Christians do not need to deny their difficulties, their inconsistencies; at the very least they remind us that our condition is no less broken with respect to our willing than it is with respect to our knowing. But there is a healing, a reconciling reality, at work. This decisiveness of the event of Jesus is realized in ongoing developments in human lives about which something waits to be said.

What reconciling capacity does Christian faith in God hold for human beings in their actual struggle with self and world, necessity and possibility? Christians find that their freedom is engaged in faith, in that they are empowered and inspired to act. Perhaps it is that the relationship to this third, the absolute God actual in Jesus, seems to offer the reconciliation in our dividedness that human freedom or history fails to yield. Perhaps it is that this third has an independence of origin. God's godness roots in God, however much God may be emphatically and inextricably for us. As such this third seems better able to resist being preempted for the internecine disputes and better able to exercise independent initiative to work for healing, though such changes do not come about without engaging that which is not God.

The matter of identity of which we have just been speaking is a case in point. To be identified by God and in relation to God frees the nervous self from other strategies for securing its identity. The self no longer needs passively to settle for or frantically to seize upon some particular constituent element—sexual prowess, intellectual acumen, social success; the weary list continues. It need not define itself negatively by focusing on what it is not, as when it seeks to control or to withdraw from the world.

This independence of identity through God would be a dangerous gift threatening dislocation, if it were not linked with a claim upon the self.[38] This gift of identity before God carries a call to full involvement with that which is not God. We have been speaking about the self's identity as given by God. That has a kind of steadiness about it that reflects its source. Rowan Williams observes that the apostles' apostasy does not take away the identity that God's purpose gives:

> Simon is still, in the eyes of God, Peter. What he has to learn is that his betrayal does not make God betray, so that his calling as Peter, as rock of the apostolic faith, is still there, waiting to be lived out.[39]

Moreover, God does not merely send the self into the world—God bestows the world (including the self) on the one called. Williams writes also of this:

> "God" is that to which all things are present, so theology traditionally affirms: so, through the mediation of God, all things can be made present to us again, present through his presence. The concept of God's "memory" as holding or keeping open the past overthrows the delusion that our violence is final and irremediable.[40]

Once again in relation to God we get further than "back to zero." The world and selves returned to us are not without change, as a final sensitive statement by Williams notes:

> [B]ecause the life of God is not a life with worldly limits, worldly constraints on its possibilities, the memory of suffering here is—we might say—embedded in an exhaustible life. So when he returns to us the memory of what has been done, it is as a memory inseparably bound to a reality which guarantees the hope of

healing because its resources and possibilities cannot be exhausted or extinguished by the world's destructiveness.[41]

My stress on understanding God's otherness as a transcendence in relationship would invite a closer formulation as to the matter of worldly constraints. But I fully agree that the resources of God's love do not run out.

I draw back from attempting to discuss specific ethical insight found by Christians in the God-relationship.[42] It is surely clear that something will follow from the fact that not only the Christian but also the world of nature and the world of the other(s) have been given an identity by God's decisive judgment. The description of just what follows surely reflects human diversity and, quite probably, human distortion. But granting that, it should still be clear that the Christian faith's relationship to ethics is not that of merely providing a conceptual schema in which ethical activity and insight make sense. Rather, the self's freedom is engaged, instruction and inspiration are added to incentive. Thus Kierkegaard could speak of the self's attaining "equilibrium" through the faith by which the self was grounded "transparently" in God.[43]

Is equilibrium to be desired? It would not be, if it meant that, with respect to human freedom, "engaged" was a euphemism for "deadened." "Equilibrium" can carry static associations, hinting at best at a third constituted by the cessation of hostilities. Perhaps Kierkegaard's nervous stress on becoming is strong enough so that few will charge him with offering the Christian faith as a soporific. But some of the objections voiced in chapter 4 are understandably made against other Christian formulations. That may be particularly true of other Christian speech about the end of history as a way of telling time's story. The issue here is not of how such speech is used. Presumably one might agree that better as well as worse ways are available to employ such a formulation. For human effort Christian hope might grant an assurance that quickens or a drug that diverts. But what of the formulation itself? Can a good account be made of this hope that is in us? That is, does Christian faith have a way of understanding its story about the end— and so about the whole—such that freedom here is truly fulfilled?

Eternity as simple persistence of identity would not do that. Despite short-sighted fantasies of this sort, we usually realize that it would not be desirable for our present existence to continue unchanged forever. Formally, such sheer extension does not offer sufficient newness to count as fulfillment. Materially, many of us would perhaps choose the grace of death over the hell held out in such a blurred vision of Christian hope. Thus in this life Christians look ahead to something different. They do so on intrinsic grounds, and not merely because of the conceptual difficulties involved in imagining finite life to be infinite ("How old will I be?" etc.). In both respects simple extension is unthinkable.[44]

It is not only theists who look for something different in looking for fulfillment of freedom. Indeed an atheist and Marxist, Vitezslav Gardavsky, attaches himself to the teaching of Jesus to formulate this longing:

Jesus is convinced that before we can come to a radical decision, before we achieve a "miracle," we must be filled with love: we must be aware—steeped in the sort of profound knowledge that governs our whole being and is sometimes felt with total immediacy—that we only exist—when we surpass ourselves: in our eyes, in the eyes of our fellow-men, and in the eyes of God; and when we know that this act of transcendence challenges our minds, our strength of purpose, our passion—both in the active and passive sense—and demands that we should bring all our senses into play.[45]

Christian faith offers a vision of such reconciling transcendence. That has not always been clear. Tempted by the lure of Platonism, for example, Augustine at times seems to state the transcendence in nonreconciling terms. What is peace for the heart that is restless until it rests in God? Augustine speaks of peace as deriving from "the ordered equilibrium" of the parts whereby "each of them is disposed in its proper place." Such peace is anticipated in earthly order and consummated in heaven, where we finally know it to be true that peace "in its final sense is the calm that comes of order."[46]

Such peace would be different enough from what we now experience to be considered transcendent. But here the sense of continuity with human striving is lost. Surely Simone Weil is closer to a characterization of the Christian hope as fulfilling in her comment:

Nothing is so beautiful and wonderful, nothing is so continually fresh and surprising, so full of sweet and perpetual ecstasy, as the good. No desert is so dreary, monotonous, and boring as evil. This is the truth about authentic good and evil. With fictional good and evil it is the other way round. Fictional good is boring and flat, while fictional evil is varied and intriguing, attractive, profound, and full of charm.[47]

How can heaven be continually fresh and surprising? It cannot be so without temporality, without activity. Indeed only as such could it carry the continuity to fulfill what we know as the restless third of history.[48]

Faith speaks more surely of God's future, as it does of God, when it speaks materially. Consider this statement by the tormented poet, John Berryman:

The only really comforting reflection is not
"we will all rest in Abraham's bosom" and rot of that purport
but: after my death there will be *no more sin*.[49]

No more sin! Every tear wiped away! But would such an issue be in fact a reconciling of what is now at odds? That reconciling is intended is clear even though Christians use such stumbling terms as "spiritual body" and "new Heaven and new earth" to speak of the ultimate future.

What is to be said of the misuse of freedom? If we will then be no longer able to sin—"non posse peccare," in the phrase of traditional dogmatics—how is that a fulfillment of present freedom's evil?[50] What must be said of the consequences of such freedom? What final consequences could fulfill such choices? This is not clear. It is clear that Christians are called to hope for the reconciliation of all. To hope for this without knowing how it can be may be precisely to give up our longing for "the tidy drama of history."[51]

May it be, though, that the fact that we will then no longer see as in a glass darkly will make a difference? Then even the rich man will know that it is better to be with God—and so to be with Lazarus! Does such clarity weaken evil's hold on the will rooted in ambiguity? Does "every knee bending and every tongue confessing" (Philippians 2) mean simply that it will then be clear to all who is God?

Is naked defiance not possible? Or may it be that even that can give itself and its efficacy to God and be fulfilled in being used up? Our victim is our hope.[52] Do we perhaps already have reason to suspect that our contingent will is only a part of our freedom's causality? May it be even a lesser part of our being's effects? As we do what we do to God, do we not thereby enter God? Surely, then, we will no longer be unchanged. Perhaps even victims and perpetrators are to be reconciled within the life of this actively suffering God. Otherwise appeals to "the meaning of history," to closure, whether by the first or second coming of this or any other Jesus must be seen to be either hollow or horrifying.[53] Athanasius long ago spoke of God's becoming human so that we might become God.[54] Something really new is being written through time's story.[55] In this may be the reconciliation of all.

Must we end with "may"? If we must, what is to be made of that? To end our commendation of intensification, comprehension, and reconciliation with the word "may" making the connection to Christian faith surely means that when we are done commending we are not done conversing. Of that continuing conversation something further must be said.

PART THREE:
CONTINUING
THE CONVERSATION

8 TO ASSESS THE CONVERSATION

HOW DO MATTERS STAND?

We are not done. Despite the last chapter's ringing sentences' carrying the promise of reconciliation, anyone who has read this book from the beginning will not expect that matters have been settled. As questions were identified in chapters 2 through 4, an effort was made to show how Christian faith could attend to these concerns. But to attend is not to answer. In the second movement of the conversation the Christian commendation of a word that intensifies, comprehends, and reconciles is further response to these questions, even though the word does not derive from the questions. Consider the contention from the first movement of questioning that the Christian claim to knowledge denies the community of knowers and the consensus of knowledge attained. Perhaps when commending the faith the Christian does respond to this concern by speaking of comprehending the world—its givenness, its directedness, its momentousness. That is a significant response. But the conversation will continue, if the person who is not a Christian finds in such a claim to comprehend, nothing other than precisely the authoritarianism earlier criticized as denying the tentativity that reflects the experimental character of our knowing.

What of the concern identified in chapter 3, that the God of the Christian faith is so other as to be simply beyond the human, or surely above the human, in a relationship that must be ruled oppressive, given the widespread human experience of suffering? Why does not a God caught in such a "can't win" situation (can't touch: any touch kills) simply in fact lose? Perhaps the Christian responds to this painfully heard question in commending a Word of God and a speaking of God that are fully "worldly" in that they meet us precisely as we seek to create and understand (chapter 6). But it may still occur to one to ask if the modest product now on display in the notion of God is not sorely overpriced. Why should one spend one's all too skimpy psychic capital for nothing more than this? Perhaps the Christian claims about reconciliation—as those earlier ones about intensification and comprehension—address that question. And what of the charge that Christian faith deceives, demeans, and tranquilizes the self in the world? The Christian responds in a word of commendation: "Yes, I hear you and I share your concern. But I have good news for you: Christian faith offers a vision of the reconciliation of self and world through an actual absolute." Well, that could make a difference surely, but one may still hear the question, Why do Christians actually so often get it wrong?

Thus the conversation runs. Neither the questioning of unbelief nor faith's quest to respond seems decisive in our time. The Christian is called to commend: faith inspires that and unfaith requires that. Yet Christian commendations may elicit genuine human interest and attention, and still fail to win assent. The non-Christian may return to some familiar objection almost as a way of remaining in relation to the Christian faith, while yet retaining unfaith's integrity. Or perhaps for some the sense of moral and intellectual grievance against the Christian faith constitutes so consuming a passion that the commendations can hardly be heard. In a sense in such a case the unbeliever does not need to hear, much less consider and far less accept, the Christian claim. One's sense of offense has been converted into a positive power. It is quite enough that this faith must be resisted.

Perhaps the reason we are not nearly done is that we are so clearly not one. To speak today of the human and the Christian is emphatically to speak of two realities. But the two realities, while two, are together. Many of us, even as individuals, live in two places with respect to Christian faith. Nearly two decades ago Dorothee Soelle spoke of two such realities, the experience of the death of God and the experience of faith in Christ's resurrection. She resisted the attempt to force a choice between these two and offered her own sense of their connectedness:

> To try to compel a choice between them—on grounds of so-called logic, traditional orthodoxy, church theology—is to do positivism's work for it and to hand over those who have this twofold experience to the self-assured smugness of people who simply *know* that there is no God and that Christ is dead; or, worse still, to those who are equally sure that God exists and that Christ is therefore alive. But Christ is not a replacement for the dead God. He is the representative of the living God. . . .[1]

I believe that today many Christians will join me in the unsettling recognition that something like Soelle's description fits: the sense of Christian identity exists alongside radical doubt or even the strong sense of the absence of God. Indeed the Christian in us and the human in us come together to resist any easy reconciliation such as may be offered in Soelle's suggestion that by God's choice God's identity is still to come. Rather the two remain two with no union in sight. We are not able to live with Christian faith and we are not able to live without it, and we do not see in the offing any change in this schizophrenic predicament.

Faith and unfaith are two today in such a way that traditional "defense" of the faith may seem both fantastic and futile. The two never seem really to meet. Thus the traditional field of apologetics seems now to be divided between those who claim too much and those who claim too little for Christian faith.[2] The term "apologetics" is now most used by those who seem to claim too much in the sense that the apologetic effort proceeds as monologue, missing the other within and outside the Christian self. The Scripture is baldly cited as divinely authoritative and no other human word can be heard. That will not do. Apologetics requires that believers and unbelievers alike possess voice and vote. On the other hand, the Christian cannot meet the human if the Christian is not present. The Christian apologist needs to recognize that what is held in common may not be what is prized in particular. One may speak of the human without speaking of God. One may put the religious question well without entering the Christian quest.

Dogmatics cannot replace apologetics. The Christian cannot assume the common human possession of some given, whose orderly development will yield the full flowering of the conversation with unfaith. Were that the case one could indeed hold out the hope of an essentially conclusive reflection on that single common reality. But two who are not one can speak together of what they separately find to be real. Indeed the conversation may be the more serious and profitable if differences are consciously acknowledged. Perhaps, then, dogmatics—the community's reflection on its specifically constituting word—can be done in an apologetic context. For that matter, if the brokenness with regard to faith is as internal as I have suggested, dogmatics will succeed in making its claim upon the humanity of even the Christian only if it is done with the apologetic agenda at hand. Moreover, as the traditional chasm between dogmatics and apologetics is bridged, it will be the more likely that apologetics will not erode into mere accommodation.[3]

How do matters stand? The conversation is begun. In the first movement it is the non-Christian's objections that set the agenda. It is not that the non-Christian asks of God and the Christian answers with the ease of authority. The questioning is not dispatched by dogmatic decree. Indeed, for three reasons the Christian does not want to dispatch the question. First, in the contentions of unfaith the Christian can recognize the question of the God for whom commendation is to be spoken in Christian terms. There is contact here. The question is useful in explicating the response. Second, the question is the Christian's own question and has its own inner source of life. There is common ground here. Third, when the Christian sets the agenda by speaking to commend, that speech is as much quest as possession. Even for the Christian such speaking is often against the grain. One needs the grain if one is to speak against it. Such speaking still carries the question of God within itself and so represents the quest for a knowledge of God, indeed a knowing God, such that the question may be satisfied.

There is more than the question in the quest. Question and quest have much to do with each other, and yet the difference in the image is instructive. The one who quests feels the question keenly, for one must bear it on a pilgrimage. One must do something with the question, or while questioning. But one who travels has not arrived. One believes there are good and sufficient reasons to be on this journey of faith, but one has not reached the destination. One sees what one is about, but one's vision is hardly beatific. Faith is not question-ending sight.[4]

I believe we have begun. In what I have written I hope that the non-Christian and the Christian can recognize themselves and recognize the conversation as important. Because we are not done we need to continue; because we have begun we can continue. As we do so, we ask two other questions.

WHAT MIGHT BE EXPECTED?

As human and as Christian we ask the question in relation to the realities of which we have spoken in these pages: self, world, history. Given our sense of self, world, and history, what expectations might we appropriately have for the conversation between faith and unfaith? In addressing this question we seek a perspective from which to evaluate the conversation and its "standing."

One thing that is becoming clear to us about the ways to truth regarding self and world is precisely that we must resist a polarization of methods that sets the knowing of self and the knowing of world against each other. There is convergence on this point. I have referred to a student of the arts, Wayne C. Booth, who has criticized the "modern dogma" that scientismically elevates a supposedly simple objective world (and the knowledge of that world) over a seemingly subjective self with its private ecstasies. I have cited the philosopher Stephen Toulmin's point that criteria for argument are "field dependent" so that the realm of reason must not be limited to work dominated by the precision of the analytic. Finally, I have introduced Richard Rorty's metaphysical point that the very process of perception that is the self's knowing of the world should not be understood as the passive reception of isolated items of the sense experience of a world residing in sovereign objectivity. Truth is found in conversation, not by correspondence.

The arguments behind these points need not be repeated. But it is appropriate to ask now about the points' bearing on expectations for our conversation. First, the observations about the knowing of self and world have relevance for theological claims in that those claims are themselves about self and world. We have spoken here theologically of the intensification of self, the comprehension of world, and the reconciliation of self and world. I will grant and even insist that the reference of theological talk is not exhausted by self and world. By that I do not deny that talk of God is always at least implicitly mediated by reference to that which is not God.[5] Perhaps some would make that denial. But even if one does not attempt such an argument, one will want to hold that speaking of God is not honorific within self- and world-talk.

Does the "more" of which one would speak theologically in relation to self and world somehow double back to affect the process of faith's knowing? That is the second matter to be considered. Since the Christian knows more than self and world, should one expect that the knowing itself is different—reflecting, as it were, the superiority of that which is known? That would alter our expectations for the conversation. Obviously, faith's claims are claims made by selves in the world. But is there a deeper side of things such that somehow the qualifications and limitations of selfish and worldly knowing are overruled? Can we expect all doubts to be swept aside? I think not. At their best, Christians know that even when they speak of God, they do not speak *as* God. Christian speech shares with other human speech in the quest for meaning. With other speech it will know change and incompleteness. The differences distinguishing speaking of God will fit within the range of differences marking human efforts to speak truly. Indeed, as that God-talk takes its place, it turns out that that human place may lead us to expect not more but less by way of verification.

What might be expected? If Christian speech is (a) about self and world, and (b) about more than self and world only in relation to self and world, and (c) by selves in the world, then we can expect Christian speech to be both possible and difficult. It will be possible, for non-Christians will be able in principle to recognize something familiar to them in the substance and style of this kind of speaking. It will be difficult, for one seeks to speak of more than what is familiar without any self-evidently superior means of access. Yet perhaps the difficulty itself need not be unfamiliar. Thus John Whittaker writes:

The substance of religious claims does not come from given facts about the world around us, but from the order and intelligibility—the sense—which can be discovered in these given facts. Religious principles, that is, are second-order claims, claims about the way in which one set of truths (the known facts of nature and of history) can be comprehended under another aspect (according to their reason for being or their ultimate purpose). To those who think that every truth or every fact must be fundamentally alike, it must seem strange to postulate such higher truths, existing beyond what we would ordinarily call the realm of facts. Yet religious assertions are not the only assertions which force us to recognize a different order of truth claims.[6]

His examples are drawn from the aesthetic field ("good literature possesses an inherent value apart from its moral or practical utility") and the scientific ("causal explanations can be traced through uniform laws of nature").[7]

Thus Christians and non-Christians can reach significant agreement in their expectations for the conversation. Obviously non-Christians should not expect (any more than they will accept) that Christian speech is granted an exemption from trials known in the struggle for significance. Christians expect there to be disagreement about whether there is a God to be known, because with the created gift of freedom comes ambiguity. If disagreement derives from the exercise of human freedom, Christians will not expect a sure-fire method of resolving such disputes. If offered a sure-fire method, the Christian will wonder if the price is to be paid in human freedom. Ambiguity and disagreement are expected.

Care must be exercised in saying this. I would not speak of a hidden God in a way that would imply divine deception or invite special pleading. Christians speak of a God who is present and who can be known. It is inappropriate to say things like "Only the future will reveal God because only then will God be God—by the will of God." Nor should one suppose that the ambiguity and indecisiveness of the "case for God" can somehow itself be converted into evidence for a self-hiding God who is nonetheless infallibly known by the Christian. Ambiguity in knowing God fits the claim about God—that is all. It does not force assent. God can be known, now and by all. That much the Christian does claim, but readily grants that such knowing does not fail to be human and earthly. Thus we say again: the conversation about faith cannot be expected to proceed any more surely than our regular debates about what (whom) we know when we know self and world.

If the Christian says that God desires to be known in a way that involves the will more than some cognitive acts do, a darker view of the disagreement about faith may be considered. Perhaps in the objections of unfaith we meet defiant will, rather than responsible doubt. Perhaps those who do not know

God simply will not know God. Perhaps. The Christian cannot be sure. But the claim is still that in faith one knows; faith has to do with something that can be got at and talked about. So, again, the Christian stands with all human beings who puzzle about how valuing and knowing connect.

How might our expectations be affected by what we know of history, that "third"? Our remarks so far in this section have stressed the "two" of self and world. One might say that we have had our hands full enough to justify this separation. But it would be a mistake all the same to leave matters so, for we know this third to be such that it reaches back to comprehend the self and the world. We seem increasingly clear not only that the knowing of self and the knowing of world must not be polarized, but also that both knowings are emphatically historical. Self and the knowing of self, world and the knowing of world, self in-the-world knowing self-and-world, these are not metaphysical universals but are historically particular. They are relative to the concreteness of historical circumstance and condition.

Such a remark is often spoken or heard as ominous. Is that assessment appropriate? To be relative is to be related. The knowing process is related to particular persons knowing at particular times; it occurs here and there, concretely. But it does not follow that what is known dissolves in atomistic isolation. Part of our developing historical consciousness is precisely a recognition of how what is past lives on to condition and in part to constitute the present.[8] As human we can understand that what is said about God is incomplete, but it does not follow that it is incorrect. It is not futile to know in part, particularly if what we do know connects with what we do not yet know.

Again here, Christian expectation agrees that all the knowing that comes into the conversation about faith is historical. The Christian, we have said, so speaks of God as to recognize the distinct reality of that which is not God—say, self and world. Thus to speak of creation is not only to speak of God but also to speak of the reality of history, which is not God. The Christian recognizes that God and all that which is not God are together in the whole, that "third" which is history. God is not outside history, awaiting its completion when the divine decrees will be effortlessly accomplished. We have spoken of God as the ground for the momentousness of history. History matters because of God, and, consistently, it matters to God. God is at risk. Yet God is not only passively present in history, helplessly suffering its energies.

How does such speaking about God in history affect our expectations for the conversation concerning faith? If God and we are in history, surely our relationship to God is also historical! Thus the Christian expects that something is coming about, something is being formed in the passing of time with respect to our relationship to God. Our knowledge of God, as part of that relationship, will undergo change. We come to know God in time. In time we will know God differently. Because of God the Christian expects history to matter for and in the conversation about God.

Something does seem to be happening in our knowing of God, although it is harder to be precise about what is happening. This does not seem to be an age of faith; at least the classic Christian faith does not obviously or explicitly "come up" when one seeks to understand the orientations and activities of many individuals and movements in life today. If this is so and if it is newly so, Christians should not be surprised. On a Christian reading of things something different and decisive can occur in history in the relationship to God. Are we living at the end of an era? Were Nietzsche and Freud, say, simply ahead of their time? Will religious faith continue to survive only in our culture's backwaters? Will the survivors have to settle for agreeing about their numerical status, adding the characterization "remnant" gladly or sadly? Elsewhere will the churches serve us only through their art and music, helping us to feel but no longer to know? Perhaps. The Christian faith is not immune to historical change. That is clear to non-Christians. It should be clear, I am saying, to Christians as well. Indeed Christians are called to seek and create change. Christian faith accepts the human sense of the decisiveness of the temporal and renders it the more momentous by refusing to grant the God-relationship an exemption. If the currents of human consciousness do continue to flow into unbelief, the Christian will not expect Christian faith somehow magically to survive.

Christian expectation may not only yield formal acceptance of historical efficacy regarding the standing of faith; it may alter our reading as we seek to evaluate any such efficacy. Ironically faith and unfaith may both have labored under an understanding of history by which change in faith is regarded as loss of faith. That common assumption may lie beneath such varying responses as exultation, despair, and nostalgia. If one rejects that assumption, what differences in expectation and evaluation might arise? Perhaps our time has become an age of faiths. It has become a truism to speak of religious pluralism. What is to be made of that? Faith giving way to faiths—that might be expected if faith is as human and historical as we have argued. After all, to speak of the human is to speak in special measure of novelty, for it is to speak of the way in which consciousness and symbol-making capacities add other layers to the reality of the given. On human and Christian grounds one can agree. We have spoken of the Enlightenment as a special time of the discovery and celebration of human capacity. We have noted that the Christian doctrine of creation speaks of the human as God's viceregent, called to cultivate the earth. We have spoken of the divine incentive to the civilizing acts of the human.

Surely part of this human development will be diversification; the creations of human historical consciousness will themselves be concrete and particular and, so, diverse. Should not the Christian expect that also for the human reality of faith? If by the will of God human initiative and historical efficacy are real, the Christian ought not be surprised by the dizzying proliferation of faiths.[9]

Should the Christian be disturbed, if not surprised? That is, of course, another question. Part of our consciousness of religious pluralism is not merely the awareness of plurality, but the sense that no single faith can appropriately order this largess. Does the Christian expect and so accept that? I defer a fuller response until the discussion of "practice" in the next section, for the Christian expects the answer to this question to emerge in the conversation. But to call for a conversation is to call for some ordering. It seems right to say here that Christian expectation approaches the development of religious pluralism as not necessarily falsifying Christian truth claims either directly or by making the effort of comparison implied in such claims a futile exercise. Perhaps the non-Christian can agree, for human development yields now, together with the proliferation of forms, some kind of convergence as the contraction of the globe is accelerated technologically.[10] The Midwestern farmer knows not only that those strangers on the next place are other; they are, so to speak, other in the farmer's own backyard.

Will the conversation be possible? After all, the principal emphasis here has been on a conversation between faith and unfaith. That is not obviously what one is talking about in considering a pluralism of faiths. I think the Christian expects that a conversation between faith and unfaith will be possible. Perhaps "expectation" is too strong a word; "hope" might be better. The Christian faith represents an affirmation of human competence for the conversation. But can one expect that competence will be earnestly exercised? I have suggested that Christian claims are "in contention" for those who do not accept them. Whether they seem irksome or winsome contenders, the claims invite consideration. Agnostics—and even atheists—may recognize with Christians that their questions can be considered in conversation with those who make the Christian quest their own. Sometimes they even sense their own somewhat strained participation in that quest. Consider Anthony Kenny's remark at the end of *The God of the Philosophers*:

One thing seems clear. There is no reason why someone who is in doubt about the existence of God should not pray for help and guidance on this topic as in other matters. Some find something comic in the idea of an agnostic praying to a God whose existence he doubts. It is surely no more unreasonable than the act of a man adrift in the ocean, trapped in a cave, or stranded on a mountainside, who cries for help though he may never be heard or fires a signal which may never be seen.[11]

Given their own life with the questions, and given what may be a grudging recognition of the inevitability of human change with respect to faith, Christians may well be slow to dismiss such cries or to require that a membership card be shown before such a cry can be considered. Perhaps we, questioners and questers alike, cry aloud by talking together.

If we are to talk, what must be expected? Three things are fundamental: (1) Each participant seeks to contribute. Belief, doubt, and unbelief all bear some witness here. (2) Each participant expects to learn. The others with whom I disagree and to whom I expect to contribute have something to teach me. (3) Given these two points, the outcome of the conversation cannot be predicted. But this much can be said: Someone—likely each one—will be changed.

WHAT IS NOW NEEDED?

Practice is. I refer not to practice for, but to practice in, the conversation. If we can expect a mutual commitment to a conversation that is possible, difficult, and important, then we had better get on with the interchange itself. This book will have reached its goal if Christian and non-Christian together read what I have written and say, "We need to talk. We can talk. Let's talk!"

It may be that no more should be said here. But I mention two other matters: world religions and feminism. Why bring these up? Why now? Very little has been said of them along the way, surely nothing near what could have been called for in view of the complexity of these matters. If these topics seem to appear here as leftovers, one will surely find their treatment to be not only too late but also too little. Yet brief reference to them may serve us well here at the end, with the agenda sketched. Here we are not hurrying to complete a conversation by covering the last stretch of ground, but pausing to offer a final comment on the proposed conversation. How, then, do these topics serve us at the end? They are illustrations, perhaps, but they count as much for method as for matter. In their compression much is brought together and so summed up.

How shall the Christian regard the other religions of humankind? They can be regarded as a problem. Do they not, at bottom, represent rivals to

Christian faith? This may seem a thoroughly radical way to state the relationship, but we shall soon see that certain feminist voices would suggest that a still more basic relationship obtains: the other traditional "high" religions are our colleagues under judgment. But if we formulate the relationship, for the time being, within the realm of the religious, another problem may arise. Suppose we settle matters by taking a stand on the issue of the rivalry between Christianity and other religions. Suppose we grant that they are rivals and then single out Christianity as humankind's proper suitor. Have we solved a problem, or created one (or more)? In some sense we can say we have the one real God. But is it not problematic that the Christian God, the true God, has no more than a minority following after all these centuries? Does this God seek nothing more than that? Is that not unjust of God? Or is God simply ineffective? Does not the Christian claim about God seem preposterously presumptuous? Ironically, thus to protect the uniqueness of the Christian God seems to be to undercut the credentials of that God. To set that God apart in such a way seems to invite us to set that God aside.

Jürgen Moltmann hints at this in noting that the "world class" status of Christianity is no longer to be assumed:

> The phrase "world religion" has hitherto been understood to cover the great supranational "higher" religions, Buddhism, Hinduism, Confucianism, Islam and Christianity. The only religions that will be able to present themselves and to maintain their ground as "world religions" in the future will be the ones that accept the "single world" that is coming into being and the common world history which can be created today for the first time.[12]

One may want to plead that the "single world" is very complex and warn against a diluting simplification. Still, the Christian's own universalistic claims about God call for some comment about the "problem" of the other religions. That call is more urgent in Christianity's case than it is in the case of a religion such as Hinduism, which has manifested more inclusive tendencies.

Those God-claims do speak of all persons without making such speaking dependent on the religiousness of the persons. That surely seems the right place to begin also in thinking about the other religions. Any glad Christian insistence that the Christian faith is *for* all the world must not be cut loose from the norming recognition that it is *about* all the world. We have spoken in these pages of how all life is grounded in the gracious will and activity of God. In that activity God works through many means, as John Taylor recognizes in reading the Hebrew Scriptures:

> The covenant with Noah embracing all the sons of men and, indeed, all creation,

reverberates through the words of much later prophets and psalmists. God has shown his particular favour in more than one exodus deliverance. "Have I not brought up Israel out of the land of Egypt, and the Philistines from Caphtor, and the Sirians from Kir?" (Amos 9:7) . . . "From the rising of the sun to the going down of the same my name is great among the Gentiles, and in every place incense is offered in my name and a pure offering. But you have profaned it." (Mal. 1:11)[13]

The New Testament builds upon this foundation and clearly declares that God's will for salvation is universal (1 Tim. 2:4). When we are speaking of salvation we are speaking of God. Moreover, we are speaking of Jesus; the Christian will want to name that name early. Is this driving together of the universal claim and the particular name a problem? It is not obviously so. After all, it should not be hard for the church to concede—indeed, to insist—that what God has done decisively in Jesus, God has done for all. There is but one God, and it is unseemly that an actual absolute should no longer be sought or claimed when the matter of the other religions comes up.

Christians may have been strangely slow in recognizing the universal import of the work of Christ. But another difficulty requires attention. To speak of salvation is to speak, after all, of humankind. God's saving will and activity are directed out to that which is not God. God is not saving God. So what will come of this activity? In this book I have stressed that when the work of God reaches that which is not God, it reaches that which is other than God is. It reaches the uncertain, the contingent. Christians have recognized that and yet have also wanted to continue to speak of God's sure will.

The church is not at the end, but lives in the middle. While the church attends to the phenomenon of religious diversity and in some way commends God's universal will and work for salvation, much is not clear. Indeed, one thing that is clear is that quick solutions must be resisted, solutions that could preempt the struggle to converse, to understand. The human phenomenon and the Christian claim combine in rejecting certain stultifying positions:

1. One position holds that the Christian faith alone is true. This can be put variously. Occasionally one still hears it suggested that Christianity is not a religion. Or one hears that it is the only true one. But parallels exist that are more than formal.[14]

2. Another position tries to retain the exclusive character of Christian faith by modifying the meaning of truth. Here there is a backing away from a "fides quae creditur," a set of truths, and a move toward a noncognitive grasping of the "fides qua creditur." Some content does remain, it seems. It is Jesus who is the way. But the way is simply naming the name in faith. No

one comes to God except by trusting in, relying upon, Jesus. This approach resembles the "Christianity is not a religion" approach in being overtly, perhaps even strictly, theological. It is on divine authority that one makes the decisive distinction in either case. But, alas, the revelation of this divine authority can effectively occur only as the revelation reaches out to articulate a view of things, to make truth claims. While there may be significant differences among religions in this respect, Christianity is clearly not the least "intellectualistic" of them. It will not work to seek to avoid bankruptcy by selling the store.

3. One of the truth claims is this: the God whom Christians worship is the only God, and that God wills to be known universally. What may the "no other name" affirmation mean within that context? Krister Stendahl has commented:

> Acts 4:12 is not a good basis for an absolute claim in an absolute sense, but . . . it is a natural confession growing out of the faith, growing out of the experience of gratitude. Also out of apostolic humility, that is, the awareness that they didn't do it themselves but that it was all in the power of the Lord. They thereby pointed away from themselves. Just as any reference to election is saying that one cannot understand how it could happen. Here is a confession, not a proposition. It is a witness, strangely enough not actually an argument, but just exactly a witness.[15]

Here we have an approach that supports the conversation in that it takes Christian claims to be about and for God and not about and against non-Christian religions. That should make sense to a Christian who recognizes how earthen the vessels of faith are. To affirm what we know is primary; to proceed to negations is to rely heavily on inference.

But this approach easily slides into a third unproductive simplification when that reorientation is in turn converted back into a claim about the relation of Christian faith to other faiths. That happens "easily"—that is, casually or carelessly—for the position implied seems hard to maintain in deliberate argument. Shall one simply say that all religions are equally true? We spoke earlier of parallels. But they exist within differences. We could then be saying that all religions are equally true in that they are all, as wholes, untrue. Or is God not one? Or is it the case, again, that to know God is not to know anything about God?[16] Is the religions' seeming self-contradictory knowledge *about* God actually a single knowing *of* God?

4. Ironically, a fourth way of closing off conversation is to concentrate on the conversation too much. That is, one may make the conversation a free-standing reality with a life wholly its own. To do so ignores the fact that the conversation depends on the life and light it draws from the primary faith orientations of its participants. The conversation between a Buddhist and a

Christian is not a new religion, though it may affect the faith of either of the participants. Thus there arises the danger of artifice and ambition joining hands in an effort to construct a "world theology," which represents a universal religion.[17] Sadly, even the most earnest of such efforts at synthesis tend to divert their laborers from conversation in the terms of the particular faiths.

I am calling for conversation: for study, for dialogue, for argument even. That is what is most needed now. To say that we do not know what will come out of this is not to retreat behind some epistemological modesty but to recall the decisiveness of historical development and to recognize the primitive state of such contact.

The process will be difficult. But it will not be impossible, if we together seek to attend to certain basic aspects of experience. Perhaps the "self and world together in history" structure of our study can provide some assistance. Eric Voegelin has identified six structures that raise religious questions for human beings:

1. The existence of the cosmos
2. The hierarchy and diversification of being
3. The experience of questioning as the constituent of humanity
4. The leap in existential truth through noetic and pneumatic illuminations of consciousness
5. The process of history in which the differentiations of questioning consciousness and the leaps of truth occur
6. The eschatological movement in the process beyond its structure[18]

One may detect here a rhythm of world (1, 2), self (3, 4), history (5, 6).

Self, world, and history are the "stuff" that receives the ministry of the faith. It is self, world, and history that are grounded, guided, healed, fulfilled, and illumined. Here there may be a basis for judgment. Does the faith manage some such relation to these structures? Does it manage the relation claimed? In these terms internal and even external criticism become possible. One will thus question religious realities that in theory or practice work against the reality of the nonreligious. Emphasis on the magical, on fatedness, on freedom-leveling harmony, or on a fundamental escape from the nonreligious will be suspect.[19]

I have spoken of evaluation, for that is implied in comparison. But the fundamental need is for understanding. Again the structures may serve us. I have sought to describe the "precarious project of the self" as a quest for coherent identity in the "manyness" of relationships, for consistency in the story of life. Do we not find such themes appearing no longer as goals but as givens in the description of God in the monotheistic Semitic tradition? We have spoken of world as a gathering structure that serves the drive to understand and create. Does not the Sinic matrix represent an affirmation of such a world, whether in nature (Taoism) or society (Confucianism)?

And history, that "third"? Christians are prone to claim historical consciousness as their special strength, though we have noted some reluctance to pay the price involved in the risk of granting some final constitutive significance to that which is not God. It does seem to matter whether or not the whole is conceived as the gathering third of self and world. Through the two this third becomes decisive. Instead one may sever the connection and speak with some forms of Buddhism of the absolutely nonfinal reality of the individual self or with some forms of Hinduism of the self as linked irreducibly with absolute reality.[20] In such Indic traditions the "whole" does not seem to be understood historically, as Eric Voegelin notes:

> In the culture of Hinduism, historical consciousness is muted by the dominance of late-cosmological speculations on the cosmos as a "thing" that is born and reborn in infinite sequence. The hypostasis of the cosmos, and the fallacious infinite of cosmological speculation, can be identified as the stratum in the Hinduist experience of reality that has not been broken by epochal events comparable to the poetic and pneumatic theophanies in Hellas and Israel.[21]

To what are we coming with this self-world-history suggestion? Are we playing precisely into the hands of those who expand the suggestion to invoke the shade of Feuerbach? If the holy has so clearly to do with self, world, and history, may it not simply be the projection of those structures on the spreading span of the unknown? Well, that has been our question earlier, and our response then perhaps can be said to have yielded a standoff. In this chapter's preceding section we have spoken of why the Christian might expect such ambiguity. In religion we are talking about self, world, and history; we could be talking about nothing more. But it should be noted that religion employs those structures, at times at least, to speak of the otherness of the holy. To speak of the reality that is worshiped as related to self, world, and history is to speak of that which is other than they are.

That otherness may be expressed in the relationship in different ways. One may speak of the "givenness" of the structure itself. Such a relationship does ground and so affirm life and yet one hears in the word "given" a note of contingency. What is given might not be. The gift of life is sweet, but in its fragility it cannot be possessed. Together these notes—that life is truly given, that life is only given—may strike the chord of transcendence. In religious faith we do not worship self, world, and history.[22]

To what are we coming? By employing the self-world-history structure in conversation with other faiths we can become clearer about our own identity. We understand the holy to be related to this structure in one way, and not in another. In the comparison a new kind of understanding is gained. As I see what you are doing, I see, or see more clearly, what I am doing.

At the same time that through comparison we become aware of the relationship of the holy to the structure we can recognize that the holy cannot be reduced to the structure. The sense of alternative descriptions evokes the sense of otherness within any particular description. Some people worship the holy as personal and others as impersonal. Some see the holy as having to do with history, but others as dissolving the distinctions that constitute history. If my human kinship with other faiths is such that we can appear together in a morphology so structured, then I may acquire some perspective on my own perspective. In the relation of the holy these two are together: connection and distinction. Through the otherness of the non-Christian the Christian may come to be aware of the otherness of God: "You are saying the holy is like this. I see that I, on the other hand, am saying that God is like this other reality. But a God who is *like* some reality is not that reality." In comparison with non-Christian religions, thus, I may recognize that I understand God to be one and personal, but I may recognize as well that God is not one and personal as human selves are. At least God is not one personal human self. "One—personal—human—self": each word will require attention. In the conversation together, therefore, participants of different faiths may recognize that what the one believes may not exclude what the other believes, and they may be provoked to work at speaking of how the holy remains other even in relatedness.

In this compressed discussion we do find an illustration of how attending (to the reality of other faiths) clarifies commending (faith in a God who is transcendent in relationship). Some voices in the feminist movement will not be surprised that different religions can serve each other so happily, for the religions are together in not serving at least half the human race. How shall one assess the role of the feminist movement in the conversation concerning faith? I find the same rhythm discerned in the relationship to other faiths: in attending to a problem that is posed the church is driven to discover or recover its own treasure. In that discovery the prospect of solidarity challenges the specter of opposition occasioned by the posing of the problem. There are important differences between the two cases. One of those differences, that feminism cuts across the distinction between the religious and the nonreligious, makes the common rhythm the more note-worthy.

In any case it is not to be doubted that we have to do here with a problem, though it may not be clear who has the problem. Sometimes it is suggested that the problem lies with Western religion and its stress on history against nature:

Many theologians have pointed out that Judaism and Christianity consider nature as inferior to "man"—as something to be conquered by "him." . . . Woman is often seen as nature in Judaism and Christianity, as an inferior being in need of taming and cultivation by "man."[23]

Different religions do indeed have different difficulties—we anticipate the christological case—but fundamentally East joins West in the dock:

Usually, a woman has gained status by belonging to a man—by being the daughter of this father, the wife of this husband, the mother of that son. Indeed, in few cultures was a woman's consent even needed for either marriage or divorce. The religious traditions of West and East, in fact, agreed that a woman should never be independent, ought always be subject. . . . Hinduism denied women the sacred thread, the symbol of religious birth. Buddhist nuns, while freed from familial supervision, were expected to serve even the youngest monk. Christian wives were taught to be silent in church and obedient to their husbands, for their husbands were their "heads," as Christ is head of the Church. Purdah kept Muslim women veiled from the eyes of all but their own men, partly because Islam measured women's salvation in terms of their submission, not to Allah, but to their husbands.[24]

Some feminist writers find the basic distinction to be between archaic religion and the so-called high, or developed, religions. Denise Lardner Carmody has written favorably of the former:

Archaic peoples . . . live in a holistic universe, where the sacred penetrates all reality. . . . In cultures where the dominant value has been union or harmony with the sacred, archaic woman's roles and images have naturally been held sacred. The principal focus of female sacrality (the power at which women's roles and images converged) has been fertility. . . .[25]

What can the church learn from those who draw this distinction? I doubt it can or should learn to discover a new primitivism.[26] The appeal that the spells of witches and the fantasy of tarot cards hold points clearly to the gravity of the problem but less clearly to anything else. In any case, we cannot know now all the changes in concept and structure that will be required. Issues of justice and truth clamor equally for attention in what the feminists are telling the church, just as they have been together earlier in this book. We can think and talk together and we can join as well in the conversation that is action. It is practice in both senses that we need. Much is not yet clear, but some directions are apparent:

1. The church needs to attend to the experience of women. There are specific lessons to be gained here, some of which I suggest below. But to make this point about empirical method in the quest for God is necessarily to broaden the point to encompass the experience of all persons. Christian faith will strive to confess one God for females and for males. That faith

calls us as well toward a common humanity. As we try to think through what this means, as we try to work for what we can see clearly or even not so clearly, we attend to all human experience, but particularly to neglected female experience.

2. Will feminist theology remain monotheist? Should it? Feminism and the church it criticizes can together learn that what is crucial is fresh and fundamental reflection together on God. Here it is particularly instructive that feminism cuts across the religious-nonreligious distinction. Perhaps it represents an outcry for the recognition of the worth of the human—the woman as human, the human as woman, the human. Perhaps the God of nonarchaic religion tends to be precisely so "high" that the human must be debased. It is not surprising that in response Mary Daly speaks of how "the ultimate power of the universe is on the side of the free self-actualization of human life"[27] or, even less subtly, that Zsuzsanna Budapest of the Sisterhood of Wicca says: "In self-blessing, you affirm the divine you."[28] It is not surprising, particularly if Kate Millett is right, that "what lingers of supranatural authority, the Deity, 'His' ministry, together with the ethics and values and philosophy and art of our culture—its very civilization—as T. S. Eliot once observed, is of male manufacture."[29] If God is against woman, will she not have to be for herself?

But need it be a self-blessing to be human-affirming? Is religion to be about the *self*-actualization of human life? Other voices in the feminist movement sound a dissenting note, refusing to accept the prescription that women must be alone, against God and against men. Thus Rosemary Radford Ruether points to a different way, a difficult but possible way:

> [H]umanity can be reconciled with God only if God is converted from "His" patriarchalism to become the ground of reciprocity in creation. The death of God the Father is the overthrowing of the alienated image of male egoism in heaven which sanctifies all relations of domination and subjugation in the world in order that the new covenant of life can appear. This is the new creation glimpsed but unrealizable under a patriarchal gospel. . . .[30]

Here the church is invited to learn a lesson about God, and about humankind. The power of God is not that of domination and control. And that is not to be the power at work among human beings made in the divine image. The feminist movement can call the church to think about "power with," "power together," and to let that replace "power over."

3. To plead for the human is to plead for the human together, and that is not to speak against God. But what of Jesus? Here the rhythm of attending to a problem with the result that a resource is commended is intensified. Statements of the problem are readily available. Here is Naomi Goldenberg's:

Jesus Christ cannot symbolize the liberation of women. A culture that maintains a masculine image for its highest divinity cannot allow its women to experience themselves as the equals of its men. In order to develop a theology of women's liberation, feminists have to leave Christ and Bible behind them. Women have to stop denying the sexism that lies at the root of the Jewish and Christian religions.[31]

Or, more briefly, recall Daly's "If God is male, then the male is God."[32]

Do women have to leave Christianity because of Christ? If women do, do not men need to as well? Perhaps the feminist movement is right in calling on the church to attend to its problem *and* to commend its treasure in the area of Christology. What will come of that is not clear for it will come in the course of the conversation. But it will not come truly without focusing on the God whose undergoing in the suffering Jesus becomes an overcoming that can avail for us all actually and absolutely.[33] Jesus is not to be set up as the sovereign example of what it is to be human. He is the singular instance in whom God's will for all humanity attains absolute confirmation in the face of full-fledged rejection. That God does this in a male is not much to the point. If anything, it may be that the lesson that a "suffering God can help" (Bonhoeffer) is taught the more emphatically in this way.[34] But God is not a male, large or small, domineering or suffering.[35]

Such is the practice we need. Persons of Christian faith, persons of other faiths, persons of no faith, all need to come together in conversation about God. It may seem chaotic; it is unpredictable. What we have set out here in some order has been an agenda for the conversation; matters to attend to and convictions to commend have been identified. I cannot claim more than that. Moreover, this bare skeleton is firmer than the living flesh of the conversation is apt to be. The book's order will not control the practice. Perhaps that has been clear in these last pages where the rhythms of attending and commending converged.

The conversation will be chaotic also in that there is no single set of Robert's Rules set for the meeting for which this agenda applies. It would be nice to be clear about such questions as who is competent to participate, when and how to close off debate, what constitutes adequate evidence and sufficient agreement on various questions, as well as who has the authority to rule on disputes about the rules themselves. Some things can be said about such questions, and we have done some of that along the way and also here in the last chapter. But no Robert's Rules is available for the meeting about God. It is in the conversation itself that the rules will have to emerge.

Why should anyone enter this conversation? In chapter 1 we talked about coming to the conversation. But the question may reappear in view of the confusing and chaotic prospects. But in spite of the difficulties and even because of them, we need and want to talk together. The Christian hears a special call: "Always be prepared to make a defense to anyone who calls you to account for the hope that is in you" (1 Pet. 3:15). There is as well the call from these other human beings with whom one shares this place. We want them to know the good we know in knowing God; we want that good tested by touching their lives. The non-Christian may not be so far from this quest. Much of the questioning we have identified here hardly seems disinterested. Question and quest do keep company as human beings think of God. Many will agree with Anne Sexton's words:

> My faith
> is a great weight
> hung on a small wire . . .
> God does not need
> too much wire to keep Him there
> just a thin vein, . . .
> and some love . . .
> even a small love.
> So if you have only a thin wire,
> God does not mind.
> He will enter your hands
> as easily as ten cents used to
> bring forth a Coke.[36]

Is this blasphemous, to speak of bringing forth a God "as easily as ten cents used to bring forth a Coke"? Well, it is human. It is human to question God. It is human to quest for God. Whatever the wire, it does not displease God. In desire and in desperation there is some earnestness, if not confidence. To call for a conversation is to call the solitary together. Together we question and quest.

NOTES

CHAPTER 1

1. I recognize that Christianity is sometimes understood to make no claim on reality, as in Hans Vaihinger, *The Philosophy of "As If": A System of the Theoretical, Practical, and Religious Fictions of Mankind* (London: Routledge & Kegan Paul, 1965), and R. B. Braithwaite, *An Empiricist's View of the Nature of Religious Belief* (Cambridge: At the Univ. Press, 1955). Even in making the reality claim the Christian may experience doubt; quest and question coexist. But both have to do with the issue of reality.

2. Philip Rieff, *The Triumph of the Therapeutic: The Uses of Faith After Freud* (New York: Harper & Row, 1966), 261. See also his "Fellow Teachers," *Salmagundi* 1 (Summer-Fall 1972): 5–85.

3. Wallace Stevens, "On the Road Home," *The Palm at the End of the Mind*, ed. Holly Stevens (New York: Alfred A. Knopf, 1971).

4. Alasdair MacIntyre and Paul Ricoeur, *The Religious Significance of Atheism* (New York: Columbia Univ. Press, 1969), 24.

5. Erich Fromm, *Man for Himself* (New York: Holt, Rinehart & Winston, 1947; Fawcett Premier ed.), 56.

6. Peter Berger, *The Heretical Imperative* (New York: Doubleday Anchor Books, 1979).

7. Jeremy Bernstein cites Rabi's remarks in *Experiencing Science* (London: Burnett Books, 1979), 45–46.

8. I have found particularly helpful Peter Gay's *The Enlightenment: An Interpretation*, 2 vols. (New York: Alfred A. Knopf, 1966–1969), Ernst Cassirer's *The Philosophy of the Enlightenment*, trans. F. C. A. Koelln and J. P. Pettegrove (Princeton: Princeton Univ. Press, 1951), and Basil Willey's several studies.

9. René Descartes, *Philosophical Writings*, ed. and trans. E. Anscombe and P. T. Geach (London: Thomas Nelson & Sons, 1954; Nelson Univ. Paperback, 1971), 13.

10. Gay, *The Enlightenment* 1:266.

11. See Karl Barth's remarkable chronicle of eighteenth- and nineteenth-century discoveries in *From Rousseau to Ritschl*, trans. Brian Cozens (London: SCM Press, 1952), 19. Cf. Gay's observation in *The Enlightenment* 2:25, that "the recovery of nerve" was "infectious."

12. Barth, *From Rousseau to Ritschl*, 14.

13. Carl Becker, *The Heavenly City of the Eighteenth-Century Philosophers* (New Haven: Yale Univ. Press, 1932), 30.

14. Gay, *The Enlightenment* 1:324.

15. Cassirer, *The Philosophy of the Enlightenment*, 139. Cf. Gay, *The Enlightenment* 1:268–70, on the affinities and differences between the Enlightenment and the Renaissance as "defined by . . . relative proximity to the Christian Middle Ages."

16. Gay, *The Enlightenment* 1:xiii.

17. Cassirer, *The Philosophy of the Enlightenment*, 13. Cf. his reference to the "logic of facts," p. 9.

18. Gay makes this point effectively by recounting an anecdote: "Voltaire, the arch-philosophe, had come back to Paris to be deified and to die, and among his carefully staged final performances was a highly emotional meeting with Benjamin Franklin in mid-February: twenty spectators, 'shedding tender tears,' were present to see Voltaire embrace Franklin and bless Franklin's grandson in English with these charged words: 'God and Liberty'" (*The Enlightenment* 2:557, citing Voltaire to the Abbé Gaultier, Feb. 20, 1778, Correspondence xcviii.110). See also the material Gay takes from Madison in the *Federalist* (2:567).

19. Peter Berger has written extensively concerning crises in the plausibility structures of religion. See, for example, *The Sacred Canopy* (Garden City, N.Y.: Doubleday & Co., 1967; Penguin Univ. Book, 1973), 157ff.

20. Gay, *The Enlightenment* 1:418–19.

21. Cassirer, *The Philosophy of the Enlightenment*, 164.

22. Basil Willey's studies make clear the deeply religious character of the work of the Cambridge Platonists. In his work of 1712, Clarke examined 1251 Scriptural texts but failed to find the "proposition" of the Trinity. See as well his *The Evidences of Natural and Revealed Religion* (facs. of 1706 original, Stuttgart-Bad Cannstatt: Friedrich Frommann Verlag, 1964), 241, 258. The assertive rationalism of the later deists is well illustrated by John Toland who subtitled his *Christianity Not Mysterious* "a treatise showing that there is nothing in the Gospel contrary to reason or above it, and that no Christian doctrine can properly be called a mystery."

23. Benedict Spinoza, *Theologico-Political Treatise* in *Works of Spinoza*, trans. R. H. M. Elwes (New York: Dover, 1951), 189. Cf. 198.

24. Spinoza, *Ethics*, esp. parts II and V.

25. Immanuel Kant, *Religion Within the Limits of Reason Alone*, trans. Hoyt H. Hudson and Theodore M. Greene (New York: Random House [The Modern Library], 1949), 396–98. Italics his. I appreciate Eugene TeSelle's caution against dispatching Kant with the label "moral idealist," but think the careful study TeSelle offers still points toward this conclusion. See his *Christ in Context* (Philadelphia: Fortress Press, 1975), 52–69.

26. In *The Christian Faith*, 2d German ed., trans. H. R. Mackintosh and J. S. Stewart (Edinburgh: T. & T. Clark, 1928), 194, Schleiermacher is very clear that the various divine attributes do not denote "something special in God, but only something special in the manner in which the feeling of absolute dependence is to be related to Him," lest there might be division and change in God. Thus, consistently, he rejects the notion of divine "Lordship," since "Lordship is connected with

independence only on the presupposition that the independent is at the same time in need of something" (p. 219).

27. G. W. F. Hegel, "The Spirit of Christianity and Its Fate," *Early Theological Writings*, trans. T. M. Knox (Chicago: Univ. of Chicago Press, 1948), 272. Cf. *The Science of Logic*, trans. William Wallace (Oxford: At the Clarendon Press, 1892), 137, 210; this is translated from *Encyclopedia of the Physical Sciences*, 2d ed.

28. Thus David Friedrich Strauss, *The Life of Jesus Critically Examined*, 2d ed., trans. George Eliot (London: Swan Sonnenschein & Co., 1892), 779–80: "If reality is ascribed to the idea of the unity of the divine and human natures, is this equivalent to the admission that this unity must actually have been once manifested, as it never had been, and never more will be, in one individual? This is indeed not the mode in which Idea realizes itself; it is not wont to lavish all its fullness on one exemplar, and be niggardly towards all others—to express itself perfectly in that one individual, and imperfectly in all the rest: it rather loves to distribute its riches among a multiplicity of exemplars which reciprocally complete each other—in the alternate appearance and suppression of a series of individuals."

29. A. R. Peacocke, *Creation and the World of Science* (Oxford: At the Clarendon Press, 1979), 59–60.

30. See Martin E. Marty, *The Modern Schism: Three Paths to the Secular* (London: SCM Press, 1969), on continental "utter" secularity, British "mere" secularity, and American "controlled" secularity.

31. I have discussed this development in nontechnical terms in *Contemporary Forms of Faith* (Minneapolis: Augsburg Pub. House, 1967), chap. 5.

32. Soren Kierkegaard, *Concluding Unscientific Postscript to the Philosophical Fragments*, trans. David F. Swenson and W. Lowrie (Princeton: Princeton Univ. Press, 1944), 191, 345–46. Cf. Jean Milet's observations in *God or Christ?* (New York: Crossroad, 1981) on the tendency in Barth toward subjectivization. In *God in Exile: Modern Atheism*, trans. and ed. Arthur Gibson (Westminster, Md.: Newman Press, 1968), part 8, Cornelio Fabro links "dialectical theology" and death-of-God theology and worries about "psychological fideism" and "ontological deism" as "antechambers of atheism."

33. In *Joyful Wisdom*, trans. Thomas Common (New York: Frederick Ungar Pub. Co., 1960), 167–68 (Bk. 3, sec. 125), Nietzsche makes the madman's message concerning the death (murder) of God eloquent, but hardly exuberant: "What did we do when we loosened this earth from its sun? Whither does it now move? Whither do we move? Away from all suns? Do we not dash on unceasingly? Backwards, sideways, forewards [sic], in all directions? Is there still an above and below? Do we not stray, as through infinite nothingness? Does not empty space breathe upon us? Has it not become colder? Does not night come on continually, darker and darker? Shall we not have to light lanterns in the morning? Do we not hear noise of the grave-diggers who are burying God? Do we not smell the divine putrefaction?—for even Gods putrefy! God is dead! God remains dead! and we have killed him!"

34. Langdon Gilkey makes this point well in *Naming the Whirlwind: The Renewal of God Language* (Indianapolis: Bobbs-Merrill, 1969), 150 and passim.

35. Even the "hiddenness of God" is not unqualified in Luther's thought. Thus in

the *Bondage of the Will* there is offered the promise of a light of grace that will show the justice of God with respect to salvation, and Luther adds an appeal that is not to the future, "as we are instructed and encouraged to do by the example of the light of grace explaining what was a puzzle of the same order to the light of nature" (*Martin Luther: Selections from his Writings*, ed. John Dillenberger [Garden City, N.Y.: Doubleday Anchor Books, 1961], 202). Cf. B. A. Gerrish, "To the Unknown God: Luther and Calvin on the Hiddenness of God," *Journal of Religion* 53 (July 1972): 273–75, on how Luther recalled his own struggle with predestination as something he had behind him and therefore as the experiential basis for his counseling of others.

36. In "Athens and Jerusalem," in *The Philosophical Frontiers of Theology* (Festschrift D. M. Mackinnon), ed. Brian Hebblethwaite and Stewart Sutherland (Cambridge: At the Univ. Press, 1982), 19, G. W. H. Lampe draws on this theme from Justin's *2 Apologiae*, 13.

37. Wolfhart Pannenberg, *The Idea of God and Human Freedom*, trans. R. A. Wilson (Philadelphia: Westminster Press, 1973), 103–4, makes the point of how the witness to Jesus needs the reference to God.

38. Charles Hartshorne, *Philosophers Speak of God* (Chicago: Univ. of Chicago Press, 1953), 7.

39. For a philosophical statement of this notion, see Frederick Sontag, *Divine Perfection* (London: SCM Press, 1962), 83–125. For a theological statement that seems parallel, see H. P. Owen, *Concepts of Deity* (London: Macmillan & Co., 1971), and, less stridently, Stephen T. Davis, *Logic and the Nature of God* (Grand Rapids: Wm. B. Eerdmans, 1983).

40. Dietrich Bonhoeffer develops this theme from Luther in *Act and Being*, trans. Bernard Noble (New York: Harper & Row, 1961), 81. He has drawn the passage from vol. 23 of the Weimar edition of Luther, p. 157 ("Dass diese Wort Christ 'Das ist mein Leib' noch fest stehen," 1527).

41. Karl Barth, *Evangelical Theology: An Introduction*, trans. Grover Foley (New York: Holt, Rinehart & Winston, 1963; Garden City, N.Y.: Doubleday Anchor Books, 1964), 8. Cf. *Church Dogmatics* 4.1.186.

42. "To come into question" is surely to understate Robert Jenson's point in *The Triune Identity* (Philadelphia: Fortress Press, 1982), 139, where others are found to support such protest: "The two most important contemporary trinitarian theorists, Karl Rahner and Eberhard Jüngel, agree on the rule . . . the 'economic' Trinity *is* the 'immanent' Trinity, and vice versa, thereby bluntly stating what the old Lutherans were gingerly approaching." Italics his.

43. George Newlands, *Theology of the Love of God* (London: William Collins & Co., 1980), raises this question effectively, for example.

44. Paul Tillich, *Theology of Culture*, ed. Robert C. Kimball (New York: Oxford Univ. Press, 1959), 10. Italics his.

45. Soren Kierkegaard, *Training in Christianity*, trans. Walter Lowrie (Princeton: Princeton Univ. Press, 1944), 134.

46. Cf. W. Pannenberg, *The Idea of God and Human Freedom*, 104.

47. Cf. *Philosophical Frontiers of Theology*, 24–29, where Lampe develops this point at some length. He recounts the patristic efforts to take the sting out of the

story of the Magi, but concludes that "taken at its face value, Matthew's story tells us uncompromisingly that the birth of the King of the Jews was revealed, like that of Alexander, by a star which was observed by magi in the regular practice of astrology, and that, after they had communicated this revelation to the people of Jerusalem, these heathen were led to the Messiah by the joint guidance of their star and the scriptural prophecy of Micah, worshipped him, presented him with their treasures, and were favored with a special divine revelation to enable them to return safely to their own country." He notes a foreshadowing in several important passages in the earlier part of the Gospel, such as the contention that the move of Jesus from Nazareth to Capernaum fulfilled the prophecy of the coming of light to those in darkness, in the land of the Gentiles; the insertion of Jesus' own prophecy concerning the admission of Gentiles to the heavenly feast (and the expulsion from it of the "sons of the kingdom") into the story of the centurion; and the use made of the Servant Song of Isa. 42:1–4 with its strong emphasis on the salvation of the Gentiles, in connection with Jesus' Galilean ministry.

48. In *Theology and Philosophy of Science*, 265, Pannenberg makes the same point somewhat differently: "Theology can do justice to Christianity only if it is not a science of Christianity but a science of God. As a science of God its subject matter is reality as a whole, even though as yet uncompleted whole of the semantic network of experience." Cf. 296.

49. This amounts to blurring the distinctions David Tracy wants to make between "fundamental" theology, "systematic" theology, and "practical" theology. See his succinct statement in *The Analogical Imagination: Christian Theology and the Culture of Pluralism* (New York: Crossroad, 1981), 54–58. Such a blurring seems to me to represent more realistically the actual situation in which the theologian as a member of the public that is the church is called upon to give an account of Christian hope to the public that is academy or society. Tracy, of course, does not let these distinctions become disjunctions and I move nearer his position with respect to tactical differences of emphasis or accessibility. I have discussed several apologetic styles programmatically in "Apologetics of the Center," *Dialog* 21 (Summer 1982): 180–84.

50. For a closely argued attempt of a very different sort to address both the meaning and truth issues, see Robert P. Scharlemann, *The Being of God: Theology and the Experience of Truth* (New York: Seabury Press, 1981).

CHAPTER 2

1. Harold Pinter, *A Homecoming* (New York: Grove Press, 1966), 27.

2. The apophatic tradition in Christian thought may be viewed as a comment on the nature and content of our knowing, not as a repudiation of it.

3. *The Ontological Argument*, ed. Alvin Plantinga (London: Macmillan & Co., 1968), and *The Many-Faced Argument*, ed. John Hick and A. C. McGill (New York: Macmillan Co., 1968), remain useful surveys of the discussion. I agree with the criticism voiced in the text, thus siding with Hume's Cleanthes: "Nothing is demonstrable unless the contrary implies a contradiction. Whatever we conceive as existent, we can also conceive as non-existent. There is no being, therefore, whose nonexistence implies a contradiction. Consequently there is no being whose existence is

demonstrable" (David Hume, *Dialogues Concerning Natural Religion*, ed. Henry Aiken [New York: Hafner, 1948], 58).

4. See Karl Barth, *Anselm: Fides Querens Intellectum*, trans. Ian W. Robertson (Richmond: John Knox Press, 1960), and Richard Campbell, *From Belief to Understanding* (Canberra: Australian National Univ., 1976).

5. Van A. Harvey, *The Historian and the Believer: The Morality of Historical Knowledge* (New York: Macmillan Co., 1966), 32.

6. Richard Robinson, "Religion and Reason," in *Critiques of God*, ed. Peter Angeles (Buffalo: Prometheus Books, 1976), 116–17.

7. John Henry Newman, *An Essay in Aid of a Grammar of Assent*, with an introduction by Nicholas Lash (Notre Dame, Ind.: Univ. of Notre Dame Press, 1979), 181. Newman indicates that assent, while in its nature absolute and unconditional, "cannot be given except under certain conditions" (p. 135). See also M. Jamie Ferreira, *Doubt and Religious Commitment: The Role of Will in Newman's Thought* (New York and London: Oxford Univ. Press, 1980), for an attempt to show that Newman's elimination of doubt from faith is neither fideistic nor voluntaristic.

8. This is a great strength of the work of Friedrich Schleiermacher (*The Christian Faith*) in the last century and of Edward Schillebeeckx (*Jesus* and *Christ*) in this century. But it is important not to limit the point to theologians who are explicit about it. Thus Peter Berger in *The Heretical Imperative* (New York: Doubleday Anchor Books, 1979), 91–93, notes how the experiential root of neo-orthodoxy can be located.

9. A biblical scholar who makes this point well is Dale Patrick in *The Rendering of God in the Old Testament* (Philadelphia: Fortress Press, 1981).

10. Ray Hart, *Unfinished Man and the Imagination* (New York: Herder & Herder, 1968), 28.

11. See my article, "The Human Venture: On Raising the Bid," *Word and World* 2 (Summer 1982): 213–16.

12. See Ronald F. Hepburn, *Christianity and Paradox* (Indianapolis: Pegasus, 1968; London: C. A. Watts, 1958), 18, 83, on the lack of ostensive reference for God-talk.

13. Wolfhart Pannenberg, *Theology and Philosophy of Science*, trans. Francis McDonagh (London: Darton, Longman & Todd, 1976), 306.

14. Cf. Hume, *Dialogues Concerning Natural Religion*, 21–23.

15. In Antony Flew's contribution to the symposium "Theology and Falsification," in *New Essays in Philosophical Theology*, ed. Antony Flew and Alasdair MacIntyre (London: SCM Press, 1955), 97.

16. Sigmund Freud, *The Future of an Illusion*, trans. W. D. Robson-Scott, ed. James Strachey (London: Hogarth Press, 1978), 24.

17. Kierkegaard, for example, remarks in his journal: "God is pure subjectivity, perfect, pure subjectivity. He has no objective being whatever in him; for everything that has such objective being comes thereby into the realm of relativities" (*Papirer* XI 2 A 54). Yet I have tried to show that Kierkegaard brings even such speech about God into (objectifying?) relation to speech about the human. See my *Kierkegaard on Christ and Christian Coherence* (New York: Harper & Row, 1968). Another instance is Fritz Buri, who stresses "the non-objectifiable," and yet asks *How Can We Still*

Speak Responsibly of God? trans. Charley D. Hardwick (Philadelphia: Fortress Press, 1968).

18. Harvey, *The Historian and the Believer*, 224. Cf. the critique of the tu quoque argument in *The Retreat to Commitment* by W. W. Bartley (New York: Alfred A. Knopf, 1962). Even broader appeals of a perspectivist nature have recently appeared, as in Colin Chapman's *Christianity on Trial* (Wheaton, Ill.: Tyndale House Pubs., 1975). Mark Hanna in *Crucial Questions in Apologetics* (Grand Rapids: Baker Book House, 1981) is concerned to avoid fideism as it offers itself in "presuppositionism," where one's initial assumptions determine the nature and applicability of all criteria, but employs all the same as his "justificational starting point" a "special cognitive revelation from God." He seeks to escape from vicious circularity by appealing to universals brought to bear upon particular truth claims, thus linking self-evidence and corroboration. David Kelsey's *The Uses of Scripture in Recent Theology* (Philadelphia: Fortress Press, 1975) remains a very helpful analysis of options in this difficult area.

19. Richard Rorty, *Philosophy and the Mirror of Nature* (Princeton: Princeton Univ. Press, 1979), is perhaps the most spectacular example. A major influence Rorty acknowledges is Wilfrid Sellars; see his *Science, Perception, and Reality* (London: Routledge & Kegan Paul, 1963).

20. Charles Taylor, "Understanding in Human Sciences," *Review of Metaphysics* 34 (Sept. 1980): 26. In *In Defense of Objectivity* (London: The British Academy, 1973) Mary Hesse suggests that the epistemological concern of the older approach can still be honored: "The guarantee of objectivity in human science is the participation in DIALOGUE between investigator and investigated, in which RECIPROCAL interaction occurs. The sanction of failure is disturbance of consensus and breakdown of communication" (p. 14, emphasis hers).

21. Wallace Stevens, *The Necessary Angel* (London: Faber & Faber, 1942), 53, 60. Cf. 40, 64.

22. The categories are from John Dominic Crossan, *In Parables* (New York: Harper & Row, 1973). Cf. Paul Ricoeur, *The Rule of Metaphor: Multi-Disciplinary Studies of the Creation of Meaning in Language* (London: Routledge & Kegan Paul, 1978), for a strong emphasis on participation. *Philosophical Perspectives on Metaphor*, ed. Mark Johnson (Minneapolis: Univ. of Minn. Press, 1981), offers a good indication of the many disciplines involved in this interest.

23. For respectively polarized truth theories see J. L. Austin, "Truth," in his *Philosophical Papers* (Oxford: At the Clarendon Press, 1961), 91.

24. See, for example, Ronald Hepburn's remarkable last chapter in *Christianity and Paradox*, where he suggests a nontheistic repossession of the experience of the numinous or holy (pp. 205ff.). Don Cupitt's *Taking Leave of God* (London: SCM Press, 1980) is perhaps similar, except that it might be better termed a posttheistic interpretation.

25. Stevens, *The Necessary Angel*, 6, suggests that the immediate effect of the imagination's attaching itself to what is unreal may be intensification, but "that effect is the maximum effect that it will ever have."

26. John Locke, *Essay Concerning Human Understanding* IV.xix.1.

27. Nietzsche's words are "streng gegen sein Herz" (*Kritische Gesamtausgabe: Der Antichrist* [Elmsford, N.Y.: Walter de Gruyter, 1969], 228).

28. Stephen E. Toulmin, *The Uses of Argument* (Cambridge: At the Univ. Press, 1964), 176. See, for a fuller treatment, his three-volume project on *Human Understanding* (Oxford: At the Clarendon Press, 1972-   ). Cf. Wayne Booth, *Modern Dogma and the Rhetoric of Assent* (Notre Dame, Ind.: Univ. of Notre Dame Press, 1974), 147. Booth cites Gödel's work as softening the dogma's paradigm appeal to mathematics, p. 66. See also Booth's discussion, p. 144, of the three kinds of proof: substantive, ethical, and emotional.

29. The classic statement is Karl Popper's *The Logic of Scientific Discovery* (New York: Harper & Row, 1965), 27ff. It is instructive that Popper found T. S. Kuhn's *The Structure of Scientific Revolutions* excessively relativistic. See his criticism in *Criticism and the Growth of Knowledge*, ed. Imre Lakatos and Alan Musgrave (Cambridge: At the Univ. Press, 1970), and Kuhn's response in the "Postscript" to his second edition (Chicago: Univ. of Chicago Press, 1970). The debate concerns whether anomalous experiences function to falsify scientific hypotheses (Kuhn, pp. 146–47), and what constitutes objectionable relativism (pp. 205–6).

30. John Wisdom's influential essay "Gods" may be found in *Religion from Tolstoy to Camus*, ed. Walter Kaufmann (New York: Harper & Row, 1961), 391–406. This passage is from 397–98 and rather reminds one of Newman's remarks about "the faculty of composition" in the *Grammar of Assent*, 42ff. The italics are Wisdom's.

31. Kelsey, *The Uses of Scripture in Recent Theology*.

32. Newman, *Grammar of Assent*, 90.

33. Alfred North Whitehead, *Process and Reality: An Essay in Cosmology*, corrected ed. by David Ray Griffin and Donald W. Sherburne (New York: Free Press, 1978), 259.

34. William James, "The Will to Believe," in *Religion from Tolstoy to Camus*, ed. Kaufmann, 237.

35. Thus a case can be made that both William James and Charles Peirce—despite clichés about pragmatist truth theory's caving in upon itself in circularity (in the absence of criteria to assess a claim's "working")—still hold a correspondence theory of truth, however dynamic that correspondence may be. Cf. John E. Smith, *Purpose and Thought: The Meaning of Pragmatism* (New Haven: Yale Univ. Press, 1978), 77: "If any novel element has been introduced, it is their insistence that 'correspondence' not be conceived as a static or timeless relation having no connection with the process of inquiry and the tracing of consequences. If a label is needed, one could do no better than to call their theory of truth a theory of 'dynamic correspondence.' "

36. Booth, *Modern Dogma and the Rhetoric of Assent*, 177.

37. Newman, *A Grammar of Assent*, 294.

38. H. H. Price in his Gifford lectures, *Belief* (London: George Allen & Unwin, 1969), 487, speaks of an effort to develop the latent spiritual capacities in a person as one crucial point where the theistic world outlook lays itself open to an empirical test.

39. Perhaps such dramatic talk of choosing is itself overdrawn. Against Newman, David A. Pailin declines to call the will so to embark an "assent": "So far as I can

tell, I can only decide to act *as if* something were true, whereas 'assent' describes a state where I accept something as true without any doubt or reservation at all. This is a state in which I find myself rather than a state into which I choose to enter" (*The Way to Faith* [London: Epworth Press, 1969], 191; italics his).

40. John Skorupski, *Symbol and Theory: A Philosophical Study of Theories of Religion in Social Anthropology* (Cambridge: At the Univ. Press, 1976), 2.

41. E. B. Tylor, "The Religion of Savages," *Fortnightly Review* 6 (1866): 86.

42. Sigmund Freud, *New Introductory Lectures on Psychoanalysis*, trans. W. J. H. Sprott (New York: W. W. Norton & Co., 1933), 221–22.

43. Alasdair MacIntyre and Paul Ricoeur, *The Religious Significance of Atheism* (New York: Columbia Univ. Press, 1969), 85–86. Cf. 64–65.

44. Ludwig Feuerbach, *The Essence of Christianity*, trans. George Eliot (New York: Harper & Row, 1957), 14.

45. Ibid., 30.

46. Ibid., 270. But theology must be negated, for here the Son of God "is not a son in the natural, human sense, but in an entirely different manner, contradictory to Nature and reason, and therefore absurd" (Feuerbach's preface to *The Essence of Christianity*, xxxvii).

47. Ibid., 13.

48. Ibid., 270. Italics his.

49. Ibid., 14; cf. 16, 21.

50. See Karl Barth's linking of Luther and Feuerbach in *From Rousseau to Ritschl*, trans. Brian Cozens (London: SCM Press, 1952), 359.

51. Feuerbach, *The Essence of Christianity*, 7. I have not stressed the notion of species, since its prominence in *The Essence of Christianity* is not essential to Feuerbach's position. Indeed in his volume on Luther, *The Essence of Faith According to Luther*, trans. Melvin Cherno (New York: Harper & Row, 1967), 14–15, Feuerbach sees the species appeal as a hangover of idealism, and prefers to stress instead the self-affirmation of the concrete sensual being. Cf. the remark "God was my first thought; Reason my second; Man my third and last" from *Philosophische Fragmente* 2:388, of *Sämtliche Werke*, 13 vols. in 12 (Stuttgart-Bad Canstatt: Fromann Verlag Gunther Holzboog, 1960–64).

52. Feuerbach, *The Essence of Christianity*, 9.

53. Ibid., 29; cf. 33. Feuerbach withdrew from Schleiermacher's courses at Berlin in the winter of 1824–25 because "to my soul which demanded truth, i.e., *unity, decisiveness, the absence of qualifications,* the theological mishmash of freedom and dependence, reason and faith was odious to the point of death" (*Thoughts on Death and Immortality*, trans. James A. Massey [Berkeley and Los Angeles: Univ. of Calif. Press, 1980], xix; italics his).

54. Cf. R. P. C. Hanson, *The Attractiveness of God: Essays in Christian Doctrine* (Richmond: John Knox Press, 1973), 2, and John Bowker, *The Sense of God: Sociological, Anthropological, and Psychological Approaches to the Origin of the Sense of God* (Oxford: At the Clarendon Press, 1973), 132–33.

55. Talcott Parsons, *The Structure of Social Action* (New York: McGraw-Hill, 1968), 431.

56. Emile Durkheim, *The Elementary Forms of the Religious Life*, trans. Joseph

Ward Swain (London: George Allen & Unwin, [1915] 1976), 225–26. Cf. 3: "In reality, then, there are no religions which are false; all answer, though in different ways, to the given conditions of human existence."

57. Ibid., 430.

58. Ibid., 431.

59. Cupitt, *Taking Leave of God* (New York: Crossroad, 1981), 20. Cf. 161.

60. See Richard Neuhaus, *Time Toward Home* (New York: Seabury Press, 1975), 9–21.

CHAPTER 3

1. See Robert P. Scharlemann, *The Being of God: Theology and the Experience of Truth* (New York: Seabury Press, 1981), 57–83, on three possible senses for "God is," and an indication of what verification would entail according to the three readings.

2. Langdon Gilkey, *Naming the Whirlwind: The Renewal of God-Language* (Indianapolis: Bobbs-Merrill, 1969), 19.

3. Peter Berger, *The Sacred Canopy* (Garden City, N.Y.: Doubleday & Co., 1967), esp. chap. 6.

4. H. P. Owen, *Concepts of Deity* (London: Macmillan & Co., 1971), 17. For a comparable stress on the cruciality and connectedness of the divine attributes, see Cornelio Fabro, *God in Exile*, trans. and ed. A. Gibson (Westminster, Md.: Newman Press, 1968), 44–45.

5. Friedrich Schleiermacher, *The Christian Faith*, 2d German ed., trans. H. R. Mackintosh and J. S. Stewart (Edinburgh: T. & T. Clark, 1928), l6. Cf. his praise of Christianity as a "teleological" rather than "aesthetic" religion: "But that figure of a Kingdom of God, which is so important and indeed all-inclusive for Christianity, is simply the general expression of the fact that in Christianity all pain and joy are religious only in so far as they are related to activity in the Kingdom of God, and that every religious emotion which proceeds from a passive state ends in the consciousness of a transition to activity" (p. 43).

6. Karl Barth, *Church Dogmatics*, 4 vols. in 13 parts; vol. 3, part 3, *The Doctrine of Creation*, trans. G. W. Bromiley and T. F. Torrance (Edinburgh: T. & T. Clark, 1960), 165–66.

7. See F. C. T. Moore, *The Psychological Basis of Morality* (London: Macmillan & Co., 1978), 82ff., for a clear rejection of any distinction between moral principles and desires, together with a specification of those desires that come to be identified as moral values. Cf. F. Nietzsche, *Beyond Good and Evil*, trans. Walter Kaufmann (New York: Random House, 1966; Vintage Book, 1966). In *108 he says: "There are no moral phenomena at all, but only a moral interpretation of phenomena." He explains the Christian creation of "good" and "evil," *260, and proposes "to translate man back into nature," *230.

8. Alasdair MacIntyre, *After Virtue: A Study in Moral Theory* (Notre Dame, Ind.: Univ. of Notre Dame Press, 1981), 81, on deontological and teleological fragments.

9. Cf. Terence Penelhum's *Survival and Disembodied Existence* (New York: Humanities Press, 1970) for the charge of unintelligibility due to the absence of grounds of personal identity.

10. Don Cupitt, *Taking Leave of God* (London: SCM Press, 1980), 20. He gives particular attention to the link between the God-concept and the understanding of the self and how the self knows.

11. David Hume, *An Inquiry Concerning Human Understanding*, ed. A. Flew (New York: Collier, 1962), 135–36.

12. David Hume, *Dialogues Concerning Natural Religion*, ed. Henry Aiken (New York: Hafner, 1948), 15.

13. Scharlemann, *The Being of God*, 122.

14. Bertrand Russell, "Cosmic Purpose," in *Critiques of God*, ed. Peter Angeles (Buffalo, N.Y.: Prometheus Press, 1976), 350.

15. Hume, *Dialogues Concerning Natural Religion*, 66. Cf. 69.

16. Fyodor Dostoyevsky, *The Brothers Karamazov*, trans. Constance Garnett (London: William Heinemann, [1912] 1949), 241, 251. See Steward R. Sutherland's *Atheism and the Rejection of God: Contemporary Philosophy and the Brothers Karamazov* (Oxford: Basil Blackwell & Mott, 1977) for a discussion of this particular form of atheism.

17. Cf. Michel Tournier, *The Four Wise Men*, trans. Ralph Manheim (London: William Collins & Co., 1982).

18. Arthur Cohen, *The Tremendum* (New York: Crossroad, 1981).

19. Jürgen Moltmann, *The Crucified God*, trans. R. A. Wilson and John Bowden (London: SCM Press, 1974), 221. Cf. Dorothee Soelle, *Suffering*, trans. Everett R. Kalin (Philadelphia: Fortress Press, 1975).

20. David Ray Griffin in *God, Power, and Evil: A Process Theodicy* (Philadelphia: Westminster Press, 1976), 173, offers a criticism not only of the annulling of such self-limitation, but of the notion of self-limitation itself: "The very idea of 'power,' so far as it has any meaning through experience, is through and through a social idea, connecting a capacity to act on or influence the action of others who also are and therefore cannot be simply powerless. Consequently, 'omnipotence' cannot possibly mean all the power there is, but only all the power that could conceivably belong to any one individual consistent with there being other individuals on whom omnipotent power is exercised and who also have power, however minimal." The problem of evil would reappear, I take it, when we talk about God's creativity and responsibility in relationship to the degree of freedom. Anthony Kenny, *The God of the Philosophers* (New York and London: Oxford Univ. Press, 1979), 60, also finds the notion of voluntary self-limitation of divine powers incoherent. Obviously, we shall need to consider (in chap. 6) the notion of creation out of nothing and that of the divine kenosis (self-emptying, Philippians 2) in incarnation. But the notion of annulling seems to speak of God's creating nothing out of something—since presumably that which God has created is indeed something "outside of" God. Without paying God such a strange compliment, one may well talk, however, about the divine freedom to act toward the creatures and the creatures' creations.

21. See Paul Ricoeur, *The Symbolism of Evil*, trans. Emerson Buchanan (Boston: Beacon Press, 1967; Beacon Paperback, 1969), esp. part 2.

22. See Dietrich Bonhoeffer's letter of July 16, 1944, in *Letters and Papers from Prison*, ed. E. Bethge (London: SCM Press, [1953] 1967), 184–89.

23. Soelle, *Suffering*, 38–39.

24. Michael Durrant, *The Logical Status of "God"* (New York: St. Martin's Press, 1973), 79.

25. Michael Durrant, *Theology and Intelligibility* (London: Routledge & Kegan Paul, 1973), 156ff.

26. Nelson Pike, *God and Timelessness* (London: Routledge & Kegan Paul, 1970), 173, 175. Italics his.

27. Ibid., 189, on "the stylish." On the second point consider Christopher Stead, *Divine Substance* (Oxford: At the Clarendon Press, 1977), 274: "The classical conception of God presents him as a substance, and also as immutable; hence it is assumed that one conception necessarily involves the other, and criticisms are made of the 'static ontology' that is thus detected. But of course God can be, and has been, represented as a changing substance, and indeed as one that is ever-changing and infinitely adaptable. . . ." Stead notes that under Platonic pressure distinctions begin to be recruited, as between God's essential nature and the divine "energies," limited and adapted and deployed for special purposes.

28. Peter Strawson's *Individuals* (London: Methuen & Co., 1959) is perhaps the best-known expression of the contemporary position that has its purest form in Ryle's attack on "the ghost in the machine." See also Strawson's critique of a Cartesian concept of soul in *Freedom and Resentment and Other Essays* (Methuen & Co., 1974), chap. 8. In the second series of his Stanton lectures at Cambridge University in 1982, A. J. P. Kenny discussed what he considers "the greatest difficulty for natural theology . . . the inconceivability of a divine mind with its alleged immateriality" (pub. pending). Cf. Terence Penelhum, *Survival and Disembodied Existence*, 108.

29. R. C. Coburn, "The Hiddenness of God and Some Barmecidal God Surrogates," *Journal of Philosophy* 57 (October 1960): 689–712, and "The Concept of God," *Religious Studies* 2 (October 1966): 61–74. Coburn asks how such a one would act or think. In like manner, Kai Nielsen, "The Intelligibility of God-Talk," *Religious Studies* 6 (March 1970): 1–21, claims there would be no truth conditions for such a divine action and such an action would not be identifiable. Compare Nielsen's "On Fixing the Reference Range of God," *Religious Studies* 2 (October 1966): 13–36.

30. Cupitt, *Taking Leave of God*, 106. Italics his.

31. In "Miracles and Actions," *Religious Studies* 11 (1975): 319–27, George D. Chryssides argues that scientific and personal explanations cannot be cleanly distinguished; at least, they cannot be if they entail the suggestion that miracles are personally explicable and scientifically inexplicable. Cf. Charles B. Fethe, "Miracles and Action Explanations," *Philosophy and Phenomenological Research* 36 (1976): 415–22. Ronald F. Marshall summarizes these and many other articles pertinent to this chapter in "In Between Ayer and Adler: God in Contemporary Philosophy," *Word and World* 2 (Winter 1982): 69–81. I have also drawn on some of Marshall's unpublished papers in this area.

32. See John Hick, "Jesus and the World Religions," in *The Myth of God Incarnate*, ed. John Hick (London: SCM Press, 1977), 178.

33. The statement of the Chalcedonian settlement is conveniently available in

John N. D. Kelly, *Early Christian Doctrines* (New York: Harper & Brothers, 1958), 339–40.

34. In *Death and Eternal Life* (New York: Harper & Row, 1976), John Hick raises this and other difficulties concerning the character and purpose of any God presiding over hell.

35. John Henry Newman, *An Essay in Aid of a Grammar of Assent* (Notre Dame, Ind.: Univ. of Notre Dame Press, 1979), 36.

36. This is the emphasis in Ian Ramsey's influential discussions of paradox. See his *Christian Empiricism*, ed. Jerry H. Gill (London: Sheldon Press, 1974), 98–142, 159–76. Michael Goulder trades on this point in objecting to the use of an appeal to paradox by defenders of the doctrine of incarnation: "[M]y impression is that these days the Chalcedonian definition discloses nothing except its defenders' wish to be orthodox" ("Paradox and Mystification," in *Incarnation and Myth: The Debate Continued*, ed. Michael Goulder [London: SCM Press, 1979], 59).

37. Soren Kierkegaard, *Concluding Unscientific Postscript to the Philosophical Fragments*, trans. David F. Swenson and Walter Lowrie (Princeton: Princeton Univ. Press, 1944), 504.

38. Hume, *Dialogues Concerning Natural Religion*, 42.

39. Fabro, *God in Exile*, 835.

40. Fedor Dostoevski, *The Possessed*, trans. Constance Garnett (London: William Heinemann, 1961), 563–64. Italics his. See also John Luce, "Literary Prototypes of Atheism," *Dialog* 19 (Fall 1980): 256–62.

CHAPTER 4

1. Kai Nielsen, *Ethics Without God* (Buffalo: Prometheus Books, 1973) has argued for the independence of ethical criteria and against a theism denying that independence. This point is supported by Gerhard von Rad's interpretation of the wisdom literature (*Wisdom in Israel*, trans. James D. Martin [Nashville: Abingdon Press, 1972], 89–90) and by a Reformation understanding of the abiding relationship to God the creator, despite the gravity of human sin. See Edgar M. Carlson, *The Reinterpretation of Luther* (Philadelphia: Westminster Press, 1948) and Gustaf Wingren, *Creation and Law*, trans. Ross Mackenzie (Philadelphia: Muhlenberg Press, 1951).

2. Alasdair MacIntyre, *After Virtue: A Study in Moral Theory* (Notre Dame, Ind.: Univ. of Notre Dame Press, 1981), 21, 56–59.

3. Simone de Beauvoir, *The Ethics of Ambiguity*, trans. Bernard Frechtman (New York: Philosophical Library, 1948), 15–16. This is, of course, *not* her explanation.

4. Erich Fromm, *Psychoanalysis and Religion* (New Haven: Yale Univ. Press, 1950), 49–51. Italics his.

5. Friedrich Nietzsche, *The Joyful Wisdom*, *319, *Ecce Homo* IV.1. Italics his. I am using Walter Kaufmann's translations.

6. Friedrich Nietzsche, *Beyond Good and Evil: Prelude to a Philosophy of the Future*, trans. Walter Kaufmann (New York: Random House, 1966; Vintage edition, 1966), *225.

7. Ibid., *212.

8. Ibid., *213.

9. Wallace Stevens, "Sunday Morning," *The Palm at the End of the Mind*, ed. Holly Stevens (New York: Alfred A. Knopf, 1971).

10. See the very thorough criticism of the aesthetic deficiencies in Christianity's approach to ethics, in Brand Blanshard, *Reason and Belief* (New Haven: Yale Univ. Press, 1975), for example, 340ff., and in Richard Robinson, *An Atheist's Values* (New York and London: Oxford Univ. Press, 1964), for example, 148ff. An autobiographical witness to the guilt mechanism can be found in *Some Day I'll Find You* (London: Mitchell Beazley, 1982) by Harry Williams, a member of the Community of the Resurrection, an Anglo-Catholic monastery at Mirfield, England. A more general statement of the effect of guilt feelings is in Walter Kaufmann's *Beyond Guilt and Justice* (New York: Dell Publishing Co., 1973; Delta Book, 1975), 115–16.

11. Fromm, *Psychoanalysis and Religion*, 53.

12. On the rebellion of the lowly see Nietzsche's *Beyond Good and Evil*, *195, 198, 199. Walter Kaufmann discusses the concept of "ressentiment" in *Nietzsche: Philosopher, Psychologist, AntiChrist*, 3d ed. (Princeton: Princeton Univ. Press, 1968), 371–78.

13. Carl G. Jung, *Psychology and Religion* (New Haven: Yale Univ. Press, 1938), 104.

14. MacIntyre, *After Virtue*, 107–8. Italics are Nietzsche's.

15. Fedor Dostoevski, *The Possessed*, trans. Constance Garnett (London: William Heineman, 1961), 561. Cf. Don Cupitt, *Taking Leave of God* (London: SCM Press, 1980), 20.

16. Karl Marx, *Toward the Critique of Hegel's Philosophy of Law: Introduction* in *Writings of the Young Marx on Philosophy and Society*, ed. and trans. Lloyd D. Easton and Kurt H. Guddat (New York: Doubleday & Co., 1967; Doubleday Anchor Books, 1967), 258. Italics his.

17. Nietzsche, *Beyond Good and Evil*, *61. On Christianity as a Platonism of the people, see the preface and *62.

18. Marx, *Toward the Critique of Hegel's Philosophy of Law*, 250. Italics his.

19. Marx, *Toward the Critique of Hegel's Philosophy of Law*, 250. Italics his. On Lenin's "opium *for*" and Marx's "opium *of*," see Nicholas Lash, *A Matter of Hope: A Theologian's Reflections on the Thought of Karl Marx* (London: Darton, Longman and Todd, 1981), 158ff. Recall Marx's famous eleventh thesis on Feuerbach: "The philosophers have only *interpreted* the world in various ways; the point is, to *change* it" (*Young Writings*, 402; italics his).

20. See James W. Savolainen, "Theology in the Shadow of Marx," *Dialog* 19 (Fall 1980): 268–73.

21. Albert Camus, *Resistance, Rebellion, and Death,* trans. Justin O'Brien (New York: Alfred A. Knopf, 1961), 222–27.

22. Morris Cohen, "The Dark Side of Religion," in *Religion From Tolstoy to Camus*, ed. Walter Kaufmann (New York: Harper & Row, 1961; Harper Torchbook, 1964), 289.

23. Basil Mitchell, "A Summing-up of the Colloquy: Myth of God Debate," in *Incarnation and Myth: The Debate Continued*, ed. Michael Goulder (London: SCM Press, 1979), 238.

24. Malcolm Hay, "Europe and the Jews," in *Religion from Tolstoy to Camus*, ed. Kaufmann, 354.

25. Kaufmann, *Nietzsche*, 326.

26. Perhaps the best-known statement is Harvey Cox's in *The Secular City* (London: SCM Press, 1965), 21–25. The contrast of the biblical understanding of nature with the Greek is discussed in M. B. Foster, "The Christian Doctrine of Creation and the Rise of Modern Natural Science," *Mind* 43 (1934): 446–68. A. R. Peacocke discusses this argument in *Creation and the World of Science* (Oxford: At the Clarendon Press, 1979), 7–14.

27. See Bradford P. Keeney, "Ecosystemic Epistemology: An Alternative Paradigm for Diagnosis," in *Family Process*, 18.2 (June 1979): 117–29, for a discussion and application of Bateson's critique of a "transitive" understanding of power. The argument is that ecological goods are often intransitive "so that the goods become toxic if they become greater than some optimum" (p. 123). Cf. Bernard Loomer, "Two Conceptions of Power," *Process Studies* 6.1 (Spring 1976): 5–32.

28. Dietrich Bonhoeffer, *Letters and Papers from Prison*, ed. Eberhard Bethge (London: SCM Press, [1953] 1967), 184–89, letter of July 16, 1944.

29. Auguste Comte, *Introduction to Positive Philosophy*, trans. F. Ferré (Indianapolis: Bobbs-Merrill, 1970).

30. Karl Popper, *The Open Society and Its Enemies*, 2 vols. (London: Routledge & Kegan Paul, 1945; rev. ed., 1962, 1966), 2:271–72.

31. Philip Rieff, *Triumph of the Therapeutic* (New York: Harper & Row, 1966; Harper Torchbook, 1968), 261.

32. Karl Popper, *The Poverty of Historicism* (London: Routledge & Kegan Paul, 1957), 159.

33. Soren Kierkegaard, *The Sickness unto Death: A Christian Psychological Exposition for Upbuilding and Awakening*, ed. and trans. Howard V. Hong and Edna H. Hong (Princeton: Princeton Univ. Press, 1980), 130. Italics his.

CHAPTER 5

1. See Wayne Proudfoot, *God and the Self: Three Types of Philosophy of Religion* (Lewisburg, Pa.: Bucknell Univ. Press, 1976), 226–31, on both the self and God as interpretations.

2. See Daniel Bell's essay, "Beyond Modernism, Beyond Self," in his collection *The Winding Passage* (Cambridge, Mass.: ABT Books, 1980), 275–302. Bell's early work (like *The End of Ideology* [Glencoe, Ill.: Free Press, 1960]) is here advanced only to end on a dark note: "The difficulty in the West is that bourgeois society— which in its emphasis on individuality and the self gave rise to modernism—is itself culturally exhausted. And it, too, now exists in a beyond" (p. 302). Cf. Robert Lifton, *Boundaries: Psychological Man in Revolution* (New York: Random House, 1967). In *The Heretical Imperative* (New York: Doubleday Anchor Books, 1979), 19, Peter Berger stresses the "pre-theoretical uncertainty which conditions contemporary choice."

3. H. Richard Niebuhr, *The Meaning of Revelation* (New York: Macmillan Co., 1967), 59. Niebuhr continues: ". . . to have a god is to have a history. . . ."

4. Alfred North Whitehead, *Modes of Thought* (New York: Macmillan Co., [1938]

1966), 114. Cf. his remark in *Process and Reality*, ed. David Ray Griffin and Donald W. Sherburne (New York: Free Press, [1929, 1957] 1978), 170: "A traveller, who has lost his way, should not ask, Where am I? What he really wants to know is, Where are the other places? He has got his own body but he has lost them."

5. Cf. Peter Strawson, *Individuals* (London: Methuen & Co., 1959), and chap. 3 above, n. 28.

6. Helpful summaries are available in G. G. Simpson, *The Meaning of Evolution* (New Haven: Yale Univ. Press, 1949; New York: Bantam Books, 1971), and T. Dobzhansky, *Mankind Evolving* (New Haven: Yale Univ. Press, 1963).

7. Arthur Peacocke, *Creation and the World of Science* (Oxford: At the Clarendon Press, 1979), 121, drawing on C. Blakemore, *The Mechanics of the Mind* (Cambridge: At the Univ. Press, 1976).

8. D. O. Hebb, *The Organization of Behavior: A Neuropsychological Theory* (New York: John Wiley & Sons, 1949), xii, 164. For a more recent statement see Hebb's "What Psychology Is About," *American Psychologist* 29 (Feb. 1974): 71–79.

9. Carl Rogers, *Freedom to Learn* (Columbus, Ohio: Charles E. Merrill, 1969), 295. For popular statements of the position, see B. F. Skinner, *Walden Two* (New York: Macmillan Co., 1948) and *Beyond Freedom and Dignity* (New York: Alfred A. Knopf, 1971), as well as Albert Bandura, *Principles of Behavior Modification* (New York: Holt, Rinehart & Winston, 1969). A typical statement is that of W. R. Hess, *The Biology of Mind*, trans. Gerhardt von Bonin (Chicago: Univ. of Chicago Press, 1964), 164: "[O]ne is led to the conclusion that the content of subjective experience is bound to the structure of the brain and the properties of its structural elements and that only those contents of consciousness can be developed that correspond to the organization of the brain."

10. James P. Chaplin and T. S. Krawiec, *Systems and Theories of Psychology*, 3d ed. (New York: Holt, Rinehart and Winston, 1974).

11. Peacocke, *Creation and the World of Science*, 154.

12. See Ludwig von Bertalanffy's remarks in *Toward Unification in Psychology: First Banff Conference on Theoretical Psychology*, ed. Joseph R. Royce (Toronto: Univ. of Toronto Press, 1970). In *Mind and Nature* (New York: Bantam Books, 1979), 127–49, Gregory Bateson speaks of a stochastic process in both evolution and thought. Such a process involves a stream of events appearing randomly with a nonrandom selective process. In individual thought perhaps the mental processes are random, generating a large number of alternatives. A selection takes place by a process "something like" reinforcement.

13. See John B. Cobb, Jr., *The Structure of Christian Existence* (Philadelphia: Westminster Press, 1967), and *Toward Unification in Psychology*, ed. Royce, 30–32.

14. D. C. Phillips, *Holistic Thought in Social Science* (New York: Macmillan Co., 1976), 36–37, 123.

15. Whitehead, *Process and Reality*, 108.

16. For a discussion of this emphasis in Kierkegaard's thought see Harold Durfee, "Metaphilosophy in the Shadow of Kierkegaard," *Kierkegaard's Truth: The Disclosure of the Self*, ed. Joseph Smith (New Haven: Yale Univ. Press, 1981), 85–118. Durfee draws comparisons to such contemporary figures as Feyerabend, Deridda, and Rorty. F. C. T. Moore in *The Psychological Basis of Morality* (New York:

Macmillan Co., 1978) discusses a new "organon" to be found in developments in phonetics, physics, mathematics, and biology, and speculates, on p. 95: "We glimpse here emerging severally in different branches of knowledge what may in due course be recognized as a new organon. The formal theory of this organon may be emerging most dramatically in the work of René Thom, whose qualitative dynamics would have two important consequences . . . first, the reinstatement of certain analogues of teleological explanation for local processes, and secondly, the rejection of a Laplacian belief in global determinism in favor of a characterisation of science—including the human sciences—as concerned to discover and analyse local determinisms within a generally rather labile and chaotic universe."

17. The classic statement in Kierkegaard is, of course, *The Sickness unto Death: A Christian Psychological Exposition for Upbuilding and Awakening*, ed. and trans. Howard V. Hong and Edna H. Hong (Princeton: Princeton Univ. Press, 1980), 13–14 for the "formula," and passim for the explication. See also Paul Holmer, "Post–Kierkegaardian Remarks About Being a Person," in *Kierkegaard's Truth*, ed. Smith, 3–22. For a statement that seeks to combine physiological and organic determinism with a notion of freedom and applies that to the discipline of medicine, see Oliver Sacks, *Awakenings* (London: Pan Books, 1983).

18. Cf. Jürgen Habermas's statement in *Knowledge and Human Interests*, trans. Jeremy J. Shapiro (Boston: Beacon Press, 1971; Beacon Paperback, 1972), 313, of the three categories of possible knowledge: "information that expands our power of technical control; interpretations that make possible the orientation of action within common traditions; and analyses that free consciousness from its dependence on hypostatized powers." The "neo-Freudians" I have in mind are Adler, Horney, Fromm, and Sullivan.

19. For a reasoned and passionate response to Sartre's famous diagnosis in *No Exit*, see Wayne Booth's *Modern Dogma and the Rhetoric of Assent* (Notre Dame, Ind.: Univ. of Notre Dame Press, 1974), 106–36.

20. James W. Fowler favors such a formulation. See his *Stages of Faith* (New York: Harper & Row, 1981).

21. Friedrich Nietzsche, *Beyond Good and Evil*, trans. W. Kaufmann (New York: Random House, 1966; Vintage ed., 1966), *188. Italics his.

22. Cf. R. W. Hepburn's warning in "Optimism, Finitude, and the Meaning of Life," in *The Philosophical Frontiers of Christian Theology*, ed. B. Hebblethwaite and S. Sutherland (Cambridge: At the Univ. Press, 1982), 119–45. Cf. Walter Kaufmann's critique of the classical conception on integrity in *Without Guilt and Justice: From Decidophobia to Autonomy* (New York: Dell Publishing Co., 1973; Delta Book, 1975), 180ff.

23. Walter Pater, "Conclusion," in *The Renaissance: Studies in Art and Poetry in Selected Writings of Walter Pater*, ed. Harold Bloom (New York: New American Library, 1974; Signet Classic ed.), 60–61. For a succinct discussion of the formalist movement in art represented by such figures as Oscar Wilde, James McNeill Whistler, Edmund Gurney, Eduard Hanslick, and Konrad Fiedler, see Melvin Rader and Bertram Jessup, *Art and Human Values* (Englewood Cliffs, N. J.: Prentice-Hall, 1976).

24. *Gorgias* 503E–4A (Jowett's translation).

25. John Maynard Keynes, *Essays and Sketches in Biography* (New York: Meridian Books, 1956), 242.

26. F. Schiller, "Letters on the Aesthetic Education of Man," in *Modern Continental Literary Criticism*, ed. O. B. Hardison, Jr. (New York: Appleton-Century-Crofts, 1962), 38. Italics mine. Cf. Charles Lamb's discussion of the way the theater lover finds "a speculative scene of things, which has no reference whatever to the world that is," in "On the Artificial Comedy of the Last Century," in *The Essays of Elia* (Totowa, N.J.: Biblio Distribution Centre, [1906] 1978).

27. Wallace Stevens, *The Necessary Angel: Essays on Reality and the Imagination* (London: Faber & Faber, 1942), 14, 139. Cf. L. Reid's discussion of the four meanings of "the real" in *A Study in Aesthetics* (New York: Macmillan Co., 1931), 272–73.

28. "Memorial Verses," April 1850, from *Poetry and Criticism of Matthew Arnold*, ed. A. Dwight Culler (Boston: Houghton Mifflin, 1961). Italics mine.

29. I cite here Rader and Jessup's description in *Art and Human Values*, 231, of Charles Lamb's moral aestheticism. The earlier passage is from p. 102 of this book.

30. See Arnold Berleant, *The Aesthetic Field* (Springfield, Ill.: Charles C. Thomas, 1972), 151, 180. Cf. Ernst Cassirer, *An Essay on Man* (New Haven: Yale Univ. Press, 1944; Yale Paperback, 1967), 148: "It is not the degree of infection but the degree of intensification and illumination which is the measure of excellence in art." In *Lost in the Cosmos* (New York: Farrar, Straus & Giroux, 1983), 120, Walker Percy gladly speaks of the transcendence known in art—that of "*seeing* and naming what had heretofore been unspeakable, the predicament of the self in the modern world," but readily grants the transience of such experience and the difficulties encountered in "re-entry." Italics his.

31. John Hospers, *Meaning and Truth in Art* (Chapel Hill, N.C.: Univ. of N.C. Press, 1946), 99.

32. Stevens, *The Necessary Angel*, 76–77. On the differences between the arts with respect to the spatial and the temporal, see F. David Martin, *Art and the Religious Experience: The "Language" of the Sacred* (Lewisburg, Pa.: Bucknell Univ. Press, 1972).

33. Michael Compton, "Peter Blake," in the catalogue published by the Tate Gallery, London, for Blake's exhibition in 1983.

34. Albert Hofstadter, "Kant's Aesthetic Revolution," a paper presented to the Pacific Division of the American Society for Aesthetics, Asilomar Conference Ground, California, April 12, 1974, cited by Rader and Jessup, *Art and Human Values*, 184ff.

35. D. H. Lawrence, *Phoenix* (New York: Viking Press, 1936), 65–66.

36. Percy Shelley, "Defense of Poetry," in his *Selected Poems, Letters, and Essays* (New York: Odyssey Press, 1944), 540.

37. Kai Nielsen makes this point emphatically, as in *Ethics Without God* (London: Pemberton Pub. Co., 1973). Cf. Simone de Beauvoir, *The Ethics of Ambiguity*, trans. Bernard Frechtman (New York: Philosophical Library, 1948), 14–16.

38. H. L. A. Hart, *The Concept of Law* (Oxford: At the Clarendon Press, 1961), offers such an understanding of natural law. For a statement of the difficulties facing

traditional natural-law theory, see D. J. O'Connor, *Aquinas and Natural Law* (New York: Macmillan Co., 1967).

39. Moore, *The Psychological Basis of Morality*, 82.

40. This is the approach of John Searle in his well-known "How to Derive Ought from Is," which is reprinted in *Theories of Ethics*, ed. Philippa Foot (New York and London: Oxford Univ. Press, 1967). Philip Hefner finds wide support for some such move and adds his own theological arguments in "Is/Ought: A Risky Relationship Between Theology and Science," in *The Sciences and Theology in the Twentieth Century*, ed. A. R. Peacocke (London: Oriel Press, 1981), 58–78.

41. For a helpful discussion of R. S. Peters's advocacy of this understanding, see A. J. Watt, "Transcendental Arguments and Moral Principles," *Philosophical Quarterly* 25 (January 1975): 40–57. David Little draws on the work of such anthropologists as Kluckhohn, Linton, and Mead to develop a cross-cultural candidate for theological appropriation in "Calvin and the Prospects for a Christian Theory of Natural Law," in *Norm and Context in Christian Ethics*, ed. Paul Ramsey and Gene Outka (New York: Charles Scribner's Sons, 1968), 188–89: "We are, then, coming close to an empirical definition of 'humanity' as distinct from the primates (to whom man is obviously similar in many respects): to be human is to order life cooperatively.... Beings become human insofar as they are capable of symbolizing and sharing. There is, as it were, a certain fixed design to the concept 'human' which designates what man must do and be, if he will survive as man."

42. Cf. Alan Gewirth, *Reason and Morality* (Chicago: Univ. of Chicago Press, 1978), on the "problem" of justification.

43. S. de Beauvoir's *Ethics of Ambiguity* depends on such an approach with respect to the reality of human freedom. See also Peter Winch, *Ethics and Action* (London: Routledge & Kegan Paul, 1972), and Philippa Foot, "Moral Beliefs," in *Theories of Ethics*, ed. Foot, 83–100, on the possibility of identifying elements of experience to which any and every morality must have reference. Cf. also W. D. Hudson, *Modern Moral Philosophy* (Garden City, N.Y.: Doubleday & Co., 1970), for a discussion of the necessity of moral discourse for a full personal life, and John Rawls's *Theory of Justice* (Oxford: At the Clarendon Press, 1972), on the roots of justice in human nature.

44. Alasdair MacIntyre, *After Virtue: A Study in Moral Theory* (Notre Dame, Ind.: Univ. of Notre Dame Press, 1981), 197ff.

45. Rader and Jessup cite this passage from the *Philadelphia Public Ledger* for January 22, 1922, in their *Art and Human Values*, 189.

46. Peter Berger considers such matters as human propensities for order, hope, judgment, play, and humor in *Rumor of Angels* (Garden City, N.Y.: Doubleday & Co., 1969), chap. 3.

47. One thinks of the use of humor in the work of Kurt Vonnegut or, less grimly perhaps, in the science-fiction satire of Alexis Gilliland in the "Rosinante" books. In such cases it seems that if one gets a glimpse of the condition of the whole of human life one will weep or laugh; redemption is not suggested. Cf. Kierkegaard's comment in *The Concluding Unscientific Postscript to the Philosophical Fragments*, trans. David F. Swenson and Walter Lowrie (Princeton: Princeton Univ. Press, 1941), 462–63: "The difference between the tragic and the comic lies in the relationship

between the contradiction and the controlling idea. The comic apprehension evokes the contradiction or makes it manifest by having in mind the way out, which is why the contradiction is painless. The tragic apprehension sees the contradiction and despairs of a way out."

48. Leo Tolstoy, "The Death of Ivan Ilyitch," in *Religion from Tolstoy to Camus*, ed. Walter Kaufmann (New York: Harper & Row, 1961; Harper Torchbook, 1964), 66–116. On the correlation of religious experience with the sense of contingency see also Langdon Gilkey, *Naming the Whirlwind: The Renewal of God-Language* (Indianapolis: Bobbs–Merrill, 1969), 261, and John E. Smith, *Experience and God* (New York and London: Oxford Univ. Press, 1974), 151. Alan Keightley in *Wittgenstein, Grammar, and God* (London: Epworth Press, 1976), 82, discusses "God" as a word for "the complex patterns of religious reactions to the contingency of the world."

49. John Bowker, *The Sense of God: Sociological, Anthropological, and Psychological Approaches to the Origin of the Sense of God* (Oxford: At the Clarendon Press, 1973), 25, 29.

50. Hepburn, "Optimism, Finitude and the Meaning of Life," 134–35.

51. Kierkegaard, *The Sickness unto Death*, 79.

52. On such a "positive" connection see also Gilkey, *Naming the Whirlwind*, 313, and Smith, *Experience and God*, 151. In *The Structure of Christian Existence*, John Cobb develops the category of responsibility as that which distinguishes the structure of Christian existence from other structures.

53. Christopher Ricks cites Eliot's praise in "The Damnation of Baudelaire," *The Sunday Times*, London (January 16, 1983), 43.

54. Wolfhart Pannenberg, *The Apostles' Creed in the Light of Today's Questions*, trans. Margaret Kohl (London: SCM Press, 1972), 76–77.

55. Kierkegaard, *Concluding Unscientific Postscript*, 288. In the *Fragments* he had put the point this provocatively: "God's presence in human form, yes in the lowly form of a servant, is itself the teaching. . . ." (p. 44), and again: "Even if the contemporary generation had left nothing other than these words: 'We believe that in such and such a year God manifested himself in the lowly form of a servant, lived and taught among us, and then died'—that would be more than enough" (p. 87).

56. Kierkegaard, *Concluding Unscientific Postscript*, 527–28.

57. Kierkegaard, *The Sickness unto Death*, 113–14. Cf. *The Concluding Unscientific Postscript*, 505–8.

58. Hans Küng, *On Being a Christian*, trans. Edward Quinn (London: William Collins Sons, 1974; Fount Paperback, 1978), 601–2.

59. Rudolf Otto, *The Idea of the Holy*, trans. John Harvey (London: Oxford Univ. Press, 1923).

60. Thus George Newlands, *Theology of the Love of God* (London: William Collins & Co., 1980), 172–76, criticizes the tendency to let the Chalcedonian formulations control christological discussion, because the affirmation of Jesus' humanity is purely formal, but also because there is no material characterization there of the love of God.

61. Kierkegaard, *The Concluding Unscientific Postscript*, 527. See Kersten Nordentoft, *Kierkegaard's Psychology*, trans. Bruce Kirmmse (Pittsburgh: Duquesne

Univ. Press, 1972), for a description of the two perspectives in Kierkegaard represented by "the anthropological model" and "the conflict model." See esp. 110ff., on the conflict model.

62. Cf. Dale Patrick's critique of salvation history thinking in *The Rendering of God* (Philadelphia: Fortress Press, 1981), 113.

63. Ibid., 127.

64. This would connect with Louis Mackey's emphasis on "alterity," not "identity," in the understanding of the human, in "A Ram in the Afternoon," in *Kierkegaard's Truth*, ed. Smith, 193–229.

65. See MacIntyre, *After Virtue*, 189, on the contemporary obstacles to the Kierkegaardian quest for unity, and Michael A. Cowan, "Emerging in Love: Everyday Acts in Ultimate Contexts," unpublished paper (March 11, 1982), for a critique of maintaining self-identity as a model of/for being human.

66. See William Kerrigan, "Superego in Kierkegaard, Existence in Faith," in *Kierkegaard's Truth*, ed. Smith, 119–65, esp. 161.

CHAPTER 6

1. See, for example, Dame Freya Stark's reflections on a half century of travel in *Some Talk of Alexander: Letters, 1952–59*, vol. 8, and in her *Traveller's Epilogue: Letters, 1960–80*, vol. 8, ed. Caroline Moorhead (Salisbury: Russell, 1982), as well as in her *Rivers of Time* (Edinburgh: Blackwood, 1982) and in Alexander Maitland's *A Tower in a Wall: Conversations with Freya Stark* (Edinburgh: Blackwood, 1982).

2. Consider, for example, the work of Abdus Salam and Steven Weinberg at CERN, the nuclear research organization in Geneva, work for which the Nobel prize was awarded in 1979.

3. Richard Sennett, *The Fall of the Public Man* (New York: Vintage, 1976); Christopher Lasch, *The Culture of Narcissism* (New York: W. W. Norton & Co., 1978).

4. See, for example, Robert C. Johansen, *Toward an Alternative Security System*, World Policy Paper no. 24 (New York: World Policy Institute, 1983).

5. See Charles Long, ed., *Alpha: The Myths of Creation* (New York: George Braziller, 1963).

6. For example, Claus Westermann, *Creation*, trans. John J. Scullion (Philadelphia: Fortress Press, 1974), John Reumann, *Creation and New Creation* (Minneapolis: Augsburg Pub. House, 1973), and Gustaf Wingren, *Credo*, trans. Edgar M. Carlson (Minneapolis: Augsburg Pub. House, 1981), make such a statement readily available.

7. I am indebted to my colleague Professor Frederick Gaiser for this discussion of the relationship between Israel's "historical" and "creation" experience. Cf. Claus Westermann, *Blessing in the Bible and the Life of the Church*, trans. Keith Crim (Philadelphia: Fortress Press, 1978).

8. Westermann, *Creation*, 11. Cf. 14–15.

9. Walter Brueggemann provides a dramatic statement of this possibility in *In Man We Trust* (Richmond: John Knox Press, 1972).

10. Langdon Gilkey's *Maker of Heaven and Earth* (Garden City, N.Y.: Doubleday & Co., 1959) remains an excellent study of this formulation. Gilkey stresses "the

transcendent holiness and power of God, who because He is the ultimate origin is the ultimate Ruler of all created things" and adds affirmations concerning human meaningfulness and obligation (p. 25). A philosophical statement that chimes with Gilkey's argument is Robert C. Neville's *God the Creator* (Chicago: Univ. of Chicago Press, 1968) with its theme that "the essential identity of the parts or finite elements consists simply in their determinate characters whereas, on the other hand, the essential identity of God transcends, because it gives rise to, all determinate relations to the characters of finite things" (p. 201). Hans Küng in *Does God Exist?* trans. Edward Quinn (New York: Doubleday & Co., 1980), distinguishes between nihilism and atheism (p. 422), but argues that while "factually" nihilism may be overcome by fundamental trust, it is not so overcome "in principle": "The reality on which fundamental trust is based seems itself to be without foundation; and it is also in fundamental trust that man must live and deal with the uncertainty of reality" (p. 477).

11. Ernan McMullin, in "How Should Cosmology Relate to Theology?" in *The Sciences and Theology in the Twentieth Century,* ed. A. R. Peacocke (London: Oriel Press, 1981), 17–57, wonders why the bang could not be merely a big sneeze: "Cosmologists who postulate a contradiction preceding the Big Bang are not indulging in 'pure speculation' . . . but are assuming that certain parameters remain invariant (total mass, for example) or are continuously traceable throughout (radius, volume, rate of change in size). Even if the progress of cosmology leads us to opt for the 'open' rather than the 'closed' expanding model, i.e., one which puts our present universe in a state of indefinite future expansion, this could hardly be said to rule out the possibility of a preceding stage of matter to which we simply have no access through the singularity." His cautious conclusions are "first, that the Big Bang model does not entitle one to infer an absolute beginning of time. Second, that there is nothing scientifically or philosophically inadmissible about the supposition that an absolute beginning *might* have occurred (though on methodological grounds such a beginning ought to be conceded only if all the familiar sorts of continuity could be excluded); and third, that if an absolute cosmic beginning *did* occur, it could look something like the horizon-event described in the Big Bang theory" (pp. 35–38, italics his).

12. Mortimer J. Adler, *How to Think About God: A Guide for the Twentieth-Century Pagan* (New York: Macmillan Co., 1980), 148.

13. Ibid., 144. Cf. Wolfhart Pannenberg, *Theology and Philosophy of Science,* trans. Francis McDonagh (London: Darton, Longman & Todd, 1976), 306–7.

14. For a thorough discussion, see William L. Rowe, *The Cosmological Argument* (Princeton: Princeton Univ. Press, 1975). Rowe concludes that the criticisms of the argument fail, but also that "the argument cannot pass muster as a proof of the existence of God. For each of its premises has been shown either to express or to rest on an unknown—if not unknowable—principle, the Principle of Sufficient Reason" (p. 266). He adds that "possibly" the argument demonstrates the reasonableness of belief in God, even though it fails as a proof. For the observation that the principle of sufficient reason is neither analytically true nor metaphysically necessary, see pp. 83–94.

15. To this end Arthur Peacocke helpfully employs the image of the fugue in

speaking of God's ongoing work as creator. See his *Creation and the World of Science* (Oxford: At the Clarendon Press, 1979), 111.

16. F. R. Tennant, *Philosophical Theology*, 2 vols. (Cambridge: At the Univ. Press, 1956), 2: chap. 4.

17. Errol E. Harris, *The Foundations of Metaphysics in Science* (New York: Humanities Press, 1965), 277.

18. See A. N. Whitehead, *Process and Reality*, corrected ed., ed. David Ray Griffin and Donald W. Sherburne (New York: Free Press, 1978), 32, for a brief statement of the argument: "In what sense can unrealized abstract form be relevant? What is its basis of relevance? 'Relevance' must express some real fact of togetherness in the formal constitution of an actuality. So if there be a relevance of what in the temporal world is unrealized, the relevance must express a fact of togetherness in the formal constitution of a non-temporal actuality. But by the principle of relativity there can only be one non-derivative actuality, unbounded by its prehensions of an actual world. Such a primordial superject of creativity achieves, in its unity of satisfaction, the complete valuation of all eternal objects. This is the ultimate basic adjustment of the togetherness of eternal objects on which creative order depends." See pp. 31–32 for the application "It is here termed 'God'; because the contemplation of our natures, as enjoying real feelings derived from the timeless source of all order acquires that 'subjective form' of refreshment and companionship at which religions aim."

19. Harris, *The Foundation of Metaphysics*, 249. Italics his.

20. See, for example, Pauline Bart, "The Myth of a Value Free Psychotherapy," in *Sociology and the Future*, ed. Wendell Bell and James May (New York: Russell Sage Foundation, 1971).

21. Alasdair MacIntyre, *After Virtue: A Study in Moral Theory* (Notre Dame, Ind.: Univ. of Notre Dame Press, 1981), 105–9, 169.

22. James M. Gustafson, in *Can Ethics Be Christian?* (Chicago: Univ. of Chicago Press, 1975), chap. 4, discusses the ethical bearing of the following senses: dependence, gratitude, repentance, obligation, possibilities, and direction. My own discussion is in chap. 7.

23. A highly readable discussion for nontechnical purposes is David Bohm's "The Implicate Order: A New Order for Physics," ed. Dean R. Fowler, *Process Studies* 8 (Summer 1978): 73–102. Cf. Henry J. Folse, Jr., "Complementarity, Bell's Theorem, and the Framework of Process Metaphysics," *Process Studies* 11 (Winter 1981): 259–73.

24. Stephen Jay Gould of Harvard has described the life of the earth as "like the life of a soldier . . . long periods of boredom and short periods of terror." On the criticism of the stress on small variation and slow change, see Brian Leith, *The Descent of Darwin* (London: William Collins & Co., 1982).

25. John Archibald Wheeler, "Bohr, Einstein, and the Strange Lesson of the Quantum," in *Mind in Nature*, Nobel Conference 17, ed. Richard Elvee (San Francisco: Harper & Row, 1982), 1–39. I link his point with Richard Rorty's critique, *Philosophy and the Mirror of Nature* (Princeton: Princeton Univ. Press, 1979).

26. It may be possible to learn too quickly, as when Richard Schlegel ponders

quantum theory and concludes, "There is now no basis for regarding freedom of the will as illusory. . . ," in "The Return of Man in Quantum Physics," in *The Sciences and Theology in the Twentieth Century*, ed. Peacocke, 150. It would seem that the very discontinuities stressed require one to proceed more carefully in moving from the microscopic to the macroscopic. Thus Walker Percy grumbles in *Lost in the Cosmos* (New York: Farrar, Strauss & Giroux, 1983), 81: "What is more boring than hearing Heisenberg's uncertainty relations enlisted in support of the freedom of the will?" On the catastrophic, see René Thom, *Structural Stability and Morphogenesis: An Outline of a General Theory of Models*, trans. D. H. Fowler, with a foreword by C. H. Waddington (Reading, Mass.: W. A. Benjamin, 1975).

27. Daniel O'Connor and Francis Oakley, *Creation: The Impact of an Idea* (New York: Charles Scribner's Sons, 1969), 8–9. Italics his.

28. Whitehead has stated the point well in *Process and Reality*, 345: "But God, as well as being primordial, is also consequent. He is the beginning and the end. . . ." Thus, by reason of the relativity of all things, there is a reaction of the world on God.

29. Neville makes this point relentlessly in *God the Creator*.

30. Stephen E. Toulmin, *The Uses of Argument* (Cambridge: At the Univ. Press, 1964), 147ff. Cf. John H. Whittaker, *Matters of Faith and Matters of Principle* (San Antonio: Trinity Univ. Press, 1981), 56, on how "second order" claims deal with how "one set of truths . . . can be comprehended under another aspect. . . ."

31. The writings of Sartre and Camus reach for a kind of lucidity even within the absurdity of our situation. Thus Camus in "The Unbeliever and Christians," in *Resistance, Rebellion and Death*, trans. Justin O'Brien (New York: Alfred A. Knopf, 1961), 73: "Christians and Communists will tell me that their optimism is based on a longer range, that it is superior to all the rest, and that God or history, according to the individual, is the satisfying end-product of their dialectic. I can indulge in the same reasoning. If Christianity is pessimistic as to man, it is optimistic as to human destiny. Well, I can say that, pessimistic as to human destiny, I am optimistic as to man. And not in the name of a humanism that always seemed to me to fall short, but in the name of an ignorance that tries to negate nothing."

32. The Council of Chalcedon (Denzinger 148).

33. Cyril of Alexandria may be linked with such a notion of the humanity of Jesus, though the fundamental tendency is already found in the "Logos-Sarx" Christology of Apollinarianism; see Aloys Grillmeier, *Christ in Christian Tradition from the Apostolic Age to Chalcedon (451)*, trans. J. S. Bowden (New York: Sheed & Ward, 1965), 410. No less a "father of liberal theology" than Friedrich Schleiermacher can compromise the full humanity of Jesus; see *The Christian Faith*, English trans. of 2d German ed. by H. R. Mackintosh and J. S. Stewart (Edinburgh: T. and T. Clark, 1928), 387: "The expression 'the existence of God in anyone' can only express the relation of the omnipresence of God to this one. Now since God's existence can only be apprehended as pure activity, while every individualized existence is merely an intermingling of activity and passivity—the activity being always found apportioned to this passivity in every other individualized existence—there is, so far, no existence of God in any individual thing, but only an existence of God in the world. And only if through vital receptivity, and this receptivity confronts the totality of finite existence (so far, i.e., as we can say of the individual as a living creature that, in virtue of the

universal receprocity, it in itself represents the world), could we suppose an existence of God in it."

34. Cf. Eduard Schweizer, *Jesus*, trans. David E. Green (Richmond: John Knox Press, 1971), 159: "It is clear beyond all doubt (I John 4:21!) that Jesus is truly a human being, not, say, an angel exempt from all human frailty. Therefore men take offense at him, because he comes from the little village of Nazareth (1:46) and is the son of Joseph, someone whose parents everyone knows (6:42, 7:27)."

35. I have this statement by Eliot from the Reverend Canon Michael Mayne in a sermon, "Who Knows," preached in Great St. Mary's Church, Cambridge, England, February 17, 1983. Cf. Russel Kirk, *Eliot and His Age: T. S. Eliot's Moral Imagination in the Twentieth Century* (New York: Random House, 1971), 212. Against the view that this is a particularly modern problem, see J. W. Rogerson, "The Old Testament View of Nature: Some Preliminary Questions," *Oudtestamentische Studien* 20 (Leiden: E. J. Brill, 1977): 67–84, on how the people of Israel's "perception of reality . . . did not obviously and inevitably point to the God of Israel."

36. Grillmeier, *Christ in Christian Tradition*, 493.

37. Terence Fretheim presents an emphatic statement of this theme in *The Suffering of God: An Old Testament Perspective* (Philadelphia: Fortress Press, 1984).

38. Gilkey, *Maker of Heaven and Earth*, 60.

39. Robert W. Jenson, *The Triune Identity* (Philadelphia: Fortress Press, 1982), 39. Note the comment on the linguistic developments leading to "paradox Christology," p. 63: "What must be said of Christ to speak the gospel is in each case the opposite of some predicate of the negative theology; the central example is 'suffered under Pontius Pilate' versus 'impassible.' "

40. Ibid., 141.

41. Ibid., 85. Italics his.

42. In "Creation as a Triune Act," *Word and World* 2 (Winter 1982): 34–42, Robert W. Jenson asks, "Does 'creates,' predicated of God, denote a particular *act* done by him, or a standing fundamental *relation* between him and other beings?" (italics his) and in effect answers, "Yes, both."

43. Cf. the formulation by H. Richard Niebuhr in *The Responsible Self* (New York: Harper & Row, 1963), 126: "I am one in many-ness in myself and so responsible as self, as I face the One action in the actions of the many upon me. . . . Responsibility affirms: 'God is acting in all actions upon you. So respond to all actions upon you as to respond to his action.' " Niebuhr's "radical monotheism" yields here a formulation that will be too ambitious to some who will yet not be able to exclude God from any event, even if God's presence is that of defeat and suffering. See Kazoh Kitamore, *Theology of the Pain of God* (Richmond: John Knox Press, 1958), where God's suffering itself is rooted in God's action.

44. Eugene TeSelle, *Christ in Context: Divine Purpose and Human Possibility* (Philadelphia: Fortress Press, 1975), 142. Italics his.

45. Gordon D. Kaufman, *God the Problem* (Cambridge: Harvard Univ. Press, 1972).

46. This is Nelson Pike's suggestion in *God and Timelessness* (London: Routledge & Kegan Paul, 1970), 175–80.

47. See the discussion by Robert H. King in *The Meaning of God* (Philadelphia: Fortress Press, 1973), 85ff.

48. In *The Meaning of God*, 84, King seems specifically to reject this notion "for it suggests a certain incompleteness on God's part." I agree and here would be closer to Peter C. Hodgson's notion of "finite transcendence" in *Jesus—Word and Presence* (Philadelphia: Fortress Press, 1971), 110.

49. See the discussion by Robert L. Wilken, "The Resurrection of Jesus and the Doctrine of the Trinity," *Word and World* 2 (Winter 1982): 24. Italics his. On the way in which Tertullian combines the eternal solitariness of God with the immanence of the Word in God, see Rusch, *The Trinitarian Controversy* (Philadelphia: Fortress Press, 1980), 10.

50. Jenson, *The Triune Identity*, 139, and Karl Rahner, *The Trinity*, trans. J. Donceel (New York: Herder and Herder, 1970). One wonders whether Jenson's formulation, whatever its other merits or demerits, is sufficiently radical to escape Michael Durrant's critique of reinterpretations of trinity teaching (like that of Macquarrie, whom he cites) as failing because that which is reinterpreted is itself unintelligible. Still, Jenson might be viewed as trying to do the impossible, to separate the formula of the trinity from its doctrine. See Michael Durrant, *Theology and Intelligibility* (London: Routledge & Kegan Paul, 1973), 188ff., and for a quite different response, C. Stead, *Divine Substance*. (New York and London: Oxford Univ. Press, 1977).

51. Paul Tillich, *Systematic Theology*, 3 vols. (Chicago: Univ. of Chicago Press, 1951–1963), 1:111–15.

52. This is E. Schillebeeckx's summary statement in *Interim Report on the Books Jesus and Christ*, trans. John Bowden (New York: Crossroad, 1981), 52.

53. Walther Eichrodt, *Theology of the Old Testament*, 2 vols., trans. J. A. Baker (Philadelphia: Westminster Press, 1961–67), 2:27. Cf. Ulrich Mauser, "Image of God and Incarnation," *Interpretation* 24 (July 1970): 336–56. Mauser stresses particularly the transcendence in relationship in Hosea, arguing for New Testament incarnation as fulfillment, while granting (p. 355) that in the Old Testament one does not claim that "an entire human life represented God to man entirely."

54. Cf. Ian D. Kingston Siggins, *Martin Luther's Doctrine of Christ* (New Haven: Yale Univ. Press, 1970), 203. That Luther was not without a decisive God at work in Jesus is reflected in the themes Siggins draws together to underline the stress on the humanity: "Christ's calling as preacher is the function of His human office, not of His divine nature. Because we could not endure the awful majesty of God, He sent us His Son, 'Who will be a human being and will speak to you in human speech and words.' The accomplishment of our salvation is likewise in Christ 'as He was and as He sojourned on earth'; He was human in His death . . . , in His Resurrection, and even in His exaltation."

55. Pannenberg, *Jesus—God and Man*, trans. Lewis L. Wilkins and Duane A. Priebe (Philadelphia: Westminster Press, 1982), 344. One is reminded of Augustine's emphasis in *On the Trinity* on God as threefold love and in *The City of God* on the nature of our being as that which seeks to cleave (*adhaerēre*, "adhere") to the other.

56. Wolfhart Pannenberg, *Jesus—God and Man*, 336. Cf. 339.

57. Whitehead, *Process and Reality*, 344. Neville finds this an insufficient statement of God's otherness, as is clear in *God the Creator*, 73, and more recently in *Creativity and God* (New York: Seabury Press, 1980). I have commented in *Faith and Process* (Minneapolis: Augsburg Pub. House, 1979), esp. 337 n. 22.

58. Soren Kierkegaard, *Philosophical Fragments*, ed. H. V. Hong, trans. David Swenson (Princeton: Princeton Univ. Press, 1962), 44.

59. See above, 90–91. In addition to the works by Langdon Gilkey and John Smith cited there, see Dale Patrick's discussion of the "evocativeness of the biblical depiction of God" in *The Rendering of God in the Old Testament* (Philadelphia: Fortress Press, 1981).

60. Rorty, *Philosophy and the Mirror of Nature*, 345, 376–77. Italics his. Cf. John Whittaker, *Matters of Faith and Matters of Principle*, 64, on how "neutral kernels of metaphysical fact" cannot sprout into the teleological truth claims of religion.

61. Peacocke, *Creation and the World of Science*, 122–24, makes the point that a new and more comprehensive paradigm must incorporate the old; thus the brain remains the basis for "mind."

62. William James, *The Will To Believe and Other Essays in Popular Philosophy* (London: Longmans, Green & Co., 1909), 41–42.

63. Arthur A. Cohen, *The Tremendum: A Theological Interpretation of the Holocaust* (New York: Crossroad, 1981), 7, 22. Italics his. For a broader sketch of desolation and dislocation in "the aftermath," see Malcolm Bradbury, *The Modern American Novel* (New York and London: Oxford Univ. Press, 1983). This is the underside of the "protean" noted by Robert Lifton in relation to such diverse figures as Saul Bellow, John Cage, and Daniel Bell.

64. Ernest Becker, *Escape from Evil* (New York: Free Press, 1975), 154, on how Christianity denies life in order to deny evil. Cf. his *The Denial of Death* (New York: Free Press, 1973). In *The Public Church* (New York: Crossroad, 1981), 8, Martin Marty worries about the emerging ascendency of such methodological "moves": "The end of the Age of Enlightenment may well be at hand. . . . Nowhere that I can think of do faiths that allow for complexity and ambiguity compete evenly with those that engage in simplisms or are authoritarian."

65. Soren Kierkegaard, *The Sickness unto Death*, ed. and trans. Howard V. Hong and Edna H. Hong (Princeton: Princeton Univ. Press, 1980), 126.

66. Thus Kierkegaard, against the Socrates he knew, finds that knowledge brings one only a *dialectical* step nearer healing. God's commitment to genuine freedom brings us beyond debates as to whether the traditional teaching of omnipotence can coherently speak of freedom and yet of God's "*over*-powering," just as it brings us beyond that minimal element of efficacy that may be required for a being to be. See the exchange between Nelson Pike, "Process Theodicy and the Concept of Power," and David Griffin, "Actuality, Possibility, and Theodicy: A Response to Nelson Pike," in *Process Studies* 12 (Fall 1982): 148–79.

67. The image is taken from Paul Ricoeur, *Fallible Man*, trans. Charles Kebley (Chicago: Regnery, 1965), though it could come as well from Kierkegaard's *The Concept of Anxiety*, ed. Howard V. Hong and Edna H. Hong, trans. Reidar Thomte (Princeton: Princeton Univ. Press, 1980), 41–46, with its reference to "the anxious possibility of *being able*" (italics his) which points to the possibility of consequence.

68. Paul Ricoeur, *The Symbolism of Evil*, trans. Emerson Buchanan (Boston: Beacon Press, 1967), 306. Cf. 309.

69. Ibid., 313, 322.

70. Harold S. Kushner, *When Bad Things Happen to Good People* (New York: Schocken Books, 1981). For an equally accessible statement of several approaches, see Daniel J. Simundson, *Faith Under Fire: Biblical Interpretations of Suffering* (Minneapolis: Augsburg Pub. House, 1980). Simundson resists making the clean choice Kushner favors, and perhaps even the cloudier one Ricoeur favors.

71. C. S. Lewis, *The Problem of Pain* (New York: Macmillan Co., 1948), 19. Cf. Tennant, *Philosophical Theology* 2:201: "If water is to have the various properties in virtue of which it plays its beneficial part in the economy of the physical world and the life of mankind, it cannot at the same time lack its obnoxious capacity to drown us. The specific gravity of water is as much a necessary outcome of its ultimate constitution as its freezing point, or its thirst-quenching and cleansing functions."

72. Dorothee Soelle, *Suffering*, trans. Everett Kalin (Philadelphia: Fortress Press, 1975), 38–39. A more leisurely discussion is available in John Hick's *Evil and the God of Love* (London: Macmillan & Co., 1966), chap. 16. For an empirical application, consider Bradford Keeney's emphasis (drawing on Gregory Bateson) on not alleviating conflict symptoms but recognizing them as a "motor for growth," *Family Process* 4 (June 1979): 38.

73. Cordell Strug, "Evil, Evolution, and the Creativity of Chaos: William James and the Human Plight," an unpublished lecture delivered at Luther Northwestern Seminary, 1982, p. 9. In *Creation and the World of Science*, 164, Arthur Peacocke remarks that natural selection is often a very peaceful process.

74. Norman Malcolm, *Ludwig Wittgenstein: A Memoir* (New York and London: Oxford Univ. Press, 1958), 70 n. 1.

CHAPTER 7

1. To accept such a theory is to refuse to explain the joint system of DNA and proteins by appealing, with Francis Crick, one of the discoverers of the structure of DNA, and the astronomer Sir Fred Hoyle, to an origin in outer space. We do not need to go even to the outer reaches of the world to explain a living cell or a living self. For Hoyle's views, see his *The Intelligent Universe* (New York: Holt, Rinehart & Winston, 1984). I have in mind the Cambridge biochemical tradition represented by the Nobel prizes awarded to Klug and Crick, Sanger (two prizes), Kendrew, and Perutz. On the clay-crystal work, see Graham Cairns-Smith, *Genetic Takeover and the Mineral Origins of Life* (Cambridge: At the Univ. Press, 1982).

2. Walker Percy, *Lost in the Cosmos: The Last Self-Help Book* (New York: Farrar, Straus & Giroux, 1983), 1, 12–13.

3. Consider, for example, Noam Chomsky's provocative return to the Cartesian tradition of inwardness in *Reflections on Language* (New York: Pantheon Books, 1975), and *Problems of Knowledge and Freedom* (New York: Pantheon Books, 1971).

4. See James Forsyth, "Tragedy and Hope: Psychoanalytic and Religious Perspectives," *Dialog* 16 (Summer 1977): 191–97.

5. See Marjorie Wallace's report on the work of Professor David de Wied at

Utrecht University's Project for Memory and Memory Disorders, presented in *The Sunday Times*, London (April 24, 1983).

6. Oliver Sacks, *Awakenings* (London: Pan Books, 1983).

7. Soren Kierkegaard, *The Sickness unto Death*, ed. and trans. Howard V. Hong and Edna H. Hong (Princeton: Princeton Univ. Press, 1980), 13.

8. Arthur A. Cohen, *The Tremendum: A Theological Interpretation of the Holocaust* (New York: Crossroad, 1981), 92.

9. See the discussion by Nicholas Lash, *A Matter of Hope* (Notre Dame, Ind.: Univ. of Notre Dame Press, 1981), 5. Compare the contemporary statement of Marxist hope by Ernst Bloch in *A Philosophy of the Future*, trans. John Cumming (New York: Herder and Herder, 1970), 144: "All earthly cultures and their inherited infrastructures are experiments, ventures and variously significant testimonies to the ultimate *humanum*: the content that must be processed out, the final and most important reference point of progress . . . nowhere as yet adequately manifest, but appropriately anticipated" (italics his).

10. Kurt Vonnegut's *Deadeye Dick* (New York: Delacorte, 1982) is an interesting metaphoric use of this apocalyptic image.

11. Carl Sagan, *Cosmos* (New York: Random House, 1980), 259.

12. A playful statement would be the Rosinante series by Alexis Gilland. But the line between science fiction and science is not so clear. Walker Percy notes that Carl Sagan appropriately ridicules the UFOers. But he wonders why "Sagan has written whole volumes promoting the probability of the existence of intelligent life on the billions of planets orbiting the billions and billions of stars in our galaxy, let alone the billions of other galaxies—this in spite of the fact that there is no evidence that life exists anywhere else in the Cosmos, let alone intelligent life." Percy is provoked to ask, "Why is Carl Sagan so lonely?" and among his answers is this one: "Sagan is lonely because, once everything in the Cosmos, including man, is reduced to the sphere of immanence, matter in interaction, there is no one left to talk to except other transcending intelligences from other worlds" (*Lost in the Cosmos*, 172–74). Very different from Gilland and Sagan is Isaac Asimov, who draws on space science to plead for "globalism," which presents humanity as a single entity, unlike "localism." Here, one may say, "outer" space is recognized as both necessity and possibility, and so as pertinent to our human freedom.

13. Robert W. Jenson, *The Triune Identity* (Philadelphia: Fortress Press, 1982), 1–2. Cf. Peter C. Hodgson's statement about how word gathers into presence temporally, constituting presence to oneself: "For presence to oneself means that the temporal modes of existence—future, past, present—are integrated, achieve mutual coinherence. Without temporal integration human life would disintegrate into an irredeemable past, an unachievable future, and a meaningless present. Such disintegration is the essence of schizophrenia—the loss of center" (*Jesus—Word and Presence* [Philadelphia: Fortress Press, 1971], 104).

14. See Eugene TeSelle's discussion of Hegel in relation to "third age thinkers" in *Christ in Context: Divine Purpose and Human Possibility* (Philadelphia: Fortress Press, 1975), 103–4.

15. In *The Christology of Hegel* (Albany: State Univ. of N.Y. Press, 1982), 56, James Yerkes makes this point, citing Hegel's *Lectures on the Philosophy of Religion*,

trans. E. B. Spiers and J. B. Sanderson, 3 vols. (New York: Humanities Press, 1962), 1:173–74, and *The Logic of Hegel*, trans. from the *Encyclopaedia of the Philosophical Sciences*, 2d rev. and aug. ed., by William Wallace (Oxford: At the Clarendon Press, 1892), 116.

16. See, for example, C. J. Jung, *Collected Works*, 20 vols., trans. R. F. Hull (New York: Pantheon Books, 1953–59), 9:2 *301. In *The Tao of Physics*, Fritjof Capra finds ethical wisdom in the Eastern notion of balance between the yin and the yang (New York: Random House, 1975), 117.

17. For two of the many statements available, see R. W. Hepburn, "Optimism, Finitude, and the Meaning of Life," in *The Philosophical Frontiers of Christian Theology*, ed. B. Hebblethwaite and S. Sutherland (Cambridge: At the Univ. Press, 1982), 119–45, and A. J. P. Kenny's Stanton lectures, 1983, pub. pending, esp. lecture 7, "The Point of History."

18. Gerhard O. Forde, "Caught in the Act: Reflections on the Work of Christ," *Word and World* 3 (Winter 1983): 28.

19. Anselm's *Cur Deus Homo*, in *Saint Anselm: Basic Writings*, trans. S. N. Deane (LaSalle, Ill.: Open Court Pub. Co., 1972), is the classic statement.

20. Thomas J. J. Altizer's early work on "the death of God" is perhaps the most striking example. Less clear is Jürgen Moltmann, who in *The Crucified God*, trans. R. A. Wilson and John Bowden (New York: Harper & Row, 1974), 249ff., emphasizes the "within Godness" of the death of Christ, with special emphasis on Jesus' God-forsakenness, and not surprisingly finds himself pressed to distinguish his position from both conventional theism and conventional atheism.

21. Yerkes, *The Christology of Hegel*, 119, 135.

22. For the statements suggesting closure, see R. Kroner's introduction to Hegel's *Early Theological Writings*, trans. T. M. Knox (Chicago: Univ. of Chicago Press, 1948). Such statements must struggle against such explicit passages as this from *The Phenomenology of Mind*, trans. J. B. Baillie (New York: Harper & Row, 1967; Harper Torchbook), 105: "Appearance is the process of arising into being and passing away again, a process that itself does not arise and does not pass away, but is *per se*, and constitutes reality and the life-movement of truth" (italics his).

23. Maurice Merleau-Ponty, *Humanism and Terror: An Essay on the Communist Problem*, trans. John O'Neill (Boston: Beacon Press, 1969), xviii and 98.

24. F. W. Dillistone, *The Christian Understanding of Atonement* (Philadelphia: Westminster Press, 1968), 410–16. Italics his.

25. Jürgen Moltmann, *The Crucified God* (New York: Harper & Row, 1974), 229–30.

26. Karl Barth, who is seldom charged with compromising divine transcendence, is nonetheless clear about the divine commitment. Thus in *Church Dogmatics* (Edinburgh: T. & T. Clark, 1957), II.2.155: "We must not allow God to be submerged in His relationship to the universe or think of Him as tied in Himself to the universe. Under the concept of predestination, or the election of grace, we say that in freedom (its affirmation and not its loss) God tied Himself to the universe." Cf. Barth's discussion of how each of the divine perfections is a form of love in which God is free or a form of freedom in which God loves (II.1.322–677).

27. George W. Stroup, *Jesus Christ for Today* (Philadelphia: Westminster Press,

1982), 86. Cf. Hans W. Frei, *The Identity of Jesus Christ* (Philadelphia: Fortress Press, [1967] 1975).

28. In *Faith and Process* (Minneapolis: Augsburg Pub. House, 1979), chap. 5, I have tried to amplify the employment of Whiteheadian resources made in this area by J. Gerald Janzen in "Metaphor and Reality in Hosea 11," *Society of Biblical Literature 1976 Seminar Papers*, ed. George MacRae (Missoula, Mont.: Scholars Press, 1976).

29. Barth, *Church Dogmatics* IV.1.567.

30. *God and Incarnation in Mid-Nineteenth Century German Theology: G. Thomasius, I. A. Dorner, A. E. Biedermann*, ed. and trans. Claude Welch (New York: Oxford Univ. Press, 1965), 67–68. Thomasius's effort reaches back behind Lutheran orthodoxy to Luther. Marc Lienhard in *Luther: Witness to Jesus Christ*, trans. Edwin H. Robertson (Minneapolis: Augsburg Pub. House, 1982), 390, notes that the orthodox theologians were ready enough to stress within the communication of attributes the "genus majestaticum," which attributed the divine properties to the human nature. But he adds: "At the same time, however, these theologians will not respect the intuitions of Luther at all points. Thus they recoil before the idea of a genus tapeinoticon, which envisages the communication of the suffering of the humanity to the divinity—an idea which was, however, already there in Luther, but will be taken up again only in the Kenotic theories of the 19th century." Again and again theologians have approached the notion of a co-constituting togetherness of the divine and the human, only to back away.

31. I have discussed some of the difficulties involved in such talk in *Faith and Process*, chap. 4.

32. John B. Cobb, Jr., *Christ in a Pluralistic Age* (Philadelphia: Westminster Press, 1975), 139–40.

33. For the former figure see Edward Schillebeeckx, *Jesus: An Experiment in Christology*, trans. Hubert Hoskins (New York: Crossroad, 1981), 652–69; for the latter ("the history of man, his free action, and the absolute climax of his freedom"), Karl Rahner, *Theological Investigations*, trans. Kevin Smyth (London: Darton, Longman & Todd, 1966), 4:130.

34. Schillebeeckx, *Interim Report on the Books Jesus and Christ*, trans. John Bowden (New York: Crossroad, 1981), 69ff., distinguishes four pre–New Testament creedal models that later came together in the New Testament: (1) Maranatha Christologies, (2) a "wonder-worker" Christology, (3) Wisdom Christologies, (4) Easter or death and resurrection Christologies.

35. Rowan Williams, *Resurrection* (London: Darton, Longman & Todd, 1982), 60.

36. In *Markings*, trans. Leif Sjoberg and W. H. Auden (New York: Alfred A. Knopf, 1964), 197, Dag Hammarskjold writes: "Forgiveness breaks the chain of causality because he who 'forgives' you—out of love—takes upon himself the consequence of what *you* have done. Forgiveness therefore, always entails a sacrifice" (italics his). Significantly, this "marking" of Easter 1960 goes on to say that the "price" to be paid for liberation is that "you in turn must be willing to liberate in the same way, irrespective of the consequences to yourself." While the direct reference is to relationships among human beings, the dating suggests a connection to the

decisive divine act of forgiveness, which yields consequences of which we speak in the final pages of this chapter.

37. Williams, *Resurrection*, 23.

38. See the concern voiced by Dorothee Soelle, in *Christ the Representative* (Philadelphia: Fortress Press, 1967), that Christ's representing us does not "replace" us, as substitution would. For a different tack, see Wolfhart Pannenberg's attempt to align Jesus' work with substitution as "a universal phenomenon in human social relationships," in *Jesus—God and Man*, trans. Lewis L. Wilkins and Duane A. Priebe (Philadelphia: Westminster Press, 1968), 268.

39. Williams, *Resurrection*, 35. Cf. 42: "We may betray, but the world characterized by betrayal is now interwoven with a reality incapable of betrayal. God's faithfulness has worn a human face, through Calvary and beyond. The incarnate truth, 'risen from the dead,' establishes that faithfulness as the ground of inexhaustible hope in the world, even in the midst of our self-deceits."

40. Ibid., 23. Cf. Jenson in *The Triune Identity*, 174: "[I]n that this Jesus is just in this very identification the creature for all others, the one whose individuality consists in surrender of all individual claims, the Father's preoccupation with him, Jesus' objectopacity to the Father's outward flight of pure knowledge and will, does not impede the way of the Father's intension to all things; it *is* the way" (italics his).

41. Williams, *Resurrection*, 23.

42. But of course such discussions are readily available, as of the bearing of faith on self-understanding, in David Baily Harned, *Creed and Personal Identity: The Meaning of the Apostles' Creed* (Philadelphia: Fortress Press, 1981), and of Christ for life in the world, in James Gustafson, *Christ and the Moral Life* (New York: Harper & Row, 1968).

43. Kierkegaard, *The Sickness unto Death*, 14. On the notion of equilibrium in Kierkegaard, see Mark C. Taylor, *Kierkegaard's Pseudonymous Authorship: A Study of Time and the Self* (Princeton: Princeton Univ. Press, 1975), 339.

44. On the conceptual difficulties, see Peter Geach, *God and the Soul* (New York: Schocken Books, 1969), and Terence Penelhum, *Survival and Disembodied Existence* (New York: Humanities Press, 1970).

45. Vitezslav Gardavsky, *God Is Not Yet Dead*, trans. V. Menkes (Baltimore: Penguin Books, 1973), 48. Italics his.

46. Augustine, *The City of God*, (Garden City, N.Y.: Doubleday Image Books, 1958), 456 (XIX.13).

47. Simone Weil, *On Science, Necessity, and the Love of God*, trans. and ed. Richard Rees (New York and London: Oxford Univ. Press, 1968), 160.

48. Similarly, Carl Braaten notes that Moltmann and Pannenberg worry about an eschatology "in which the horizon of the future is swallowed up by the eternal blitzing in from above" ("The Kingdom of God and the Life Everlasting," in *Christian Theology: An Introduction to Its Traditions and Tasks*, ed. Peter C. Hodgson and Robert H. King [Philadelphia: Fortress Press, 1982], 291). That worry is a well-placed one, but only if there is a genuine openness to the future. Langdon Gilkey questions whether the eschatological theologians actually do have an open future, if they do not recognize the role of present causality (including nondivine

causality) in constituting that future. See his discussion in *Reaping the Whirlwind: A Christian Interpretation of History* (New York: Seabury Press, 1976), esp. 233–36.

49. John Berryman, "Surveillance," *The Ohio Review* 15 (Winter 1974): 45. Italics his. This posthumously published poem begins, "Almost the only place I really enjoy praying is hospital."

50. Heinrich Schmid, *The Doctrinal Theology of the Evangelical Lutheran Church*, trans. Charles A. Hay and Henry E. Jacobs, 3d ed., rev. (Philadelphia: Lutheran Pub. Society, [1875] 1899), 268.

51. Williams, *Resurrection*, 85. See Schillebeeckx, *Interim Report*, 138, for an interpretation of the descent into hell as God's action to claim all, to reconcile all—including the past.

52. Williams, *Resurrection*, chap. 1, offers a moving discussion of this theme.

53. See Robert S. Frey, "Issues in Post-Holocaust Christian Theology," *Dialog* 22 (Summer 1983): 227–35. Frey asks, "[H]ow can one place the terror and suffering of Jewish children within the scheme of a forward-looking theodicy? What goodness inherent in heaven can atone for such unwarranted pain?" and responds, "We submit that ultimately no event on any plane can redeem such suffering as was the Holocaust, neither the creation of the State of Israel nor the attainment of a distant heaven."

54. Athanasius *De Incarnatione* 54.

55. We are then here following the second of the major tendencies Dillistone discerns in the tradition concerning the atonement. See above.

CHAPTER 8

1. Dorothee Soelle, *Christ the Representative: An Essay in Theology after the "Death of God,"* trans. David Lewis (London: SCM Press, 1967), 134. Italics hers.

2. On the one hand, I think of the influential work of Francis Schaeffer, who argued that it is the possession of an absolute that enables one to proceed confidently by the method of "antithesis"; see his *The God Who Is There* (Chicago: Inter-Varsity Press; London: Hodder & Stoughton, 1968), 14. Or one might consult Josh McDowell's *Evidence That Demands a Verdict* (San Bernardino, Calif.: Campus Crusade for Christ, 1972) or Colin Chapman's *Christianity on Trial* (Wheaton, Ill.: Tyndale House, 1974). In his recent "evangelical" critique of fideism, *Crucial Questions in Apologetics* (Grand Rapids: Baker Book House, 1981), Mark M. Hanna claims a nonarbitrary starting point, which turns out to be fivefold: ontological (the triune God), epistemological (personal awareness), justificational (given cognitive revelation), interpretive (the Christian credenda), and methodological (the culture's chief focus). On the other hand, I am thinking of those who build their apologetic work on the common ground found in metaphysical analysis. Notable instances are Schubert Ogden, *The Reality of God and Other Essays* (New York: Harper & Row, 1963), and David Tracy, *Blessed Rage for Order* (New York: Seabury Press, 1975). See also n. 49 to chap. 1, above.

3. An eloquent statement of this concern is to be found in the work of C. S. Lewis. See Paul L. Holmer's discussion in *C. S. Lewis: The Shape of His Faith and Thought* (New York: Harper & Row, 1976), 8: "There is, indeed, an argument and a strong plea for rationality; but it is also the case that one must realize a sense of dismay and

see Christian things in that qualified way so that the teachings begin to make sense. Also one must correct self-conceit and self-will by becoming a repentant subject before one can see some things to be the case." While "we do have to be converted, even in thought" (p. 116), that occurs on earth and not in heaven: "Until the language of faith can begin to construe the manifold of the human heart, it can never quite match up humankind and God. Lewis managed that" (p. 109). I grant that Lewis yet holds apologetic work much further apart than I do from the dogmatic givenness of what he calls "mere Christianity." Cf. p. 34: "I am not yet within a hundred miles of the God of Christian theology." I certainly do not claim to travel faster than Lewis; perhaps it is that I am not trying to get as far.

4. Cf. John H. Whittaker, *Matters of Faith and Matters of Principle: Religious Truth Claims and Their Logic* (San Antonio: Trinity Univ. Press, 1981), 138: "The believer who 'leaps' into the domain of teleological judgment by adhering to some religious principles does not discover on the far side of the leap the compelling evidence he lacked on the near side. He may or may not acquire an increased capacity to make some sense out of life's brute facts; but his insights will remain so informed by the concepts and principles by which he took hold of his experience that they will never be translatable into independent arguments of belief, even for himself."

5. Perhaps the most extended recent statement of this point is Gordon D. Kaufman's *The Theological Imagination: Constructing the Concept of God* (Philadelphia: Westminster Press, 1981). Indeed, to speak of something as strong as the "mediation" of God-knowledge through self, world, and history may be to overstate Kaufman's point. While "speech about the Christian God as 'real' or 'existent'" does require "a substantial metaphysical foundation—the belief that there are cosmic forces working" toward humaneness (p. 49)—conventional Christian speech about God would seem too concrete and too confident on this account. *What* one knows in faith is pulled severely back to *how* one knows.

6. John Whittaker, *Matters of Faith and Matters of Principle*, 57. Italics his.

7. Ibid., 54–55.

8. To argue in this way for the possibility of significant but finite interconnectedness is to stop short of Kaufman's contention that "a radical and genuine doctrine of finitude can be made fully intelligible only in partnership with a correlative concept of an 'absolute' which sustains the finite" (*The Theological Imagination*, 91). Our argument that faith "comprehends" the world of reason (chap. 6) is softer than that, and so here we settle for saying that relativity does not render futile our claims for God; we do not try to convert that recognition into an argument for the claims.

9. For an emphatic development of Thomas's "The thing known is in the knower according to the mode of the knower" (*Summa Theologica* II/II Q.1, art. 2), see John Hick's *God Has Many Names* (Philadelphia: Westminster Press, [1980] 1982). I am arguing that our principled expectation renders the empirical conversation crucial. It is not crucial if one knows in advance that the plurality of faiths must be in conflict or that conflict is in principle impossible.

10. See Teilhard de Chardin's discussion of the role of "the roundness of the earth" in "forced coalescence," in *The Phenomenon of Man*, trans. Bernard Wall (London: William Collins Sons, 1959; Harper Torchbook, 1961), 239–43.

11. Anthony Kenny, *The God of the Philosophers* (Oxford: At the Clarendon Press, 1979), 129.

12. Jürgen Moltmann, "Christianity and the World Religions," in *Christianity and Other Religions*, ed. John Hick and Brian Hebblethwaite (Philadelphia: Fortress Press, 1981; London: William Collins & Co., 1980), 192.

13. John V. Taylor, "The Theological Basis of Interfaith Dialogue," in *Christianity and Other Religions*, ed. Hick and Hebblethwaite, 219. Taylor comments on the Malachi passage: "Does it not seem likely that this haunting reference to the rising and going down of the sun was in the mind of Jesus when he pointed to the faith of the Roman centurion saying: 'Many shall come from the East and from the West and shall sit down with Abraham and Isaac and Jacob in the Kingdom of heaven, but the sons of the Kingdom shall be cast into outer darkness' (Matt. 8:11–12). The Church cannot read those words today without applying them to itself, and, indeed, they strike at the heart of all exclusive religious claims" (219–20). See also Taylor's *The Primal Vision: Christian Presence amid African Religion* (London: SCM Press, 1963). Given my approach's emphasis on the actual conversation, it is worth noting that Taylor taught for many years in Africa before becoming general secretary of the Church Missionary Society.

14. See Friedrich Heiler, "The History of Religions as a Preparation for the Co-operation of Religions," in *The History of Religion: Essays in Methodology*, ed. Mircea Eliade and Joseph M. Kitagawa (Chicago: Univ. of Chicago Press, 1959), 139. Heiler identifies seven principal areas of unity spanning the "higher" religions. While the points are indeed areas and as such are very general—(1) that there is the reality of the transcendent; (2) that this transcendent reality is immanent; (3) that this one is the highest good for humankind; (4) that this one is love; (5) that the way to this one is the way of sacrifice; (6) that the way to the neighbor is the way of love; (7) that the highest way to God is love—presumably something must be made out of them. Among the more detailed studies, see Geoffrey Parrinder's *Avatar and Incarnation* (New York: Barnes & Noble; London: Faber & Faber, 1970), 263, 278, which supports the linkage noted in the title but qualifies it by observing strongly docetic tendencies in the non–Christian formulations.

15. Krister Stendahl, "Notes for Three Bible Studies," in *Christ's Lordship and Religious Pluralism*, ed. Gerald H. Anderson and Thomas F. Stransky (Maryknoll, N.Y.: Orbis Books, 1981), 14–15. C. S. Lewis in *Mere Christianity* (New York: Macmillan Co., 1964), 43, suggests that the existence of the religions poses a greater problem for atheists than it does for Christians: "If you are an atheist you do have to believe that the main point in all the religions of the whole world is simply one huge mistake. If you are a Christian, you are free to think that all these religions, even the queerest ones, contain at least some hint of the truth." It would seem, though, that the problem of pluralism would remain, not the least since Lewis was confident that "of course, being a Christian does mean thinking that where Christianity differs from other religions, Christianity is right and they are wrong." That seems less clear to me, as the discussion below will indicate.

16. See, for example, Sallie McFague's discussion of "The Christian Paradigm," in *Christian Theology: An Introduction to Its Traditions and Tasks*, ed. Peter C. Hodgson and Robert H. King (Philadelphia: Fortress Press, 1982), 323–36.

McFague argues that the consciousness of pluralism can free "the essential core of Christianity to live once again in people's lives," for "this essential core is not any book or doctrine or interpretation, but the transformative *event* of new life, a new way of being in the world that is grounded in the life and death of Jesus of Nazareth" (p. 324, italics hers). It would seem that describing and defining the family of ways of making the connection would be an essential task.

17. In *Towards a World Theology* (Philadelphia: Westminster Press, 1981) Wilfred Cantwell Smith moves from "A History of Religion in the Singular" (chap. 1) through a recognition of the personal, particular, historical, and communal character of faith to this statement of hope: "[T]hat relation of the specific to the generic, although itself specific, is conceptualised generically; or so intellectuals—theologians—hope and strive. The move, accordingly, is in our day through and beyond the several theologies of comparative religion or their counterparts that might be essayed towards something still more universal (and therein more accurate also to interpreting the specific)" (p. 181).

18. Eric Voegelin, *The Ecumenic Age of his Order and History*, 5 vols. (Baton Rouge: La. State Univ. Press, 1956–), 4:326–27.

19. I have developed this suspicion somewhat in "The Knowledge of God," in *Christian Dogmatics*, 2 vols., ed. Carl E. Braaten and Robert W. Jenson (Philadelphia: Fortress Press, 1983) 1:193–268, esp. 242–45. It is striking that some support for the work of evaluation can be found in the religious-studies field. In "History of Religions: Conditions and Prospects," *Bulletin of the Council on the Study of Religion* 13 (December 1982): 129–33, Frank E. Reynolds notes what may be said to be analytical support, in commenting on the recent "systematic" studies of Jonathan Smith (*Map Is Not Territory* [Leiden: E. J. Brill, 1978]), Bruce Lincoln (*Priests, Warriors, and Cattle* [Berkeley and Los Angeles: Univ. of Calif. Press, 1981], and *Emerging from the Chrysalis* [Cambridge: Harvard Univ. Press, 1981]), and Wendy O'Flaherty (*Women, Androgynes, and Other Mythical Beasts* [Chicago: Univ. of Chicago Press, 1980]). In a later issue of the *Bulletin*, Arvind Sharma advocates the candid adoption of "not merely evaluative but judgmental procedures" ("Playing Hardball in Religious Studies," 15 [February 1984]: 1–4). He proposes that the effort be located in the field of the philosophy of religion.

20. I am very much in debt to my colleague Paul V. Martinson for his reflections in this area. One of the regular contributors to this kind of analysis has been Ninian Smart, most recently in *Worldviews: Crosscultural Explorations of Human Beliefs* (New York: Charles Scribner's Sons, 1983), esp. "The Structure of Worldviews," 54–61. In *God, Christ, Church* (New York: Crossroad, 1982), 151–60, Marjorie Hewitt Suchocki employs Whiteheadian categories to discuss Christianity ("one"), secularism ("many"), and Buddhism ("creativity"). This is helpful, but it is not clear on what grounds she can elevate one of the three in saying that "God" uses these "three basic modes."

21. Voegelin, *The Ecumenic Age*, 321.

22. In this threefold way of speaking ("the given," "the reticent," "the transcendent"), I am again in debt to Paul V. Martinson. As a sample of his rich discussion in a forthcoming publication, *Between Matter and Mystery*, consider this on the first theme: "The Buddha, Confucius and Marx all began with empirical life, with our

corporeality. This is correct, for the first irreducible fact with which we have to do is the givenness of life. I am born with a world. . . . For the Buddhist *karma–samsara* and its subtle workings is one symbol for expressing this givenness; for the Confucian one such symbol is *t'ien–ming* (heaven's mandate); for the Marxist it is dialectics" (ms. pp. 47–48).

23. Naomi R. Goldenberg, *Changing of the Gods: Feminism and the End of Traditional Religion* (Boston: Beacon Press, 1979), 111–12. A. T. van Leeuwen, *Christianity in World History: The Meeting of the Faiths of East and West* (London: Edinburgh House Press, 1964), 67–70, stresses the connection between biblical "theocratic" motives and the Western technological way of life, as over against the "ontocratic" culture of the East. See the discussion and the criticism from within the religious realm in Carl Hallencreutz, *Dialogue and Community: Ecumenical Issues in Inter-religious Relationship* (Uppsala: Swedish Inst. of Missionary Research; Geneva: World Council of Churches, 1977), 27–28.

24. Denise Lardner Carmody, *Women and World Religions* (Nashville: Abingdon Press, 1979), 16–17.

25. Ibid., 35–36.

26. See, for example, Vicki Noble's *Motherpeace: A Way to the Goddess Through Myth, Art, and Tarot* (New York: Harper & Row, 1983). In introducing their collection of feminist readings, Carol P. Christ and Judith Plaskow note that "freedom from the past does not guarantee freedom from the influence of sexist culture" and argue that "a relation to the past seems necessary to feminists who are beginning to create a new religious future." See their *Womanspirit Rising* (New York: Harper & Row, 1979), 11. In this matter also, one does well to distinguish the postmodern from the premodern. Cf. Sallie McFague's specific criticisms in *Metaphorical Theology: Models of God in Religious Language* (Philadelphia: Fortress Press, 1982), 159ff., for balanced comment: "While Goddess religion rightly criticizes the Western tradition for its overriding transcendence and its masculine models, the solution does not lie in a total immanence or in identification of women as divine. Nor does an elevation of female qualities, either biological or culturally stereotypical, aid the liberation of women. . . . One of the basic difficulties with contemporary Goddess religion is that it is anachronistic . . . agrarian religion, thriving in cultures prior to the time when human beings were fully cognizant of the role played by the male in generation."

27. Mary Daly, *Beyond God the Father* (Boston: Beacon Press, 1973), 36.

28. Zsuzsanna E. Budapest, "Self-Blessing Ritual," in *Womanspirit Rising*, ed. Christ and Plaskow, 271.

29. Kate Millett, *Sexual Politics* (Garden City, N.Y.: Doubleday & Co., 1970), 25. Cf. 20, 28, 46–54, and this: "Patriarchy has God on its side. One of its most effective agents of control is the powerfully expeditious character of its doctrines as to the nature and origin of the female and the attribution to her alone of the dangers and evils it imputes to sexuality" (p. 51). She stresses the judgment against Pandora and Eve and sees in both "the vestigial traces of a fertility goddess overthrown." That a different reading of the text (Gen. 3:12: ". . . she gave me fruit of the tree, and I ate") can be argued for (see Phyllis Trible, *God and the Rhetoric of Sexuality* [Philadel-

phia: Fortress Press, 1978] 105–15) perhaps leaves the feminist point about the *use* of the text in no weakened a position.

30. Rosemary Radford Ruether, "Christology and Feminism: Can a Male Savior Help Women?" (an occasional paper issued by the United Methodist Board of Higher Education and Ministry as vol. 1, no. 13, December 25, 1976), 9. Cf. her discussion of "the prophetic iconoclastic Christ" in *To Change the World: Christology and Cultural Criticism* (New York: Crossroad, 1981), 53: "This reversal of order is not simply a turning upside down of the present hierarchy, but aims at a new order where hierarchy itself is overcome as a principle of rule."

31. Goldenberg, *Changing of the Gods*, 22.

32. Mary Daly, *Beyond God the Father*, 19.

33. This is not the "Jesus was the first feminist" theme. Note Mary Daly's response, "Jesus Was a Feminist, but So What?" in "Theology After the Demise of God the Father: A Call for the Castration of Sexist Religion," in *Sexist Religion and Women in the Church: No More Silence*, ed. Alice Hageman (New York: Association Press, 1974), 125–42. Her critique centers in her judgment that the "traditional idea of imitatio Christi seems to be the not-so-hidden agenda of this method" and includes the suggestion that "the very idea of model, as commonly understood, is one of those conceptual tools of patriarchy that we need to wrench from its old semantic field" (pp. 139–40).

34. Madeline Nunn suggests as much in "Christology or Male-olatry?" *The Duke Divinity Review* 42 (Fall 1977): 144: "There is nothing unusual about a woman as servant, a woman refusing to accept a position of authority, either military or as a political queen; a woman weeping over a city; a woman bending down to wash a friend's feet; a woman making the ultimate sacrifice for those she loved." Robert Jenson offers a creative turn on this theme in pondering male language for God in *The Triune Identity* (Philadelphia: Fortress Press, 1982) in discussing how the biblical writings disturb "the direct religious analogy from human perfections to divine characteristics": "Israel was not permitted to grasp God's ways by ours, and specifically not to grasp God's creativity by ours; thus her God was understood to be sexually transcendent. Therefore, in Israel when a filial term of address is needed it is the ontological inferiority of the male, the fragility of his sexuality, that offers 'Father' rather than 'Mother' as the proper term of address" (pp. 14–15). One can imagine that Jenson has heard from some women who are wondering what their ontological superiority has to do with life in church and world.

35. Krister Stendahl has a special warning for liberal theology here, "for it tended to increase the anthropomorphism of Christian language. In moving away from the deeper aspects of trinitarian speculation, it centered more and more on the idea of God as the Father and made the imagery of Fatherhood the overarching metaphor for God. One started with the idea of 'Father' and blew it up into divine proportions." See his "Enrichment or Threat? When the Eves Come Marching In," in *Sexist Religion and Women in the Church: No More Silence*, ed. Hageman, 120. Perhaps, but liberal theology should be able to find a material corrective in the theme of God's affirmation of humankind. Thus Sallie McFague, who seems to write in the liberal tradition, has addressed these concerns in *Metaphorical Theology*. Stressing that metaphor combines the "is" (which by itself would yield idolatry) and the "is not"

(which by itself would yield irrelevance), she advances "the thesis that by attending to the relationship between God and human beings rather than to descriptions of God, it is possible to find sources within the Christian paradigm for religious models liberating to women" (p. 167). She takes the root metaphor to be the "kingdom of God"—hardly a congenial choice for some feminists—but proposes subordinately the non-gender-related metaphor of "friend." By this she does not intend some "easy empathy," but surely the note of affirmation is heard (pp. 178–85).

36. Anne Sexton, "Small Wire," in her *The Awful Rowing Toward God* (Boston: Houghton Mifflin, 1975), 78. For Sexton's recognition that need is not belief, see "With Mercy for the Greedy," in her *All My Pretty Ones* (Boston: Houghton Mifflin, 1962), 22.

INDEXES

INDEX OF SCRIPTURE REFERENCES